The SWEETNESS *of* GRACE

Stories of Christian Trial and Victory

CONSTANTINA R. PALMER

ANCIENT FAITH PUBLISHING ✠ CHESTERTON, INDIANA

The Sweetness of Grace: Stories of Christian Trial and Victory
Copyright ©2017 by Constantina R. Palmer

Published by:
  Ancient Faith Publishing
  A Division of Ancient Faith Ministries
  P.O. Box 748
  Chesterton, IN 46304

Unless otherwise noted, Scripture quotations are taken from the New King James Version, © 1979, 1980, 1982 by Thomas Nelson, Inc. Used by permission.

ISBN: 978-1-944967-04-8

Printed in the United States of America

Abba Lot went to see Abba Joseph and said to him, "Abba, as far as I can I say my Little Office. I fast a little. I pray. I meditate. I live in peace and as far as I can, I purify my thoughts. What else can I do?"

Then Abba Joseph stood up, stretched his hands towards heaven and his fingers became like ten lamps of fire, and he said to him, "If you wish, you can become all flame."[1]

I would like to dedicate this book to all the struggling and holy monastics, priests, and laypeople who, like Abba Joseph, showed me by means of their own bright and brilliant example that if only I wish, I too can become all flame.

Contents

Introduction

IN A WORLD where love has grown cold, where hatred has replaced love and pleasure has replaced meaningful joy, we must cling to the little love we have for Christ in order to cultivate it. We must nourish this love to make it grow, holding in our heart every kind word, every spiritual instruction, every good homily we've heard. We must "speak about our Christ, about our Orthodoxy. We will preach Him in our home, on the way to work, on the bus, at work, in the country, everywhere, every place, at every hour."[2]

And by *preach* I don't mean merely through word but by means of our lifestyle, our deeds, our humility, our holding fast to the Faith. It is through clinging to Christ in all we do that we sow genuine seeds, in our relationships and in the world around us. Sowing is all we can do, all that is asked of us. God reaps.

This is how Christ was shared with me, through the words and deeds of others. This is what I wish to share with you in this collection of stories. But first let me introduce myself.

My husband, Fr. John, and I were blessed to live and work in Seoul, South Korea, for one year (2006–2007) teaching English as a Second Language, having followed my brother and sister-in-law (now Fr. Matthew and Presvytera Catherine) to the Asian peninsula. While there, we attended the Korean Orthodox Church. Afterward we moved to Thessaloniki, Greece (2007), to learn Modern Greek and study theology at Aristotle University (Fr. Matthew and Presvytera Catherine joined us a few years later). Fr. John was ordained to the holy diaconate by His Grace Archbishop Irénée of Ottawa and Canada in the summer of 2011 and served in Greece for a subsequent two years, while he finished his PhD in Theology and I finished my Master's in the same field.

While in Greece, I took advantage of the Orthodox environment as much as possible and took classes to learn the technique of Cretan-style icon-painting as well as Byzantine chant. We made numerous pilgrimages to various holy sites and monasteries. I wrote a book about my experiences visiting women's monasteries in particular: *The Scent of Holiness: Lessons from a Women's Monastery* (Ancient Faith Publishing, 2012). And in a sense this book, *The Sweetness of Grace: Stories of Christian Trial and Victory*, is a sequel. Although it can be read independently, a number of the themes and a few of the people I wrote about in *The Scent of Holiness* make appearances in this book. This second book, however, does not have a women's monastery as its primary setting. Rather, it is a collection of stories about Orthodox Christians—monastics and laypeople alike, along with my experiences while teaching English in South Korea, living and studying theology in Greece, as well as a few stories from life here in North America.

In 2013 Fr. John and I returned to Canada from Greece, and that spring he was ordained to the holy priesthood. Since the fall of 2013 we have lived in St. John's, Newfoundland, serving the Orthodox community here. Our mission parish is the only Orthodox church on the whole island, which is 108,860 square kilometers (42,030 square miles), not much smaller than the entire country of Greece. The population on the island of Newfoundland is half a million. It is situated in the Atlantic Ocean, northeast of the Maritimes, where my husband and I grew up in New Brunswick. The city of St. John's is on the eastern end of the island, making us almost as close to London, England, as we are to Toronto. After seven years of living abroad, we were blessed to return to our homeland, and although moving to this isolated island from the great Byzantine city of Thessaloniki was difficult, this is where God led us, so this is where we find ourselves— modern missionaries in the New World.

This book is a recollection of my travels and the great lessons I learned on the journey. Despite having a Master's degree in theology and being married to an Orthodox priest, I feel I do not have the necessary prerequisites to teach theology nor even to write about spiritual subjects, since I still have so much to learn. The only talent I feel confident I *do* have is as a storyteller. And so, just as I did in *The Scent of Holiness*, I offer a collection of stories that have greatly informed and helped me and which I hope you, my reader, will find enlightening, inspiring, and even to an extent entertaining. The stories are examples of the sweet and difficult aspects of Christian life; they are a petition to take life in Christ seriously; they are a challenge to put into practice the Gospel precepts exactly in the life circumstances in which we find ourselves.

When our Holy Lord stood on a hillside in front of a great crowd and gave His famous Sermon on the Mount, He listed qualities despised by the world and told us it is by means of these that a person will be called blessed and will become holy. He taught us:

"Blessed *are* the poor in spirit,
    For theirs is the kingdom of heaven.
Blessed *are* those who mourn,
    For they shall be comforted.
Blessed *are* the meek,
    For they shall inherit the earth.
Blessed *are* those who hunger and thirst for righteousness,
    For they shall be filled.
Blessed *are* the merciful,
    For they shall obtain mercy.
Blessed *are* the pure in heart,
    For they shall see God.
Blessed *are* the peacemakers,
    For they shall be called sons of God.
Blessed *are* those who are persecuted for righteousness' sake,
    For theirs is the kingdom of heaven."
(Matt. 5:1–10)

In honor of this recipe for holiness, this book has eight sections, each named after one of the eight Beatitudes. The stories are arranged according to these themes, each story representing an aspect of the beatitude—either the virtue, the reward, or both. Each section is joined to the next as each link in a chain connects with the next. For, according to St. John Chrysostom, in the Beatitudes Christ not only gives us a perfect guide to the Christian way of life, but He forges a gold chain, demonstrating that each virtue, each beatitude, has as a foundation the one preceding it:

> Thus, first, he that is humble, will surely also mourn for his own sins: he that so mourns, will be both meek, and righteous, and merciful; he that is merciful, and righteous, and contrite will of course be also pure in heart: and such a one will be a peacemaker too: and he

that has attained unto all these, will be moreover arrayed against dangers, and will not be troubled when evil is spoken of him, and he is enduring grievous trials innumerable.[3]

Since the Beatitudes are a perfect summary of the spiritual life, I wanted to convey elements of the spiritual life by means of various stories. When my family and I first became Orthodox, I devoured Orthodox books with powerful examples and intriguing stories. Books like the *Gerontikon* and the *Evergetinos*, the lives of contemporary elders, and the letters of holy ascetics—books that deepened my understanding of the Orthodox Faith—inspired me to struggle to live the Orthodox life and shed light on how to lead a healthy prayer life. I look for life's great lessons in the little things, and it is through story that I share what I've learned.

Although my own stories are simple and based on my personal experiences, encounters, and conversations with monastics and laypeople throughout the world, I feel they capture aspects of Christ's call to blessedness. By means of example, they show us the various ways in which we can acquire grace and avoid spiritual traps through our battle to reach and remain on the straight and narrow path.

I've called this collection of stories *The Sweetness of Grace* because I feel this title captures the one element of Orthodoxy that does not change, whether one lives in Asia, Europe, or on a Canadian island. Whether one is a priest, monastic, or layperson, the sweetness of grace is offered to us all: through the trials, through the victories, we struggle to acquire and hold onto it, and when we taste it, we want to share that sweetness with others. By sharing these stories I hope to share the sweetness I was blessed to taste.

These stories are meant to remind us that the rewards for fighting "the good fight" (1 Tim. 6:12) are very great. We are given the means to become saints; the sweetness of grace is offered to each one of us. But I also hope these stories highlight that the onus is on us. The medicine is there for the taking; the question is, will we swallow it? Will we do what is necessary to become receptive to His grace? Will we become poor in spirit, meek, pure of heart, peacemakers? Will we not only read the Gospel but live it and allow the light of Christ to shine through us?

"The soul must war," the ever-memorable Gerontissa Makrina of the Holy Monastery of Panagia Odigitria in Portaria taught, "and when it wars [against sin and the passions] it will see God come and enthrone Himself in the heart."[4] This is the goal of our Christian life. The goal of this simple book is to demonstrate that holiness is attainable, that all may taste of the sweetness of grace and live a life of blessedness—if only we struggle.

✠ONE✠

Blessed Are the Poor in Spirit
for theirs is the kingdom of heaven

Apples from Paradise

IT WAS THE BEGINNING of summertime in Newfoundland—
though you wouldn't have known it by the two sweaters I was
wearing—and I was doing schoolwork, reading about important
social issues for my social work degree. And yet I couldn't help but
think how all that I did, both as a social worker and as a missionary,
paled in comparison to the important work I once participated in
while living in Greece.

I remember during the last summer we lived in Greece, while Fr.
John was in England for a conference, I was working in one of the
monastery's large stairwells with the windows open, trying to catch
a breath of air in the intensely humid heat. I was taking pre-folded
boxes that had been thrown into garbage bags in a disordered way
and repacking them in a stacked, orderly fashion. (Anyone who visits
monasteries—particularly women's monasteries—will not be surprised

by this attention to detail. They need those boxes to be in order so they can quickly and orderly package their baked goods.)

So there I was for hours and hours, stacking boxes and praying. I prayed for my family, my reposed relatives, for our future. Occasionally a sister would come by on her way upstairs, or the guest-mistress would bring me fresh juice. Other than these brief encounters, I worked and prayed on my own, and I loved it. Despite the monotony of the task, not to mention the awful heat, I look back on that memory with great nostalgia and fondness.

There is something to feeling as though you are contributing to an important goal, that you are a part of something, even if only by means of a simple task. That's what it was like when I would help out with the sisters' work at the monastery. Just sweeping leaves from the cobblestones was enough to make me thankful, thankful to be playing a role (even an insignificant one) in the life of the monastery. St. Paul says although the Body of Christ is one, it has many members. At best I could perhaps be considered a pinky toe of the Body when I helped out at monasteries, but what a blessing it was.

I consider the time I spent in Greece, not only at monasteries but also in the company of struggling laypeople and holy priests, to have been like years spent visiting Paradise. I look back on the hundreds of photographs we took of churches, icons, monasteries, friends. I listen to the recordings I made of monks reading the epistle, nuns singing the supplicatory canon, the local chanter chanting a vigil service in the middle of the night for St. Savvas the Sanctified, and I try as hard as I can not to cry.

For I live in a form of exile now. A bit of a dramatic comparison, perhaps, but not totally. When you live on an island (a twelve-hour boat ride from the nearest point of mainland), and you belong to the only Orthodox parish on the whole island (which, for the record, is roughly the size of Spain), and you literally live on the edge of the world in the farthest-eastern city in all of North America, you feel your isolation in a real sense. This exile, my husband assures me, can be for the benefit of our souls if only we make appropriate use of it.

"Not only," he informs me, "does St. John Climacus say it's the fastest route to humility, exile is a means to remember we are all foreigners and our true home is heaven." He's right, of course.

St. John Chrysostom says:

> The one who is a stranger here will be a citizen up there; the one who is a stranger here will not be happy to live among present realities, will not be concerned for dwellings, money, food, anything else of that kind. Instead, just as people living in foreign parts do everything and busy themselves with a view to their return to their homeland, and daily strive to see the land that bore them, so too those in love with future realities are neither dejected by present griefs nor buoyed up by success, but ignore both like a traveler on the road.[5]

And so, reflecting on my time spent in Greece as a taste of Paradise, I try to keep the longing, the nostalgia I have for all the monasteries, the frescos, the chanting, and redirect them toward my yearning for our eternal home in the heavens.

St. Euphrosynos the Cook of Alexandria was a monk in a Palestinian monastery who, on account of his great obedience and humility, was blessed to visit the true Paradise. In his collection of the lives of the saints, St. Dimitri of Rostov says that St. Euphrosynos even distributed fruit from Paradise. Once, he gave three apples to a priest of his monastery, a sweet and fragrant blessing.

I, on the other hand, was only blessed to visit what I *consider* Paradise. Yet I look on my experiences as great blessings. I give you these stories of mine, simple as they may be, just as St. Euphrosynos distributed those apples. This is my attempt to share with you the sweetness of grace that God bestowed on us and to remind myself, as much and as frequently as possible, of the day when His Kingdom will come, in hopes that I will ever preserve the longing for our true home in the heavenly Kingdom. It's easier said than done, of course, but I suppose the point is to try.

Visitations of Grace

WE WERE GATHERED for a lecture, and when the conversation was opened for discussion, the topic turned to the practice of ceaselessly saying the Jesus Prayer. A senior layman spoke then, and while what he said was instructive, his facial expression conveyed more to the listening crowd than his beautiful words.

"When we keep the name of the Lord on our lips, when we say 'Lord Jesus Christ, have mercy on me,' His name becomes sweet like honey in our mouth." Here he made an indescribable face, as if he had to pause his discourse on account of the "sweet honey" he was himself tasting at that very moment. "His name is sweet, and we must keep it on our lips at all times, as much as possible."

"St. Symeon the New Theologian had experiences of the Uncreated Light while still a layman," Elder Ephraim of Katounakia once said. "How many laymen appear as such on the outside, but deep down are monastics!"

A CERTAIN PRESVYTERA, on account of the great number of souls seeking commemoration by her husband, a senior and holy priest, was required to help him during the service of the Proskomidi. (During this service the priest prepares the prosfora for the Divine Liturgy and commemorates a list of Orthodox faithful.) The presvytera would stand outside the north door of the iconostasis (behind which the priest stands at the Altar of Preparation), and he would give her a stack of papers so she could help him read all the names. Once, as she stood reading the names and praying with her whole heart, she rose into the air and prayed in an elevated state, as did St. Mary of Egypt.

OUR PRIEST IN GREECE would offer a class on various themes each Sunday following Divine Liturgy. One year he decided to dedicate our classes to the study of Christian almsgiving. He read various Fathers and patristic texts concerning almsgiving. The method of almsgiving that seemed to resonate most with our priest was indiscriminate giving. I don't recall now whether it was St. John Chrysostom or one of the Gregorys who strongly encouraged Christians to simply pull whatever they had out of their purse or pocket and give without question, without attachment, without discretion to anyone who asked.

While we always had a few gypsies waiting outside our church seeking alms each Sunday, it was as though word got out Father was teaching us to give alms indiscriminately, because suddenly we noticed the number of gypsies showing up at the conclusion of our class had increased tenfold. And fully charged with zeal, all those who had listened to Father's inspirational words would step out of class and give indiscriminately. We couldn't help but chuckle that alms-seekers came just in time, but it was beautiful to witness so many putting into practice what they had been taught.

A HOLY ATHONITE FATHER was traveling with a group of men in a car. They had asked the elder monk if he would bless them to record the conversation; however, the elder withheld his blessing. Despite this, one of the men decided to record the conversation secretly.

The party drove for quite some time, talking about various spiritual topics. The elder had shared quite a bit about himself personally, and the disobedient man was delighted that he was recording all of this.

Afterward the man hastened to listen to the recording to make sure he had captured all the wonderful, spiritual things the elder had said during their trip. To his utter astonishment, the recording captured everything the other men said—every word with clarity—but, whenever the elder spoke, not a word he said was recorded. During the times the elder was speaking, the recording only captured the noise of the running car, the traffic sounds, and other background noises. Without a blessing, the man's secret recording amounted to a fractured conversation but a perfect testament to the futility of disobedience.

WHILE VISITING a women's monastery, a young pilgrim was sleeping in the guesthouse attached to the monastery's chapel. She had been staying for a few weeks, so she was accustomed to the sisterhood's typicon of rising in the middle of the night to do the Matins service in their chapel. Once in awhile, if the sisters had a particularly long day of work, the abbess would allow them to say Matins on their prayer rope (a monastic practice of replacing the service with a set number of Jesus Prayers).

One night when such a blessing had been given, the young woman was awakened by the sound of a censer outside her bedroom door. It sounded as though someone was censing the whole hallway. She assumed the nuns must have ended up doing Matins after all and had decided to cense the guest house.

The next morning she commented to one of the sisters, "I didn't realize you were doing Matins last night, but I got woken up by the bells on the censer one of the sisters was using to cense the guesthouse."

"We didn't do Matins last night," the nun said. "And nuns don't use the censer with the bells on it; that is only used by the priest. But we didn't have a priest here either. Sometimes our spiritual father visits the monastery spiritually. Perhaps he was the one censing."

WHILE WAITING FOR THE SERVICE of monastic tonsure to begin, the novice nun stood praying before the icon of the Mother of God, for whom she had a great devotion. For reasons known only to God, at that moment the oil lamp burning before the icon tipped over and poured olive oil all over the praying novice.

Oil has great significance in the Orthodox Church. Not only are our lamps in church lit with oil, the light of which diminishes physical and spiritual darkness; not only are we covered in oil before baptism, but even the Greek word *eleios* (mercy) has ties to the word "olive." And so, to request God's mercy is to request the healing ointment, the balm of our souls. Olive oil was once used for medical purposes, to soothe and anoint the sick.

The novice stood covered in olive oil, and her spiritual father told her, "Here is a sign you will receive great mercy."

A New Name Known Only by Him Who Receives It

HE SAT ON A STASIDI* in the church, his black monastic robes brushing the ground, his head bowed in prayer. The small, worn knots on the prayer rope dangling from his lap ran rapidly through his fingers.

He was preparing for monastic tonsure, an event he had anticipated for years. He had decided to go into the church to pray a little before the service began, and thus he sat saying the Jesus Prayer.

"Lord Jesus Christ, have mercy on me!" he whispered again and again.

Parthenios, he internally heard his prayer interrupted.

"Parthenios?" he questioned. "Why would that name come to mind?"

"Lord Jesus Christ, have mercy on me!" he began again. And again he was interrupted by the mental formation of the name Parthenios.

Again he returned to prayer and yet again he heard *Parthenios*.

One of the fathers was passing by just then, and the novice asked, "Is the name Parthenios in honor of the Holy Virgin?" The Greek word for virgin is *parthenia*.

"No," the father answered. "There is a Saint Parthenios, a bishop from Lampsakos in Asia Minor."

"Oh, okay," the novice answered and returned to his prayer.

Later that evening, during the service of monastic tonsure, after his hair was cut crosswise, the novice heard his spiritual father pronounce his new monastic name: Parthenios.

---

* A *stasidi* (plural: *stasidia*) is one of the large throne-like chairs that line the walls in some Orthodox churches.

In the Book of Revelation it is written, "To him who overcomes . . . I will give . . . a white stone, and on the stone a new name written which no one knows except him who receives *it*" (Rev. 2:17).

Making Use of the Mammon of Unrighteousness

IN THE GOSPEL OF LUKE we read a seemingly peculiar passage in which Christ encourages us to use the mammon of unrighteousness for our own personal gain. Of course, He is speaking in a poetic manner, teaching us what it means to be merciful while acknowledging man's propensity to love wealth. But I believe the injunction to "make friends for yourselves by unrighteous mammon" (Luke 16:9) is not limited to this parable alone. There are many things in our lives, even simple everyday activities, that can be used to our spiritual benefit.

Years ago I heard a homily by Fr. Andreas Konanas (a well-known Greek homilist) in which he made reference to spiritualizing domestic tasks in our quest for sanctity. He described, for instance, how when we are in our kitchen cutting an onion and our eyes begin to water on account of the vapors, we should use this for our own gain. Even though the tears are not proceeding from a contrite heart in actuality, we can use them for our own devices and reflect on our sins, "cry" for our sins, as Fr. Andreas said. He mentioned using simple things as opportunities for prayer, such as taking off our coat. When we take off our coat, we can say an internal prayer: "Just as I take off this coat, so remove my sins from me, O Lord."

Similarly, I once heard a talk by a spiritual daughter of the newly canonized St. Porphyrios. She said the elder once asked her if she did prostrations as a part of her daily rule of prayer.

"No, Geronda, I thought prostrations were just for monastics and clergy," she responded.

"I know you did, that's why I asked you! You should do prostrations because they are an external posture of humility. Even when you are cooking and your fork falls on the floor, instead of becoming irritated you should kneel to pick it up, make a prostration, and thank the Lord."

In his commentary on the Gospel passage concerning the mammon of unrighteousness, St. Cyril of Alexandria says the following:

> The Lord of all therefore requires us to be thoroughly constant in our exertions after virtue, and to fix our desires upon the better and holy life, setting ourselves free from the distractions of the world . . . that we may serve Him continually, and with undivided affections.[6]

This is, in essence, what Fr. Andreas's and St. Porphyrios's advice is directed toward: fixing our desires on a holy life in all circumstances that we may serve the Lord continually.

There are so many opportunities in life to take advantage of "unrighteous mammon," of the mundane, the seemingly insignificant. To become virtuous, to become holy, takes a great deal of effort, but it can be accomplished so long as we "make friends" with all manner of opportunities presented to us—so long as we take a creative approach to our pursuit of the Kingdom of heaven.

Confess Thoroughly

A FEW MONTHS AFTER I moved back to Canada from Greece, I was speaking with an abbess on the telephone. She told me one of her nuns, one I knew well and loved, had decided to leave the monastery and return to the world. I felt horrible when I first heard the news. In fact, I felt sick to my stomach and asked, almost in despair, "How can this happen?"

The abbess's response was enlightening. She said, "This happens when a person begins to believe his thoughts."

Gerontissa Makrina of blessed memory explains this in great detail in the following passage:

> When we don't confess our thoughts to [our elder and eldress], the devil will war against us; he will put us outside the gates of the monastery, and the matter is finished. Why don't we confess our thought? We [should] say, "Gerontissa, this temptation fights me; help me, relieve me." Gerontissa will keep vigil, she will pray, she will do whatever she can to help you. For this reason God placed guides in the coenobia, the elders, the eldresses, in order to relieve and help the disciples by the grace of God. For this reason we examine which thoughts we fought, which were destroyed, and which remained without our having told them to our guides. When we don't confess our thoughts, we are harmed. The devil ruins the world and shakes with fear so as to keep us from confessing our thoughts to the eldress.[7]

"So, we avoid these things by making a thorough confession regularly?" I asked the abbess.

"Exactly," she responded.

She went on to explain that it's all about free will. It is our choice which path we take and which path we continue on or turn away from.

"God doesn't want us to be monastics out of compulsion or force; He wants us to follow Him freely," she told me.

More surprising than learning that my dear friend had turned away from the monastic life was the fact that the abbess never once conveyed feelings of having been personally affronted. She conveyed no resentment or bitterness in what she said or how she spoke.

If someone backs out of the simplest agreement we planned together, we often become upset; we can even become personally offended. Yet, here in this family dynamic in which a vital member just turned her back on the community and walked away, the abbess fully believed it to be a matter between the nun and God and not one of personal offense to the sisterhood.

Truly, a monastic is a *monachos*, that is, "one who is alone." He or she may live and pray in community, but at the end of the day the monk returns to his monastic cell alone, and it is in this personal relationship with God that he truly lives and moves and has his being (Acts 17:28). And it is *this* personal relationship that the monk is obligated to uphold, not out of compulsion, nor out of a commitment to a community, but out of pure love and devotion to God.

What a lesson I learned that day!

This is not to say that leaving monasticism is a light matter; on the contrary, it is very serious. But let us not think monastics are the only ones who can and do fall. We Christians in the world also need to freely and continually follow Him; we need to rise to the position to which He has called us.

One of the best ways to do this is to confess thoroughly. What does this mean? It means taking the time to take stock of our daily sins and tempting thoughts, writing them down if need be, and making sure to confess them to a priest. Forget about being embarrassed; push those thoughts far away. Forget about being self-willed; push those feelings far away. Just say it like it is and receive absolution. What does it matter if we confess even the most sinful, most distorted sins and thoughts? Once we confess them, we are free from their bondage. We receive healing. So we might as well reveal the festering wounds to the doctor. He will give us the appropriate medicine, and our health will be restored.

Acquiring humblemindedness is a close second to confessing thoroughly and regularly. And so, more than anything, when I reflect on my friend's departure from monasticism, I say to myself that wonderful saying of the desert fathers: *Today her, tomorrow me. She for certain will repent; I, however, will not.*[8]

Let us, then, look to our own lives, our own commitment to Christ, for He alone can keep us from stumbling on the path laid out before us and make us stand blameless before His awesome presence on the fearful Day of Judgment.

The Poison of False Belief

MANY PROTESTANT MISSIONARIES go to Greece thinking they need to save Greeks from their "idolatry," and so they proclaim their falsehoods to anyone who will listen. Unfortunately, sometimes they are successful in their attempts to convert Orthodox Christians to their errant belief systems. Often the new convert becomes a missionary himself and embarks on an overzealous attempt to coerce others into receiving his newfound faith.

I have been on the receiving end of this type of conversation more than once while living in Greece. From speaking with a few of these Greek missionaries, I have found that they often convert in reaction to their misunderstanding of the Orthodox Faith. What they often fail to see, however, is how the unhealthy fruit of their labors testifies to the unhealthy state of the tree from which it proceeds: the false faith they adhere to. And unfortunately, in their blindness they try to share their rotten fruits with many others, thus doing damage to them and inflicting more harm on their own souls.

While I lived in Greece, such missionaries would frequently approach me on the street. Before they could draw me into conversation while offering me their pamphlets, I would usually tell them, "No, thank you. I'm an Orthodox Christian." But there were a few times when I was caught off guard and a conversation began. Not being one to naturally shy away from a debate, I would explain why I wasn't interested in their belief system. Of course, if you allow even the smallest conversation to take place, they listen to you briefly and then begin their rehearsed discourse.

This only happened a few times, though, because when I told Gerontissa Philareti of this, her response was, "Don't engage in dialogue with them. They may say something to you that will cause you harm in the long run."

When I heard these words, I could feel the snake of pride rising up inside me. *I have a Master's degree in theology!* I could faintly hear my internal voice protesting. But instead of listening to my own will, I listened to her sound advice. At that time I had even been in an ongoing written correspondence with someone, but when she said, "Sever all ties. Tell her you're not able to help her and that she should find a spiritual elder to speak to who will know more than you," I swallowed my pride and did as she suggested.

Afterward I understood her advice and saw its wisdom. Deception comes about through many avenues. In speaking with individuals dwelling deeply in false beliefs, I can see that it is safer (for myself as well as others) to remember I am not an illumined elder, nor am I immune to the poison of heresy, even if I have studied theology.

One whispered suggestion was all it took for our Mother Eve to fall: one dialogue, one thought, one inadvertent acceptance of what the snake was telling her. Am I stronger than Eve? No. So I heed the advice of my spiritual mother with gratitude; I am happy to have someone I love and trust who can tell me when it's better for me to act like the psalmist: "But I, like a deaf *man,* do not hear; / And *I am* like a mute *who* does not open his mouth" (Ps. 37/38:13).

It's not as easy as it sounds—not for someone who likes to talk as much as I do. But it's better for myself and for others if I silently pray instead of publicly arguing. There is much wisdom in spiritual advice, especially the kind that deflates our ego. We can never be too cautious about the evil one's means of deceiving through the use of the spoken word.

Radiating Grace from the Kliros

MY DEAR FRIEND SR. SARAH once told me that every time she heard a certain holy monk chant the hymn during the Consecration, "We praise Thee, we bless Thee . . . ," she would be filled with compunction. Having heard many good chanters, she couldn't understand why this particular monk's voice moved her so intensely, so she asked her abbess about it.

Gerontissa responded, "When this monk chants, he doesn't merely chant with his voice but with his whole heart, and this is why his chanting makes the listener feel so compunctionate."

Concerning such holy chanters, the newly canonized St. Porphyrios once said, "You might have the voice that can move others, but he who is truly holy when he chants has something else. He does not have his voice alone. Together with his voice, which radiates with sound waves, he radiates grace with other mystical waves, which reach the souls of men and move them even more deeply."

There is little in this world that can move one's soul and soften one's heart as much as a holy chanter. Every time I heard a dearly beloved abbess in Greece chant the epistle during Divine Liturgy at her monastery, I would marvel at the quality of her voice. Perhaps it wasn't the quality of her voice that affected me so much as the spiritual sentiment conveyed along with her voice. It was so moving, I used to tell my husband I believed Paradise would smell like the fragrant myrrh that runs from the relics of St. Demetrios and sound like Gerontissa's voice when she chants the epistle.

It is difficult to convey just how grace-filled the environment of a church becomes when the chanter is holy and conveys this with his voice. If only I could pass along to you with my words the feeling one gets when, as St. Porphyrios says, grace is radiated with mystical waves. It is as if in those moments one tastes, briefly and perhaps insufficiently, the sacredness of holy things. Like Moses in front of the burning bush, something in one's soul understands, *this is holy ground upon which I stand.* If you have firsthand experience of this, then you know for yourself just how powerful a holy chanter's voice can be.

And this is why chanters have very significant roles in the Church and ought to strive to become holy—so that they will inspire people not only with their musical talent but with their love for God.

Gerontissa Makrina was very clear about how important the conduct of a chanter is in church. She taught:

> When you chant well, with meaning, with fear of God, with solemnity, the name of God is hymned and a person will pour out tears. [For this reason] do not speak, do not laugh, and do not converse at the *analogion*; it is not permitted, for it is a great sin. . . . A professor we know told me, "We leave the churches and come to the monasteries to hear humble chanting, to see the attentiveness of the priest, something which gives us joy and life." You see how psalmody—without discord and without disorder—contributes to the mentality of people? For this reason the world runs to the monasteries. [Chanting] requires earnestness, it requires zeal, it requires love of Christ. . . . When a person has love in his soul, it is a very serious and holy thing![9]

Gerontissa speaks here of the chanting in a monastery because it sets the standard we strive to attain in the parish: to communicate the same compunction, grace, and zeal communicated by monastics with hearts full of love for the Lord. Is this possible in the parish? By all means! What does it require? The same attentiveness, the same seriousness, and the same piety given to it by a monk who sings from the depths of his heart. And what is the result? Man is moved to tears, to prayer, to repentance; his heart is changed, and he—if only for a fleeting moment—lays aside all earthly care so as to receive the King of all.

Contemplating the Virtue of the Theotokos

DURING THE WINTER MONTHS, the sun had already set by the time I reached the Holy Dormition Monastery of the Mother of

God. Vespers was most often held in the large catholicon outside the monastery gates.

Entering the outer narthex, I would light a beeswax candle in front of the festal icon the sisters had set out on the icon stand. As soon as I opened the large wooden door to the nave, I would be greeted by the sound of the nuns' melodic chanting and surrounded by the sweet fragrance of burning incense. I would then proceed to the large icon of the Mother of God depicted with the Lord on her lap.

In those sacred if fleeting moments, I felt genuinely connected to the Mother of God. In the dim light of the church, I could even supplicate her with tears and be noticed by no one. As far away as she seemed out in the world at times, she seemed very near in the sacred space of her holy monastery.

To stand in the presence of a holy icon is to stand in the presence of the person depicted therein. Whether we stand before a large icon encased in an elaborately decorated wooden frame or before a paper icon taped on the refrigerator, we are in the presence of the holy person whose countenance is painted in line and color. But in the peaceful, prayerful atmosphere of a holy monastery, we are often more attuned to the spiritual reality surrounding us, which makes our prayer flow more readily and brings the contemplation of holy mysteries within our grasp.

It is in moments such as those that I contemplate the person of the Most Holy Theotokos. Thinking on her life and works, her sufferings and sacrifice, I feel she offers us the answer to all our problems. The example of her life is the cure for our illness, the source of joy to heal our sorrow. By means of merely two of her countless virtues—obedience and purity—she teaches us everything. In her obedience to God, she shows us that perfect freedom and the attainment of our full potential are found in submitting our fallen and corrupted will to the all-good Father. Thus we mold our will into His will and therefore become able eventually not only to know the good but to will it and do it.

With her outward and inward purity, the Theotokos points us to the easy path of sanctification. By keeping our souls and bodies pure, by not even accepting corrupted thoughts, we maintain the ability to hear and communicate with God and thus learn how to live in conformity to His will. If we have long ago lost our mental, spiritual, and/or physical purity, we have the opportunity to restore them through confession and repentance. These are our constant means of imitating her virtue and, as she does most of all, pleasing her Son and our God.

And so, no matter how ill we are, no matter our upbringing, no matter the genetic weaknesses of body and soul we have inherited, no matter the state of the world around us, we have the opportunity, by God's grace and through the prayers of the Theotokos, to become healthy. We too can, in our own dormition, pass from life to life through a mere falling asleep, if only we will imitate her virtue.

The Holy Spirit and Fat Dwelling Places

MY SISTER WAS VISITING a monastery for a few months during her summer vacation, so my husband and I flew in to see her, as well as to meet the abbess and her sisterhood, on our way home from South Korea.

Pulling into the parking lot, we saw large tents set up, as it was just a few days before the monastery's feast day. We went into the first building looking for my sister and were led by one of the nuns to a nearby tent. On our way we ran into my sister helping with the work. She was so excited to see us, she grabbed our hands and said, "Come meet Gerontissa!"

She took us into a tent in which some sisters were setting up tables and chairs and hastily announced, "Gerontissa, this is my sister. But she's lost fifty pounds!"

Meeting the abbess for the first time, I was a little embarrassed by my sister's remark—although I *had* lost a lot of weight living off rice in Asia, I hadn't lost fifty pounds.

In my embarrassment I joked, "Well, it's like Saint Silouan says, 'The Holy Spirit doesn't want a fat temple for His dwelling place.'"

To this the abbess quickly and wittily replied, "Yes, well, we could lie flat on the ground and be as thin as possible, but we won't attract the grace of the Holy Spirit!" We all laughed.

This was our first visit to a women's monastery. It's no wonder we barely stepped off monastic grounds after that: the abbess's charm, generosity, and wit won us over immediately. After our brief exchange, I never cited that saying by St. Silouan again in defense of my weight loss. She's correct—in some circumstances, being thin is no more an indication of ascetic endeavor than lying on the ground is a means of acquiring grace.

Humility: Our Sure Guide

AFTER I FINISHED my Master's dissertation, I went to my advisor's office to have some papers signed, and a conversation unfolded. My advisor knew St. Paisios of the Holy Mountain personally and would often draw on his experiences with the elder for his theological lectures. This particular day he told me, "Geronda Paisios said that love cannot be our guiding principle. Love can err; it can lead us astray, because love can be wrong. People do all sorts of things in the name of love. Humility, on the other hand, ensures that we follow the Church: humility must be our guiding principle." Thus my professor condensed in a few words all I had learned about Orthodox theology while listening to his lectures during my years as a student at Aristotle University in Thessaloniki.

He would often say the phrase "in my opinion" has no place in Orthodox theology, because it is not about what we think, but about what the Holy Spirit has revealed to the Holy Fathers. The Church has entrusted us with a great inheritance, the Orthodox Faith, and we are obligated, as the Seventh Ecumenical Council decreed, to "keep unchanged all the ecclesiastical traditions handed down to us, whether in writing or verbally."

Obedience to the Tradition handed down to us, whether written, verbal, or pictorial, is humility. Humility is perfect acceptance of all that the Holy Spirit does through the Church. Humility is remaining faithful to the Church, no matter how many theologians, professors, or even hierarchs teach something contrary to the Tradition handed down to us. For the Church functions in accordance with Christ's commandments. Christ is the same yesterday, today, and tomorrow, and what the Church taught yesterday will still be true tomorrow, because what the Church teaches is the Truth made flesh, the Truth made Man. And what that God-Man teaches us is to follow Him (John 1:43).

We read in the Gospel that Christ pushed out Nathaniel's doubt concerning who He truly was when He first encountered him on the road. He told him, "Follow Me." With these same words Christ pushes out all our doubts. He tells us, "Never mind what the world around you is saying or believing. Follow *Me!*"

And who wouldn't want to follow Him—the God who chose not only to save us but to make us like Him? Who wouldn't want to follow Him who humbled Himself and became Man so that we could become gods? "Who *is* so great a God as *our* God? / You *are* the God who does wonders" (Ps. 76/77:13–14), we chant in the Great Prokeimenon.

Without Christ we "can do nothing" (John 15:5). Without the Church, we do not have Christ. To follow the Church is to follow Christ. The proud man places himself before the Church and says, "I know better." The humble man, the publican, says, "Christ, my sweet Lord, without You I am nothing; without the Church I am lost. Save me; I will follow You even unto death!"

In obedience we fast. In obedience we feast. In obedience we accept everything in the Gospel, in our Orthodox Faith, and in the writings of the Church Fathers, even when they are difficult for us to accept—because this is humility. And humility is the greatest virtue, our sure guide, because it leads to perfect union with God.

Let's place our hope, our faith, and our trust in the Church, the only path to salvation (John 14:6), so that by following the Church we may follow Christ, who is our hope, our faith, our salvation. Through the prayers of the newly canonized Saint Paisios, may we put his spiritually insightful words into practice and make humility our governing principle throughout our life.

Obedience Is Better than a Pure Sacrifice

MRS. A HAD RECENTLY begun seeking counsel from a spiritual father for the first time when she found herself questioning whether she would be able or even willing to take up the yoke of obedience; it didn't exactly appeal to her straightaway.

During prayer one evening, she was praying over this dilemma when suddenly she found herself noetically on Mount Athos. Standing before her was a venerable-looking elder, and in his hand was a dirty, worn-out, old-fashioned woolen sock. He stretched out his hand to her, offering her this sock.

She was initially repulsed by how dirty it appeared. She thought, "How am I going to take this filthy sock in my hands?" But out of politeness she felt compelled to accept. Holding the sock, she noticed it gave off such a pleasant, sweet aroma that she wanted to put it in her mouth, such was its appeal. And she did, in fact, put it in her mouth and tasted its ineffable sweetness.

When she came to, back in her own home, she hastened to tell all this to her spiritual father, who on hearing the story simply laughed and said, "I can't believe you put such a dirty old sock in your mouth."

When Mrs. A told me this story, I was awestruck, and although she didn't offer an explanation, I understood the sock in her vision to be a representation of obedience to her spiritual father. Obedience may appear old and dirty, repulsive even, but the sweetness that comes from it is indescribable. Elder Joseph the Hesychast says, "As much love, and respect, and *obedience* you have toward your elder, that much and more grace you will receive."

When Elder Joseph left the world for the monastic life on Mount

Athos, he went seeking a man of God who could inform and instruct him, whom he could obey and from whom he could receive spiritual guidance. Through his ardent search he found some hidden gems who matched the caliber of the spiritual fathers of days gone by. And thus it was that he found an elder to subject himself to, and through his obedience he acquired much grace.

Describing Elder Joseph's experience of discipleship, his own disciple Elder Ephraim writes, "It was not long before they [Elder Joseph and his co-struggler Elder Arsenios] saw the fruits of their obedience. Because of their obedience, it was natural that they found great ease in prayer. In this way, Francis [Elder Joseph] began to understand why the holy Fathers praised holy obedience."[10] And again, Elder Ephraim writes, "it is completely impossible for a disciple, who with humility pleases his spiritual father, to fail in the spiritual life. It is even more impossible for him not to obtain the Kingdom of God."[11]

There are countless stories of the miracles and spiritual gifts associated with the simple but fundamental Christian virtue of obedience. Perhaps one of the most famous stories, taken from the *Sayings of the Desert Fathers*, tells of how St. John the Dwarf's elder wanted to test his disciple's obedience. He told John to plant a dry stick in the earth and water it every day. Although John had to walk a great distance each night to water the stick, he obeyed his elder, and eventually the stick bore fruit. When his elder heard the stick had actually produced fruit, he collected it and gathered the fathers in the surrounding area of Sketes, saying, "Come and taste of the fruit of obedience." With this he gave them the literal fruit that had sprouted on account of St. John's obedience.

We have access to countless stories about monastics and the grace they receive through obedience. But does this mean a layman can't also receive grace through obedience to his or her spiritual guide? No, of course not! What is good, praiseworthy, and beneficial in monasticism is also good, praiseworthy, and beneficial in a layman's life. The simple difference is that while a monastic obeys his elder even regarding when and what he eats, a layman obeys his guide regarding the spiritual life: how he'll fast, what prayers he'll say each day, and so forth.

Wanting to differentiate between secular obedience and spiritual obedience, someone once asked the renowned Elder Epiphanios Theodoropoulos, "What is the difference between a communist's obedience to his party and a Christian's obedience to his spiritual father?"

The elder replied, "In the second case, we are set free from our passions."

Our relationship of obedience to our spiritual guide is a visible image of our relationship with Christ. The closer we draw to Him, the more we strive to obey His commandments, and the more we love Him and show Him our love in action, the more we are set free from our passions.

Our spiritual father is our own personal icon of Christ, given to us as our direct link to God. Therefore, our obedience to our guide is a visible image of our invisible obedience to Christ. In obeying our spiritual guide, we seek to please Christ by showing Him, whom we cannot see, our love and devotion through the love and devotion we show toward our spiritual father, whom we can see. Thus, gradually we are set free from the sins and passions that bind us and distance us from Christ.

So, while Mrs. A was initially unsure of the merit and worth of obedience, she was given to taste of its sweetness—a sweet grace offered to us all, whether monk or layman. Let's not leave it only to monastics to win crowns and receive riches. Let's also acquire the Kingdom of heaven through obedience.

The Virtue of Virtues

WHILE I WAS YET A CATECHUMEN, I mistakenly thought spiritual progress was quantifiable. I figured there must be some blueprint for acquiring virtues. My mindset was: I've done this many prayers, fasted this many days, and confessed my sins this many times, so that means I ought to have attained this virtue, and that, and must be fast approaching the next. Unfortunately, the spiritual life doesn't work that way. I learned this when I went to my spiritual father, inquiring how I might learn what virtues I should expect to have acquired by that stage in my spiritual life.

"Virtues don't matter. None of that matters," he said, shaking his head. "The only thing that matters is humility: acquiring humility."

At the time, I accepted his answer, but I did not understand it because of my worldly mindset. Seeking self-assurance rather than humility, wanting an excuse to be pleased with myself, I was looking for a pat on the back rather than for true instruction.

My approach to the spiritual life was similar to baking a cake: I have this recipe I want to make, so I buy the necessary items, and once I have them, all I have to do is put them together, and voila! I'm a spiritual person.

The spiritual life doesn't work this way, and thank God it doesn't, because no sooner would I take the cake out of the oven than my soul would be lost on account of the pride with which I would swell up seeing my accomplishment. I would give myself all the glory and would never once give a thought that it was God who had given me the recipe, supplied me with the ingredients, and made the cake to rise. Thus, I slowly (and I mean *slowly*) have begun to understand what my spiritual father meant when he said acquiring humility ought to be my goal.

A wonderful Russian abbot, Elder Nikon, offered a similar sobering response in a letter to his own spiritual child:

> The measure of a man's spiritual growth is his humility. The more advanced he is spiritually the more humble he is. And vice versa: the more humble, the higher spiritually. Neither prayer rules, nor prostrations, nor fasts, nor reading God's Word—only humility brings a man closer to God. Without humility, even the greatest spiritual feats are not only useless but can altogether destroy a person. In our time we see that if a person prays a little more than is customary, reads a little of the Psalter, keeps the fast—he already thinks of himself as better than others, he judges his neighbors and begins to teach without being asked. All this shows his spiritual emptiness, his departure from the Lord. Fear a high opinion of yourself.[12]

The success of the spiritual life, the measure of virtue, is not dependent on spiritual feats, which can easily put us in danger of acquiring a high opinion of ourselves; rather, it is measured by the depth of our humility. And the interesting thing about that is, the more humble a person becomes, the less spiritual he considers himself to be and the more protected and virtuous he will be. Elder Nikon taught that humility guards a person from falling and brings him spiritual gifts. The royal path to acquiring virtue consists in keeping our gaze fixed only on acquiring the virtue that bears all others: humility. " A broken and a contrite heart— / These, O God, You will not despise" (Ps. 50/51:17).

Where the Morning Dawns

IN SEPTEMBER OF 2013, we moved to Newfoundland to serve the Orthodox faithful at the Holy Lady of Vladimir Mission. Immediately Fr. John set his heart on offering as many divine services as possible. However, for the first eight months we did not own a car, so we walked everywhere we went. Thus, I found myself waking before five AM on Tuesdays and walking a half hour (at the time our apartment was 3.6 kilometers from the chapel) to chant the Matins service before our choir director would chant the Divine Liturgy.

A self-professed night-owl, I found this insanely early wake-up call a bit much. You know, reading about barefoot ascetics living on greens in the wilderness and keeping vigil all night is awfully romantic. . . . At least that is what I thought until I was forced into this itsy-bitsy form of asceticism.

Looking up at the towering trees as we walked along the path leading to the chapel, I compelled myself to think of the monks on Athos arising for vigil. But the truth is, it was cold, I was tired, and my feeble attempt to replace negative thoughts with positive ones had me nearly cursing the day we decided to come to this cold, windy island.

In those dark, frigid early mornings, my thoughts would flutter to my beloved sisters, the nuns in Greece. "You're like monastics now. You no longer have a will; you obey your bishop. What he says goes,"

Sr. Evphrosini told me just before we left Greece. "So, you cry a little and then you obey. That's the life of obedience."

This obedience of walking to the chapel for services before the crack of dawn wasn't easy, but it became a lot easier when it was brought to my attention that St. John's, the city of St. John the Forerunner (where we live), is the furthest eastern city in all of North America. It's just a hop, skip, and a jump to Cape Spear, the most eastern point in the whole continent. In fact, the island is located so far east we have our own time zone, Newfoundland time. This means that when the sun rises in North America, it rises first here in the city of St. John's. And on Tuesdays the sun would rise and be greeted by the Divine Liturgy, or more properly, would rise to greet the Divine Liturgy. When I realized this, I began to drag my feet a little less (but only a *little* less) on those mornings. What a blessing it was to chant the Matins service, to attend the Divine Liturgy at the first break of dawn in all of North America.

Those sisters were right—a priest is like a monastic, and his wife and family are too in a sense, if only by default, because obedience becomes the rule by which we govern our lives. We may cry a little, we may drag our feet, we may even be overwhelmed by grumbling thoughts at times, but there are blessings, too—blessings that sometimes require a little struggle to obtain.

Amma Theodora, a desert-dwelling holy mother, said, "Let us strive to enter through the narrow gate. Just as the trees, if they have not stood before the winter's storms cannot bear fruit, so it is with us; this present age is a storm and it is only through many trials and temptations that we can obtain an inheritance in the kingdom of heaven."[13] Not only is this saying poignant, it puts a smile on my face, because in St. John's (the third windiest city in the world!) many trees are permanently slanted. Some have branches growing in only one direction on account of the strong winds.

This present age *is* a storm, but if we can withstand the trials, the difficulties, those dark, cold mornings, what will be our reward? The Kingdom of heaven! So, we cry a little, but we obey, and the eternal reward far surpasses the temporary trial. The sun comes up to warm us—even in St. John's!

✠TWO✠

Blessed Are Those Who Mourn
for they shall be comforted

Hope in Eternal Life

I HAD THE GREAT PLEASURE of meeting a wonderful woman while waiting in line with some friends to speak with an elder. Her name was Mrs. Katerina. While we waited, she entertained and inspired us with various stories, one of which was about her poor, sick, suffering sister who had since reposed.

Mrs. Katerina informed us that her sister, Elpida (which means "hope"), suffered from a horrible disease (the name of which I did not understand) that produced sores, in particular all over her back. They were open wounds, it seemed, and caused her a great deal of pain.

At some point during her illness, Elpida began having the persistent thought that she would not be saved. This thought so thoroughly wove itself into her way of thinking that it produced a great deal of suffering on its own account.

She would say to her sister, Mrs. Katerina, "Maybe, because I have suffered much, because of my illness, the Lord will grant me a small place in Paradise."

As if it wasn't enough that Elpida suffered such physical pain, she was suffering spiritually as well. It was clear from everyone's pained expressions that we all felt deep compassion for Mrs. Katerina's sister.

"I felt she should talk to someone about this thought of hers," Mrs. Katerina told us. "I took her to the monastery of St. John the Theologian in Souroti, where Elder Paisios of the Holy Mountain was staying for some time."

Mrs. Katerina and her sister arrived at the monastery and saw hundreds of people waiting for the opportunity to speak with the God-illumined elder. After some time had passed, a nun came out to the crowd and announced that the elder was not feeling well and that the rest of those waiting were permitted to see him but only to take his blessing, not to speak with him.

At this Mrs. Katerina threw up her hands before her. "Obedience!" she told us. "That was it, we weren't going to say a word. Obedience!" She drew her hand up to her mouth, making as though she were locking her lips with an invisible key.

"I just whispered to Elpida, 'We'll just take his blessing.' When our turn arrived, we went into the room where the elder was sitting. My sister went first. She bowed down, and the elder grasped her and drew her close. 'Elpida'—he called her by name despite not having been introduced to her—'you're going to *run* into Paradise!' Thus he answered her tormenting thought."

At this Elpida burst into tears and started joyfully exclaiming, "Glory to God! Thank you! Thank you, Geronda! Glory to God!"

Here at the end of her story, Mrs. Katerina wiped away tears—as did all her attentive listeners. Glory to God indeed!

Harnessing an Experience of Grace

THE FIRST TIME SR. EPHRAIMIA stepped out of Vespers at the monastery she later called home, she felt as though her heart would burst open with spiritual exaltation. The grace of the monastery was so strong it overwhelmed her. Hidden from the exiting crowd by the shadow of one of the buildings, she sat down.

Tears poured from her eyes just as the rushing water poured from the stone beast's mouth in the monastery's courtyard fountain. How much longing filled her heart then! It spilled over; she couldn't contain it any longer, having struggled to restrain herself during the service. She sat there alone and hidden from the world, giving thanks to God for having brought her home, to the one place in the world she felt she could live in Paradise. And just as she poured out tears, so she poured her heart out to the Lord. She confessed her longing, her unquenchable thirst to live for Him. As St. Silouan beautifully describes in the following quotation, this sister longingly cried out to God, thanking Him for His mercy and sweetness, asking for His governance, and begging Him never to forsake her. St. Silouan writes:

> My soul yearns after the Lord and I seek Him in tears. How could I do other than seek Thee, for Thou first didst seek and find me, and gavest me to delight in Thy Holy Spirit, and my soul fell to loving Thee. Thou seest, O Lord, my grief and my tears. . . . Hadst Thou not drawn me with Thy love, I could not seek Thee as I seek Thee now; but Thy spirit gave me to know Thee, and my soul rejoices

that Thou art my God and my Lord, and I yearn after Thee even to tears.[14]

Having all this described to me, I was left with a strong image—a paradisal image. It reminded me of a line I read in a Chronicles of Narnia book a long time ago, referring to the "New Narnia," to heaven: "I have come home at last! This is my real country! I belong here. This is the land I have been looking for all my life, though I never knew it till now."[15] This image of "coming home" is what we are always seeking, what the human heart truly longs for. It longs to dwell in God's country, to be at home, to rest, as St. Augustine so perfectly described it: "Our hearts are restless until they rest in Thee."

Sr. Ephraimia told me after this experience she would call to mind the strong feelings she felt that evening and use them for good. Like Adam standing opposite Paradise, naked and lamenting, "Woe is me!" for having been banished from his paradisal home, she kept the memory of this moment close to her heart: the memory of heartfelt longing, of perceiving her monastery as Paradise. Having been given a small taste of the sweetness of heaven, of spiritual joy and longing, she would think of all her friends and family, all those she loved and who loved her, dwelling joyfully in the monastery together as in Paradise for eternity, and her alone being shut out of the Kingdom (Matt. 23:13). She did this, she told me, as an inspiration to work harder at acquiring virtue and avoiding vice. By this she both exhibited her gratitude toward God for bringing her to the "place of her repentance" and also used the experience so that she would never forget how wonderful it felt to feel truly at home.

Balaam's Donkey:
Prayer as a Means to Divine Enlightenment

WHEN I WAS A CHILD, I had a really difficult time in school. I struggled so much, it's hard for me to even put into words how difficult this struggle was. By grade four, my parents decided to hold me back so I could repeat the year. It was at that point they also arranged for me to be assessed by a specialist. The results revealed I had a learning disability.

But even before this diagnosis, I remember my faithful Roman Catholic grandmother telling me, "Now Con, every morning when you wake up you should say, 'Holy Spirit, enlighten my mind,' just five simple words." With her encouragement, this phrase became my childhood prayer rule. Every day I prayed those words, before every test, every assignment, every time the teacher called on me to give an answer, these words were silently whispered in my heart.

And then one day my prayers were answered. I remember the exact moment the clouds darkening my thoughts began to part.

It happened at the end of grade eleven, while my mother was helping me study for my final exam in modern history. All of a sudden I could see what I was studying clearly; there was a cohesiveness of thought I had never known. Everything clicked, like puzzle pieces fitting together, and I understood what I was studying as a unified whole, not fragmented as my studies had always been. I truly felt as though my mind was enlightened—the darkness dispersed.

From then on I progressively became a better student. I went on to receive high academic distinction in my undergraduate studies, learn the Modern Greek language (and this after retaining virtually nothing from over ten years of French language studies), obtain my Master's degree in theology, become an author and subsequently a social worker. No one would have believed I would be able to accomplish so much, least of all myself.

When I read of St. John of Kronstadt's learning difficulties in his childhood, I feel as though I am reading about my own personal experience. St. John writes concerning himself:

> When the time was ripe for me to begin my schooling—I was brought to school, studies were unintelligible to me. . . . I was aware of and felt my helplessness, jealousy regarding the successes of my classmates—and began to ask for help and understanding from God. . . . and the Lord opened my mind: I was enlightened by Divine Light, reading and writing became clear to me, and I began to advance in my studies in proportion to my age and the educational aim.[16]

Although, like St. John's, my mind was enlightened, I also had to work very hard. Even after my prayers were answered, I struggled to do well in school, and especially to learn Modern Greek. In fact, my experience learning Greek was quite similar to my childhood experiences at school. I cried practically every day after Greek school. I prayed and begged God to enlighten me and asked others to pray as well. Eventually, through the prayers of many saints, I managed to become fluent in Greek, although it took one full year of studies before I could even begin to carry on an elementary conversation.

More than anything, this experience—along with the many like it I've gone through in life—has taught me the importance and power of prayer. Now, whenever I am in great need, I call out in prayer immediately, because I know from experience that God is a liberal giver.

The Scriptures say, "If any of you lacks wisdom, let him ask of God, who gives to all liberally and without reproach, and it will be given to him" (James 1:5). My own experience has confirmed this and has helped me become who I am today. I try hard not to take anything for granted, and especially the talents God has given me, because I know with my whole heart that I too can "do all things through Christ who strengthens me" (Phil. 4:13).

This is also why I've come to refer to myself (in jest) as Balaam's donkey. Balaam was an unwitting prophet described in the Book of Numbers in the Old Testament who was instructed by the Lord God not to do something, but he persisted. Although an angel blocked his passageway, preventing him from going where he was not blessed to go, Balaam was blind to the angel, while the donkey on which he was travelling was not. Finally, God allowed the donkey to speak to Balaam, and it told him of the angel blocking the way. Hearing the donkey speak enabled Balaam to see and understand that what he was doing was not God's will.

And so, when I am invited to speak at retreats and parishes, I qualify what I am about to say with the words, "Although what Balaam's donkey said was instructive, it was, nevertheless, spoken by an ass." While I say this with a smile and a laugh, the image is a valid one.

On my own account I couldn't think properly, let alone obtain university degrees and write books, and neither could Balaam's donkey speak except when the Lord willed it. Just as the Lord allowed Balaam's donkey to speak in order to instruct Balaam, so I write books. I am not worthy to instruct, but because I have had the privilege of experiencing Orthodoxy throughout the world, meeting many struggling Christians and encountering a few living

— 49 —

saints, I simply try to recount what I was blessed to see and hear.

"Without Me you can do nothing," Christ tells us. But with Him, even an ass can speak and instruct. All we have to do is ask, through prayer, and miracles happen. I am an example of a person who might not have amounted to much in the way of knowledge if it hadn't been for the simple prayer I was taught to say from childhood. And because the Lord heard my prayer, I have gone on not only to learn many things, but to teach as well (though it is one thing to teach and quite another to put those teachings into practice). But truly, the Lord has allowed me to "become rich in wisdom," as an abbess once encouraged me to do.

May the Lord continue to enlighten me, because surely without Him I am nothing.

On the Feast of St. Spyridon

ONLY A HANDFUL OF PEOPLE went to the monastery's dining hall for coffee after the Divine Liturgy for the feast of St. Spyridon. My husband, Fr. John—a deacon at that time—had served that morning in one of the monastery's small chapels.

As was the custom at the monastery, the priest sat in the front of the room next to the abbess (as did visiting clergy and monastics). We laypeople gathered round, with our small Greek coffee cups nestled in our palms, to hear what spiritual word he might share with us that day. Since he spoke only briefly, a woman asked for his blessing to share a miracle St. Spyridon had performed for her and her family on his feast day some years back.

"My husband and I were driving somewhere on icy country roads when our car went out of control, spun around, and flipped a few times, finally landing on its roof in the adjacent field," she began.

"I always wore my seat belt—always. But this particular night, neither I nor our two-year-old was buckled in, and I was pregnant. When the car finally stopped, I remember reaching for the door handle, trying to open the door. It didn't occur to me that the car had landed on its roof. I had just started going back to church, so I knew I ought to start praying. We managed to get out of the car, and my husband—his face full of cuts—walked to the road and tried to flag down a car. Someone eventually stopped and we went to the hospital," she went on, growing more emotional.

"I was afraid for the baby I was carrying, but when we spoke with the doctor, he told me, 'It's a good thing you weren't wearing a seatbelt when the car crashed, because you would have lost the baby,' he told me.

"No one was seriously injured. The worst was that my hand was broken. And once I found out whose feast day it was, I attributed the miracle to St. Spyridon. And the miracle wasn't only that we survived, but that there was no other car on the road when our car went out of control, that we managed to flag someone down, I didn't lose the baby, and everyone was okay. Since then I have a great devotion to the saint," she said, wiping tears away.

"Forgive me for sharing something about myself, for talking about myself," she said. "But I speak about the miracle in order to glorify God."

"No, no, it is good for you to talk about the miracle the saint performed," the priest reassured her.

St. Spyridon is a remarkable saint, born at the end of the third century in Cyprus. Although initially married, after the death of his wife he became a bishop. He was truly all things to all people: a philosopher, a theologian, a miracle-worker, a gracious host, a defender of the Faith, a husband to widows and father to orphans. To the dead he restored life; to the spiritually deluded he taught the truth of our Faith; to strangers he was a kind friend. And even to us in our days he demonstrates the boldness he has before God. It was kind of the woman visiting the monastery to share his miracle with us so that we might be reminded that to the righteous God gives power to become the sons of God (John 1:12).

> You were a champion of the First Council and a wonderworker, O God-bearing Father Spyridon. You spoke to one dead in the grave, and changed a serpent to gold; and while you were chanting the holy prayers, the angels were serving with you. Glory to Him who has glorified you; glory to Him who has crowned you; glory to Him who works healing for all through you. (Troparion of the Saint)

Panagia Malevi

AT THE HOLY MONASTERY of Panagia Malevi there is an icon— the icon the monastery is named after—which depicts the Dormition of the Theotokos. It is believed to be one of the seventy icons St. Luke the Evangelist painted. Since 1362 it has had a silver casing over it, revealing only the faces of the figures, which have become considerably darkened with age now.

In 717 a monastery was built on the site that is now the Holy Monastery of Panagia Malevi, but only ruins remained by the time monks from the Holy Mountain came to re-establish the monastery in 1116. They brought the aforementioned icon with them. Although always greatly revered, this icon became an even greater source of spiritual joy when in 1964 it began giving off a strong, unearthly aroma during Great Lent, and streaming myrrh on the fifth Friday in Great Lent during the service of Salutations to the Theotokos.

Despite examinations by police officers and even chemists, this miracle could not be explained, and unending crowds of visitors came to the monastery to venerate the icon and receive cotton soaked in the myrrh that ran from it. To my knowledge, the icon has not ceased to stream myrrh and work miracles of healing since that time.

Living in Greece for nearly six years, I visited many places and venerated many icons, but I regret that I never had the opportunity to venerate the holy icon of Panagia Malevi. And yet, I had a relationship with this icon from the beginning of my days as a catechumen.

I was given a medallion of the icon by a Greek-Canadian woman the first time I visited an Orthodox monastery in the States. I wore it every day until I received my baptismal cross. Then, when I lived in Seoul, a parishioner who faithfully attended church at St. Nicholas Orthodox Cathedral gave me a small sewn-up pouch that contained cotton soaked in the myrrh of the icon.

And finally, before I moved back to Canada from Greece, a presvytera gave me a copy of the miracle-working icon of Panagia Malevi. This same presvytera had herself experienced a great miracle by the grace of the Mother of God through this holy image. Her daughters, who are nuns, told me the story.

We were washing dishes in the monastery's kitchen when somehow we turned to talking about miracles of healing. "You know, Constantina, when our family lived in Athens, something happened to our mother's back, and she couldn't stand upright," Sr. Raphaela began. "It got to the point where she couldn't walk. Our father was so worried! At that time there were seven of us children—Marina wasn't born yet—and our mother couldn't even take care of us. And so, one day our father told us, 'We can't go on with your mother like this.'

"It was time for us to seek help from God, so he decided to take us all to pray for healing in front of the miracle-working icon of Panagia Malevi. The only thing is, we were such a large family, and we didn't have a car. Our father hailed a taxi, and before the taxi-driver could refuse, we all jumped in," she said with a laugh.

"Seven of us kids and our mother were all squished into the back—there were arms and legs everywhere," her sister interjected, giggling.

"And our father just yelled from the front passenger seat, 'Sir, step on it for Malevi!'"

"Do you remember, Paul's foot was sticking out between the two seats and the driver said, 'Young man, can you move your foot a little please?'" Sr. Raphaela asked her sister with a laugh.

"Someone else had their foot next to the driver's neck, and he couldn't start going until we got readjusted!" the other sister joyfully added.

"And Dad kept saying, 'Step on it! Step on it!'"

We were all laughing now.

"When we finally arrived at the monastery we all came out of the taxi like clowns spilling out of a clown car. We went into the church, and our father told us, 'Everyone get down on your knees and beg Panagia to heal your mother!'

"So there we were, seven young children sprawled out on the church floor crying and praying," they continued, laughing. "But

Panagia worked her miracle! Our mother's back improved, and she was able to walk and take care of us all just as she always had."

To Be "of God"

WHEN ON PILGRIMAGE with our Byzantine chanting class, some of the girls would bring along their guitars so we could sing together. One of the songs they taught me was about becoming "of God": what it means to live for Christ and be blessed by Him. The melody is simple, and the message is heartfelt. Here is an English translation:

> For you to be of God is a martyrdom;
> For you to be of God is joy;
> For you to be of God is a mystery;
> For you to be of God is everything.
>
> For you to be of God is a Cross;
> For you to be of God is a path to Light;
> For you to be of God is Resurrection;
> If you are of God, you live without asking "why."
>
> For you to be of God is a wondrous foolishness;
> For you to be of God is a deliberate choice;
> For you to be of God is heavenly anticipation;
> May you be of God, and may it be enough.
>
> For you to be of God is wonderful;
> It costs much, but it is worth the taste.

Whenever I sing this simple little song, I'm reminded of something an abbess once preached concerning trials. She was speaking in reference to the three youths from the Old Testament who refused to worship the pagan idols and thus were put in a fiery furnace by King Melchizedek:

"God was able to interfere so that the three youths would not enter the furnace, and would that not have been a miracle? But there! He let them fall into the forty-some–foot furnace. This makes an impression on me. Not that God didn't act in time to keep them from falling in, but we fall so that we become of God. To face our struggle, to convince God that we are His even while in the furnace, even while in the lion's den. See, it doesn't say, 'in the fountain of flames they were not burnt.' It could have, but it doesn't say, 'in the fountain of flames they were not burnt,' but rather, 'they rejoiced in the fountain of flames as though in the waters of rest.'

"The great miracle is that [even in the midst of] trials we offer a fountain of rejoicing, of joy, of elation. It is not a great miracle to be thrown to the lions and for them not to eat you. It is, of course, a miracle, but a great miracle is for the lions to become sheep! There-fore, for you to be of God is wonderful, even if it is a martyrdom!"

May the abbess's holy words and the message of the little folk song penetrate our hearts so that we not only contemplate them but put them into action: that we may learn to rejoice even in the midst of a furnace of temptation.

The Subway-Station Publican

WE STEPPED OFF THE SUBWAY and onto the multicolored tile floor of the station. As we were swept along with the surging crowd, my eyes fell on a beggar. To see a beggar in a subway station was not strange in Seoul, South Korea, but to see a beggar lying prostrate, his face to the ground, was.

I don't definitively remember us giving him change; I only remember his hands, cupped and poking out in front of his head. He didn't even raise his eyes to those passing by. He simply and humbly begged.

A sight such as that would most likely have stayed with me in any case, but on that day it did all the more because of what day it was. We had just come from the Korean Orthodox Church, St. Nicholas, having celebrated the Sunday of the Publican and the Pharisee. When we saw the man lying prostrate on the ground, our minds were immediately drawn toward the icon of the publican: prostrate, humble, not daring even to raise his eyes as he supplicated for mercy. Here in front of us was such a one. What an example of humility right before our very eyes.

We walked up the staircase leading to a different subway line, discussing among ourselves the sheer coincidence that we would see such a beggar on the Sunday of the Publican and the Pharisee.

Some eighty days later, we again encountered our subway-station publican. It was Pentecost Sunday, and we were again transferring to the next line. This time I distinctly remember giving him change. First my brother, then my sister-in-law put money into his cupped hands. I reached into my pocket and saw that I only had 300 *won* (about 30 cents). I cringed that that was all I had, but still I reached down and put the nearly useless amount of money into the beggar's hand. To my shock, he grabbed my hand, pulled it close to his lowered head, and kissed it. A kiss from a lowly beggar: perhaps not something most would consider a great gift—or so it might seem to one not on the receiving end of such a gift. I pulled my hand back in surprise.

He raised his eyes and I saw he was crying. Tears began to well up in my own eyes.

Some man who misunderstood the situation, thinking I was distressed by this beggar, began to come toward us. I made some gesture to show him everything was all right, and I turned to go.

The feeling that energized in me the moment the dear beggar kissed my hand is something very difficult to express. It is humbling to have one's hand kissed, and even more so considering all I gave to the poor beggar was a mere 30 cents. But that is life in Christ: all we have to offer God is a few cents, and He gives us back one hundredfold.

I never saw our friend again, but I have never forgotten him. Every Sunday of the Publican and the Pharisee, he is brought to mind, and I reflect on how much his humble gesture, his humble kiss, made me feel like I had received the blessing of a great saint. Truly, angels are disguised in many forms, and encounters with seemingly insignificant people can be as special as those with angels.

The Light of Life

OUR DEAR FRIEND from Thessaloniki was a smoker for many years. Desperately wanting to break this bad habit, she prayed a great deal for God to deliver her from this strong passion. She was especially grieved that she could not even go without smoking before church on Sunday mornings. This was a cause of great sorrow for her as she felt terrible guilt receiving and eating the blessed bread (antidoron) after smoking a cigarette, since—as she herself described—it was like breaking the fast we keep before partaking of blessed bread at the end of Divine Liturgy.

Thus, she struggled with this passion, praying and supplicating various saints to intercede that God would grant her the strength to overcome this habit. At long last her prayers were answered while she was on a pilgrimage to the site of Ss. Raphael, Nicholas, and Irene's martyrdom, on the island of Mytilene (also known as Lesvos).

Although these holy saints of God were brutally tortured and killed in the fifteenth century, the location of their relics and the full story of their martyrdom was not revealed until recent years. For some five hundred years, locals would make a pilgrimage to the site of the Holy Monastery of the Nativity, where St. Raphael lived with his disciple St. Nicholas and their brotherhood. However, no one remembered the details of their martyrdom, only that the monks had at one time been kidnapped and tortured by invading Turks.

In the 1960s a faithful man decided to build a church on this site, the construction of which led to the holy remains of three martyrs being discovered. At last the long-forgotten story of their Christian heroism was revealed. In the spring of 1463, Turks invaded the monastery and tortured the monks from Holy Thursday until Bright Tuesday. Even the village mayor and his family, who had come to warn the monks, were martyred. The mayor's daughter, a twelve-year-old girl, was among them and was burned in front of her own parents in an earthen vessel. The vessel is still preserved today as a remembrance that she, like a pure lamb, became a living sacrifice, a whole burnt offering, and is now glorified in the heavens for all eternity as Saint Irene.

This friend of ours who struggled with her smoking habit had gone with her nephew on a pilgrimage to the monastery. They stayed the night in the guest house, and early the next morning, while the stars and moon still dimly lit the sky, she and her nephew exited the monastery so she could have her morning cigarette before the divine services began.

While they stood looking toward the monastery, they both saw a pillar of light reaching up from the ground to the sky, bright, beautiful, and inexplicable. A miracle was unfolding before their very eyes. The grace and glory God accords to those who love Him was being displayed on the very site on which Christian bodies were put to death, but their souls received the light of life. Seeing this incredible miracle was enough to enable our friend to quit her smoking habit and preserve a special place in her heart for the holy martyrs Raphael, Nicholas, and Irene.

May this simple story remind us that "The LORD *is* near to those who have a broken heart, / And saves such as have a contrite spirit" (Ps. 33/34:18). There is no bad habit too strong for Him to deliver us from. May we have the blessing of the holy martyrs, Ss. Raphael, Nicholas, Irene, and those who perished with them!

Our Family Saint: St. John Maximovitch

"PRAY TO ST. JOHN of San Francisco for your husband. St. John was a very holy man," the priestmonk told me as I turned the door handle to leave the room, having finished our private conversation.

"Okay," I said, shrugging, not fully realizing just how holy St. John was.

I had wanted to become Orthodox for a couple of months at that point but was wary of converting while my husband was a candidate for ordination in the Anglican church. Thankfully, he had agreed to accompany me to a monastery in America for Pascha, but my struggles with remaining Anglican were the source of much tension in our sixth-month-long marriage.

I vividly remember explaining to my husband why I thought it was best for him to wait to be ordained: I felt I was not mature enough to be a priest's wife. And although I truly didn't feel mature enough at that stage in my life (I was only twenty-two years old), the real reason I wanted him to wait was that I secretly wanted us to convert to Orthodoxy together. John humbly put aside his four-year-long desire to be ordained and agreed to wait for me to be "ready." I too waited. I waited for him to become Orthodox. I prayed and kept my mouth closed to the best of my ability.

On our way from the monastery to our home in the Province of New Brunswick, we were asked if we would be willing to take a later flight in exchange for a flight voucher. We had a long layover at our next stop, so we didn't mind sticking around the airport a bit longer. I thought nothing of the voucher, since we would be moving to South Korea to teach English in a few months, and I didn't expect to fly anywhere in North America in the meantime.

Once we arrived home, I started reading the biography of St. John of Shanghai and San Francisco. Lying in bed one night, I read a story about a nurse who started to go blind and began faithfully visiting St. John's tomb and praying to him. One evening, filled with despair, she prayed fervently and opened her Bible at random to the Gospel passage about Christ healing the blind man, instructing him to wash his eyes with water from the pool of Siloam. The nurse felt that if only she could put some water from the pool of Siloam on her eyes, she'd be healed. The next day, while she was visiting St.

John's tomb, an unknown woman approached her and said she had just returned from Jerusalem and brought with her a small bottle of water from the pool of Siloam. The nurse put the water in her eyes while standing over St. John's tomb and was healed. The water was brought to her through St. John's intercession.

Having finished reading the story, I suddenly had this strong feeling that if only I could visit St. John in San Francisco, my John would become Orthodox. Then I remembered the flight voucher we had received a few months before. I was doubtful there would be any available flights to California, since the voucher seemed quite limited despite its claim of available flights "anywhere in America." I wanted to get out of bed and check online for a ticket right then, but I made myself practice a little self-control and wait until morning.

To my surprise, the next morning I found an available flight to San Francisco that the voucher covered. We were about three weeks away from moving to South Korea, so I knew I needed to act fast. I checked the dates for that coming weekend, and found I would arrive on July 2. I was flabbergasted—this was the saint's own feast day. I felt, without a doubt, that was the work of the saint. I couldn't believe it: truly I was being shown just what a wonderworker this holy man was!

I arrived in San Francisco and spent as much time as possible— whenever the doors were open—at the new cathedral of Our Lady, Joy of All Who Sorrow, where the saint's incorrupt relics are housed. I prayed and lit candles, I lovingly kissed the saint's relics, and I simply stood and looked on him with a great deal of awe and admiration. I felt reassured that through the prayers of this great saint, my husband's heart would be softened, and his mind would be enlightened to embrace Holy Orthodoxy.

On my last visit to the cathedral, I met a wonderful priestmonk, Fr. James, and even greater blessings unfolded. He was hosting a Greek family from Montreal, and he invited me to accompany them to the old cathedral (the church St. John served in). In the old cathedral he served a *moleben* with the Greek family and me in attendance, after which he prayed over us individually with St. John's hierarchical mantle. Even though my trip thus far had been more than enough to convince me of how holy and great a wonderworker St. John is, yet more blessings were to come.

I was taken to St. Tikhon's orphanage, where I was able to see St. John's cell, sit in the chair he slept in each night, and venerate the holy icons in his chapel. I was overwhelmed with all the blessings St. John sent me. How could I doubt for a second that my husband would be completely transformed through this saint's prayers?

Of course, as it is with those of us of little faith, in the weeks and months that followed I was impatient and discouraged that my husband didn't seem changed. I didn't understand that when we have timelines and expectations of others, we become blind to the spiritual transformation of the person taking place right before our eyes.

I prayed frequently to St. John—the paper on which I had printed his akathist hymn quickly became worn around the edges, and I'm sure showed faint traces of despairing teardrops. To this day I have kept that copy of his akathist, and when I look at it I remember all the times I begged St. John to help my husband. Truly he was a holy man, for although it took John longer to come around than I wanted, the day I saw him using a prayer rope as we walked home from work in Seoul was the day I realized St. John's prayers had fully penetrated his heart. I was ashamed I had ever doubted the saint, that great wonderworker and superb servant of Christ.

I wish I could say my "unbelieving" husband was sanctified by his "believing" wife, but in truth my husband was sanctified by the prayers of one who became sanctified even in our latter times, even while living in contemporary America. And that is how St. John Maximovitch became, or rather offered himself as, our family saint. May we have his blessing!

The Holy Monastery of St. George

SITTING ON THE COUCHES lining the walls in the guest dining hall, we all listened attentively to the woman explaining how she and her mother came to be regular visitors at the monastery. There were not many of us there that day—a weekday Liturgy—but those who had come welcomed the hot coffee and homemade cheese pitas that awaited us in the trapeza.

As we enjoyed the monastery's hospitality, conversation about the intercessions of the saints came up, and a woman decided to share her own experience. She began by saying that although she did not live far from the monastery, she had never heard of it until the incident she spoke of. Some years before, she told us, her mother had been suffering from depression and was on about twenty different medications for her various problems. No one in the family was particularly faithful, so it came as a surprise when this woman had a dream one night that told her to take her mother to visit the Monastery of St. George. Since neither she nor her mother knew of a monastery named for St. George, they were at a loss where to go. Time passed, and while the woman was chatting with a friend, the friend mentioned she had recently visited the Monastery of St. George.

Learning of the monastery, the woman and her mother set out to light some candles. They arrived, took a tour around the monastery, perused the book store, and returned home. That evening, the mother suddenly felt as though all the turmoil she had within her, her depression, her illness, all felt as though it were being drawn out of her through her head. "Like a vacuum was sucking out the illness," the daughter described it to us as her mother nodded in agreement. After that experience, her depression left her, and subsequently, so did the other ailments she had once required medicine to treat. The family returned to the Church and became frequent visitors to the Holy Monastery of St. George.

"And the greater miracle is that we returned to the Church and became faithful," the daughter finished.

Giving the Saints Something to Do

WHEN I NEEDED A BREAK from my studies during the years we lived in Thessaloniki, I would walk down to the sea. There is a boardwalk that spans the length of the city's harbor where I liked to walk and look out at the bluish-green water, admire the sailboats, and sometimes—on a very clear day—even catch a glimpse of Mt. Olympus on the other side of the bay.

The massive gold dome of the church of Ss. Cyril and Methodios— located one street up from the water—always enhanced the beauty of my walk. One October evening, I decided to stop by the church to attend Vespers. Every parish in Thessaloniki offered the Vespers service every evening.

Arriving at the church, I was surprised by the decorative streamers and the large crowd gathered outside. I found out the church had a small side chapel in honor of Ss. Cyprian and Justina, and they were doing the festal Vespers service for the patrons of the chapel, whose feast was the following day (October 2).

Coincidentally, I had been praying to St. Cyprian for about a month or so for a close friend who was suffering great mental and spiritual temptations. I was quite moved to find out not only was there a chapel to him a mere ten-minute walk from my apartment, but I happened to discover his chapel on the evening before his feast. Of course, I say "coincidentally," but we know there are no coincidences—only providential encounters.

During Vespers, I prayed for this friend of mine and watched with pain of heart as a woman—clearly tormented in body and soul—repetitively venerated the same icons in a peculiar manner for about five minutes. I don't believe it was by chance that she was also at the church for the Vespers service of St. Cyprian.

You see, St. Cyprian is a great intercessor for those who suffer from demonic temptation and influence, since he was once himself under severe demonic influence. He was a renowned sorcerer before his conversion to Christianity. Regarding his past, he says in his own words:

> I have seen the prince of darkness himself, for I propitiated him by sacrifices. I greeted him and spoke with him and his ancients; he liked me, praised my understanding, and before everyone said: "Here is a new Jambres, always ready for obedience and worthy of communion with us!" And he promised to make me a prince after my departure from the body, and for the course of [my] earthly

life to help me in everything. And he gave me a legion of demons to serve me.[17]

It was through the prayers, nobility, and virtue of the young maiden Justina that Cyprian was enlightened and renounced his dealings with evil spirits, later becoming as great a Christian as he had previously been a servant of the devil. He went on to become a bishop and eventually was put to death by the local governor, together with St. Justina, for their faith in Christ.

Having combated the evil one in his own life, he continues to combat him after death on behalf of all who cry to him for help. He is not the only saint who is a special intercessor for those suffering torments in body and soul. St. Arsenios the Cappadocian (who baptized St. Paisios of the Holy Mountain when he was an infant) is another mighty intercessor in such circumstances.

The holy relics of St. Arsenios are located at the Holy Monastery of St. John the Theologian in Souroti, just outside Thessaloniki. We used to visit this monastery not only to venerate the saint's relics, but to venerate the holy grave of Elder Paisios. Although the elder lived on the Holy Mountain, he died and was buried in the world: a great blessing for those of us who cannot visit Mount Athos!

Once when my mother was visiting us in Greece, we took her to St. John's Monastery for Vespers, held in the church dedicated to St. Arsenios. The church was overflowing with people, mostly youth, many of whom exhibited signs of psychiatric illness. They had come on buses to venerate the holy relics of St. Arsenios and the grave of Elder Paisios. I have no doubt they received the comfort they were seeking.

There are so many saints waiting to intercede on our behalf for the numerous things that cause pain and suffering, torment and worry, those things that cast shadows over our lives and souls and make us think the darkness will never depart. All we have to do is cry out; they are waiting for us to do so. St. Nektarios of Pentapolis once said (after his repose), "It's as if we saints are in retirement. . . . The people don't pray to us, don't entreat us, don't ask us for anything, don't give us any handiwork to do. They don't give us the opportunity to pray to God for them."

Ss. Cyprian, Arsenios, and Nektarios are just three of a whole host of saints waiting to help us.

A Miracle of St. John the Russian

WHILE STAYING AT A MONASTERY one weekend, I had the blessing of bunking with Sr. Xenia's mother, a presvytera. I had heard so much about her, I was very excited to have the pleasure of meeting her in person. When we weren't helping the sisters with work, praying in the church, or sitting in the courtyard for an evening chat with the abbess under the star-filled sky, I was listening to her stories in the guesthouse.

One such story occurred in a hospital in Athens not long before we met at the monastery. "The priest of St. John the Russian church on Evia noticed a man wearing pajamas venerating the relics, and so he approached him and asked if he needed help," Presvytera began.

"'I've just come from the hospital, having suffered from paralysis for the last twenty years,' the man told the priest and proceeded to tell him the whole story. The man had spent many years in the hospital, for he was, as I said, paralyzed. His wife would often visit and sometimes stay the night. One night she awoke to see a young man whom she took to be a doctor treating her husband. The next day, little by little, her husband began to move until he was able to walk completely on his own.

"News of this great miracle spread quickly. Many doctors came to witness this miracle for themselves. The man's wife, wanting to thank the doctor who treated her husband, asked for him and described what he looked like. No one, however, could understand who she was talking about. There was no such doctor who worked at that hospital. One doctor, however, told her the description she gave sounded an awful lot like St. John the Russian. Understanding that what had occurred to the paralyzed man was not a medical miracle but a spiritual one, he urged them to go immediately to his church in Evia, the island on which the holy incorrupt relics of St. John the Russian are housed."

St. John the Russian, my dear reader, is a beloved saint of the seventeenth century. He was originally from Southern Russia and was blessed to have pious Orthodox parents. In 1711 he took part in a battle against the Turks, and he and many Russian soldiers were captured in the city of Procopion (near Caesarea) in Asia Minor. Wanting to coerce the Christians into denouncing their faith, the Turks inflicted great tortures on the soldiers; many died a martyr's death.

St. John, neither renouncing his faith nor succumbing to bodily torture, was sent to work in a stable of a Turkish *agha* (master). Calling to mind the lowly cave in which God Almighty was born in Bethlehem, the young man rejoiced in this humble abode. St. John exhibited such virtue and steadfastness that the agha and his wife gradually grew to love their meek and humble slave. When not laboring for his master, St. John labored for the Master of all with prayer and good works, being sure to attend Divine Liturgy every week to commune of the immaculate Body and Blood of our Lord. Over time his agha grew very rich and had no qualms about acknowledging it was on account of his good and faithful slave that he gained such fortunes. The agha even offered the saint better living quarters, but the saint refused, choosing instead his ascetical lifestyle in the stable.

At some point the agha traveled to Mecca, a sacred city for Muslims. While he was on pilgrimage, his wife was at home in Asia Minor, serving her husband's favorite dish to visiting guests.

"I'm sure my husband would love to eat this right now," she said aloud in earshot of St. John, who was serving the table.

Taking heed of his mistress's words, the saint said, "I will take it to him." Those in attendance laughed at the saint's seemingly foolish claim, but the mistress told the cook to give St. John a plate of the pilaf, thinking he would give it to some poor Christian family, as was his custom. But in fact, after the saint prayed in secret, the plate appeared full of hot pilaf in the room in which the agha was staying in Mecca. If there was any room for doubt, the plate even had his name on it (as did all the dishes in his home). The agha brought it home with him on his return, and the whole house marveled at the miracle. The saint's love knew no bounds!

At the age of forty, St. John became ill, and knowing his end was approaching, he called for a priest, who brought him Holy Communion. Receiving the immaculate Mysteries, the saint reposed in peace. Just a few years later, many witnessed a light appearing on his tomb. The saint appeared to his spiritual father and told him it was the will of God to exhume his relics, since they were incorrupt.

In 1924, during the Exchange of Populations between Turkey and Greece, the holy relics of the saint were transported to the island of Evia, along with many faithful from Procopion, to the city of New Procopion. A church was built in the saint's honor, and it was to this church the previously paralyzed man had come, offering thanks for the miracle the saint had worked.

"That is why the priest saw the man standing in his pajamas, because they wasted no time in coming to offer thanks to God for the saint's intercession," Presvytera finished the story.

You see, dear reader, how great God is? We suffer much in this life, but there is no need for us to mourn as one without hope, as the Apostle Paul says. Whether in this life (as in the case of the paralytic) or in the next (as in the case of St. John the Russian), temporal pain, trial, and tribulation pass away, but not before God brings good out of evil: offering eternal and heavenly comfort to those who mourn.

The Good Shepherd

A COMMON COMPLAINT in our times is that God is not a God of love, which is supposedly illustrated by the many hardships, sorrows, sicknesses, and even death He permits. In truth, God, who loves mankind, who sacrificed Himself for our sake and was crucified with His arms wide open—an image of His love—does all He can to draw all men unto Himself (John 12:32). While our human vision is limited and cannot always perceive the reason God sends such hardships and sorrows, He does so to guide and encourage us to follow the correct path in this life. I heard the following story and its spiritually insightful interpretation in a homily by Fr. Theodore Zisis (an archpriest and well-known Greek patristic scholar). It is a perfect example of the great measures God goes to, out of love, to save the souls of His servants.

There was a couple who loved their only daughter very much. Their one thought and their one care was directed toward their daughter, but not in the right way—not in order to save her soul. Their love was exaggerated, and their expression of this exaggerated love was to make sure she had every temporal good: she was always well-dressed, went to the best schools, and was never refused anything she wanted. However, the couple was less concerned about her spiritual well-being. At some point the young girl became sick and died, and a priest was called to the house to pray the Trisagion service for the soul of the departed child.

The parents, however, in a state of great grief and anger, protested and asked, "What kind of God of love is this, the One who took the object of our love away from us? He is not a God of love, but a harsh God!" The priest, who was wise and discerning and understood that their words were a result of their great grief, did not respond but simply said he would speak a few words at their daughter's funeral.

At the funeral the priest told a story, a great parable. There was a good shepherd who always offered his sheep the best food inside the sheep pen. However, there was one undisciplined sheep who disregarded the shepherd and the safety of the flock. She would wander with her lamb outside the sheep pen, where they were in want of food and in danger of being eaten by a wolf. What was the shepherd to do? He needed to protect them from these evils. And so, in order to encourage the sheep to enter into the sheepfold, he took the ewe's beloved lamb and tethered her in the middle of the flock so that the ewe, wanting to be near her lamb, would follow the flock into the sheep pen.

Christ, who is the Good Shepherd, has built a sheep pen for us and offers us the necessary spiritual food. But many of us do not want to enter the sheep pen nor eat of the clean, nourishing food Christ has prepared for us, and so we wander outside the pen. And the wolf, who is the devil, comes to eat us. Out of His great love and care for us, Christ, wanting us to enter into the sheep pen, which is the Kingdom of God, took the child so that the parents, desiring to be with their child in Paradise, would follow after the Good Shepherd and enter into the safety of the Church.

Blessed Contemporary Co-Strugglers

ONE SUMMER DAY, while my godmother was visiting us in Greece, she invited me to come along with her to meet Elena and Dimitra, two friends she knew from her days studying at Aristotle University. Elena lived a daily martyrdom, for not only did she have a congenital disease that caused her to be born without fully formed legs, she was abandoned at birth. Thus, she had grown up in an orphanage. She was a lovely, peaceful person. Dimitra was similarly endowed with great virtues. From the time she met Elena at university, she took it upon herself to take care of her friend, and so they lived together, like an eldress and a cell attendant, united in love and Christian struggle.

As time passed, Elena's health continued to deteriorate. She had nerve and lung problems, a weak immune system, constant infections, and near the end of her life, cancer. But despite all her pain and suffering, she would write and speak with others as only the spiritually experienced and wise know how, communicating grace along with her instructive words. Being in their presence was a great blessing. While my godmother massaged Elena's sore arms, she translated Elena's instructive stories for me, as my Greek was very limited at that time.

Hearing of my struggles to learn Greek, Elena had her co-struggler and sister in Christ, Dimitra, open the little reliquaries they had been given over the years so I could venerate the holy relics of numerous saints. I remember Elena told me to bless my head with the relics of St. Nektarios of Pentapolis so that I might be enlightened to learn Greek. Then it was Dimitra's turn to instruct me in a more practical way. While she was showing me the beautiful garden she had grown on their small balcony, she gave me a Greek language lesson. She began picking up random objects, in particular small stuffed animals she had collected. She would tell me their Greek names and prompt me to repeat after her. She was as sweet and kind as Elena was patient and wise.

They lived this mutually sacrificial life—one on account of great illness and the other on account of selfless care-giving—for some thirty years or so, until Elena was diagnosed with cancer. Seeing that the end might not be far away, they decided to move to a monastery, where Elena lived as a tonsured great-schema nun. She reposed at the age of fifty-five on January 26, the feast of Ss. Xenophon, Maria, and their children, Arcadius and John (all of whom became monastics after suffering a great deal of hardship).

Elena was tonsured with the apt name Philareti (which means "lover of virtue"). A lover of virtue is exactly what she was, and not only a lover but a possessor of virtue: of patience, forbearance, fortitude, and endurance. Having lived an angelic life, she is now accounted blessed to live a life amidst the angels, as she has been enrolled in their ranks as a nun of the angelic schema. Sister Philareti, pray to God for us!

No Distance in the Spiritual Life

WHEN THE DAY FINALLY ARRIVED to say goodbye to my beloved nuns in Greece, I was surprisingly peaceful. The truth is when you are moving, especially internationally, there are so many things occupying your mind that you don't feel the full impact of the sorrow until you have settled down. Only then the reality hits you that an entire ocean separates you from those you not only love and cherish but look up to and have relied on for your own spiritual growth.

We visited the monastery for the last time, venerated the beautiful icons in the temple, and ate a wonderful meal prepared by the sisters. As we sat together, Gerontissa Philareti told me, "We won't cry, Constantina. There is no need to be upset," she said with a look that conveyed her own sober sadness. "There is no distance in the spiritual life. We part now with the hope that, through the prayers of the elder, we will be together in Paradise."

I smiled, though tears were beginning to wet my cheeks. "Amen," I said. "May it be blessed."

"By means of love you will teach the people to love God, to love His Holy Mother," Gerontissa said as we stepped out of the chapel.

At this point the sisters had all gone to their cells for the afternoon siesta. Only three sisters were there to see us off.

"You know, if you find yourself missing us, there is a great book you can read about women's monasteries. I think it's called *The Scent of Holiness*," Sr. Nektaria teased me.

I later learned that the sisters didn't realize we were leaving before Vespers. After their afternoon break, they had all come out to the gate to say goodbye only to realize we had already gone. But it was for the best that we did not really say goodbye. Goodbyes are final. Goodbyes emphasize impending separation. I tried to take Gerontissa's words to heart: There is no distance in the spiritual life, and so there was no need to say goodbye, because I must struggle to stay spiritually connected with the sisters through prayer.

I found the most difficult part of my last visit to be the drive back through the mountains. Each bend in the road seemed to bring with it a different memory, a lesson learned. Now the tears ran freely.

That sorrow was just a foretaste of all the times my heart would ache for my sisters, all the tears I would shed—especially when I first moved to Newfoundland. Even now I still deeply miss the monasteries and the sisters' quiet, compunctionate services chanted in the night, in an oil-lamp-lit, icon-covered nave. Grief and sorrow are a reality, a result of the Fall. But joy and hope are also a reality, a result of Christ's Resurrection and Ascension into heaven.

"Therefore you now have sorrow; but I will see you again and your heart will rejoice, and your joy no one will take from you" (John 16:22), Christ told His disciples when it came time for Him to depart this world. I cling to the same hope, that through the prayers of holy ones, I will be with the sisters again, with Gerontissa, in Paradise. Amen, so be it!

✠ THREE ✠

Blessed Are the Meek
for they shall inherit the earth

Do You Want to Meet a Holy Elder?

WHILE WALKING ALONG a windy path through the brush on Mount Athos, our dear friend, a Romanian priestmonk, asked the small band of pilgrims, "Do you want to meet a holy elder?"

What does one respond to that if not, "Of course!"?

Thus, they made their way to Panagouda to request a word from the holy, clairvoyant Elder Gabriel, a disciple of the newly canonized St. Paisios the Athonite, who reposed in 1995 and whose hermitage was also in Panagouda.

It wasn't long before the pilgrims arrived at the skete. Fr. G., our dear Romanian friend who had just been ordained a priest, entered the vestibule first. Fr. John, who had recently been ordained a deacon, entered next, and my brother Matthew and our Nova Scotian friend Matthew (both still laymen at that time) followed after them.

The petite elder opened the door. His white hair was disheveled, and the button at the collar of his cassock was unfastened. He invited the men in, and once they were all seated, he lay back on his bed. Picking up a large tome of the *Minge* (patristic writings), he lay flat on his bed and held the book above his face, beginning to "read" aloud. He talked about the great virtue of humility, all the while tracing his pencil along the text as if reading from the Fathers. No one was fooled by this attempt to hide his virtue: all quickly realized he spoke from his own knowledge and experience rather than from the text he held in front of him.

What meekness! Not wanting those around him to know he himself had the words of life, wanting and striving to hide his virtue, he acted as a "deceiver, and *yet* true" (2 Cor. 6:8). He pretended to read from the Fathers lest anyone see his gifts and think he acquired them without the help of God.

After speaking for some time, Elder Gabriel invited the pilgrims to venerate the myrrh-streaming icon in his chapel. They entered the tiny chapel, which had barely room enough for them all to stand inside at the same time. They saw the cotton lying on the icon collecting the myrrh, but, as the men related to us later, the presence of the holy elder was so strong, the fragrance of the myrrh seemed muted in comparison.

As they were beginning to take their leave of the little elder, Fr. G. asked to speak with him in private. Thus began a trend, and each one spoke with the elder privately. Fr. John tells me that Elder Gabriel told him something personal about himself the elder never could have known by natural means, though he has never told me what exactly that was.

The pilgrims left the skete not only uplifted in spirit but each with a face expressing joy and spiritual sobriety. They had been in the presence of a saint and spoken to a true elder, whom they recognized as one endowed with gifts from the Holy Spirit. Although Elder Gabriel is neither a priest nor a great abbot, he is full of grace, for as we learn from St. Zosimas in the Life of St. Mary of Egypt, "Grace is recognized not by one's orders, but by gifts of the Spirit."

When the pilgrims returned from the Holy Mountain and relayed this story to us, their wives (who had eagerly anticipated all the details of their Athonite pilgrimage), they all claimed to have greatly benefited from the spiritual words spoken by the elder that day. However, they agreed that what he said was not so impressive as his own person. For it is one thing to speak with wisdom and quite another to shine with wisdom, and we know from the Scriptures that a spiritual man's wisdom "makes his face shine" (Eccl. 8:1).

Let it never be said saints only existed in olden times. Even today there are those who, like the Patriarch Jacob, are accounted worthy to speak with God "face to face" (Gen. 32:30) and in turn relate to those dwelling in darkness as much about the glory of God as they can bear to receive. May we have Elder Gabriel's blessing!

From East Asia to Eastern Europe: A Saint Not Bound by Space

ON OUR LAST SUNDAY in South Korea, we went to St. Nicholas Orthodox Cathedral as we always did, only this time there was a reliquary on a table in the middle of the church. Inside was a holy relic of St. Luke of Crimea. This was the first we had heard of the Crimean saint.

We were told the holy relic had been given as a blessing by a

Greek monastery to the Korean-Russian priestmonk of the Moscow Patriarchate who held services downstairs in the chapel of St. Maximos the Greek, across the courtyard from the Cathedral. The priest, Fr. Theofan, had just finished a Korean translation of St. Luke's life. It was printed in pamphlets and distributed to the faithful, so that along with venerating the holy relic they could read the life of the saint in their own language. We were delighted with the opportunity to venerate the holy relic and receive a paper icon of him as well. From that time on, we felt an affinity for the saint.

St. Luke was born in Crimea in 1877. From his youth he cherished the Christian Faith. As a young man, he first studied fine arts and went on to study medicine, eventually becoming a renowned surgeon. He married a nurse, Anna, and they had four children. In imitation of the many holy unmercenaries who went before him, St. Luke never requested money from his patients but treated all with the love and care of a true Christian. He also never operated without an icon of the Mother of God with him in the operating room.

After the repose of his wife, he entrusted his children to the care of a surrogate mother and went on to become a monk, taking the name Luke since, like the Evangelist, he was an artist and a physician. He was ordained a priest and eventually a bishop.

During his bishopric he was imprisoned three times under the atheistic communist regime, revealing himself to be not only an unmercenary but a confessor of the Faith. Toward the end of his life, he became blind and dedicated himself even more to the preservation of the Orthodox Faith in his ministry to his many spiritual children. He reposed in the Lord on June 11, 1961.

Even at that time, his holiness was recognized, and his funeral was attended by scores of people despite the dangers of doing so under communist rule. In 1996, when his relics were exhumed, the saint's heart was found to be incorrupt—a testament to his holiness and the ability of the all-good God to preserve incorrupt both the physical and the spiritual heart of man.

A few days after venerating the saint's relics, we returned to Canada and began preparations for moving to Thessaloniki, Greece, to learn Modern Greek and study theology. Before flying off for the Mediterranean, I had a conversation with a friend of mine, an American nun, who distinctly told me, "As soon as you get to Thessaloniki, go up to St. Demetrios's basilica and ask his permission and blessing to live in his city."

St. Demetrios is considered the patron of Thessaloniki. Having served in the imperial military, he was arrested for his Christian faith and put to death in the third century, on the very site where his church was later built. Soon after the legalization of Christianity by the Roman emperor and saint Constantine, in 313, a chapel was built on this site. Since that time it has gone through many reconstructions. Today the holy, fragrant, myrrh-streaming relics of St. Demetrios are housed in the church, a beautiful basilica.

I took the nun's advice to heart and considered it a commandment. From the moment we set foot in Greece, I waited for the opportunity to go to the saint's church, venerate his relics, and ask his blessing to live in his city.

On our second or third day in Greece, we made it to St. Demetrios's basilica. It was incredibly beautiful, large, open, and bright. We entered through the narthex, where an icon of the Mother of God of Jerusalem is located in the corner. Encased in an intricately carved wooden stand with a massive oil lamp burning in front of it, this particular icon is believed by St. Paisios of the Holy Mountain to be the most accurate depiction of the Theotokos's likeness. (He knew this because she had appeared to him.)

There was a great deal to see in the basilica, and not knowing precisely where the relics of the saint were located, we proceeded to the front of the church in order to venerate the icon on the icon stand. We did not realize the icon on display was that of St. Luke of Crimea until we were very close. To our great surprise, not only was his icon on display, but his holy relics were also. We were in awe. Just two months earlier we had first learned of him and venerated his relics in Seoul, on our last Sunday in Asia, as though he were bidding us farewell. Now here we were in Thessaloniki, Greece, being greeted by the saint, as if he were welcoming us to our new home.

It turned out the abbot of the twelfth-century Holy Monastery of the Transfiguration in Sagmata, Greece (possibly where our dear Korean-Russian priest received the relic of St. Luke), was traveling around with St. Luke's holy relics and had come to St. Demetrios's basilica that day. We spoke with him briefly and told him we had just come from Korea, where we had also venerated St. Luke's relics. He smiled at the divine "coincidence" and gave us another paper icon of the saint. I made my way over to St. Demetrios, feeling as though our prayers were already answered, as though we had already received a blessing to live in his holy and ancient city.

Reflecting on this event now, nine years later, I smile to myself and think, *Yeah, that about sums up our life in Greece: blessings from beginning to end. There were temptations, but boy, so were there miracles!*

Be Angry and Sin Not

SITTING IN A dangerously overcrowded room, my sister-in-law and I quickly scooped up a few small plastic cups of Greek coffee for ourselves and those sitting near us as a parishioner struggled to squeeze through rows of tightly crammed chairs to distribute the coveted caffeine. We were waiting for the priest, sitting at the far end of the room at a slightly elevated table, to begin speaking.

This was a ritual we participated in for two hours every Sunday after Divine Liturgy. The priest, a retired patristic scholar, offered an informal class to as many people as could fit in a rather small room (by North American standards) in the basement of a residence for theological students. Many times even the stairwell served as seats for the overflowing crowd. Of course, this sort of thing is completely illegal in places like Canada and the US—fire codes and all that—but in Greece overcrowding was a common occurrence, and no one seemed to think twice about it.

The priest began with current events. Something had recently happened in the Church of Greece, and he was expressing, in his deep and passionate voice, his disapproval of the situation, explaining what he believed would be an appropriate response from those in authority. Hearing his words and tone of voice, I considered him to be quite upset, angry even. That is why what happened next shocked me so much.

Instead of waiting for the appropriate and appointed time to ask questions, a man in the crowd interrupted the priest's rant with a question, and I thought, *Oh no, he's going to get it!* Contrary to my expectation, the priest turned to him, calmly answered his question, and went right back to yelling passionately about current events.

I was stunned, because I had naively assumed that since the priest was fired up about contemporary theological errors, his anger would slip over into other matters. Because I am myself a passionate and quick-tempered person, I anticipated his response to be one of anger, as I would have responded if I were upset about something. I would easily snap over an unrelated issue on account of being in an agitated state. From the priest's reaction, I instead understood what the Psalmist means when he writes, "Be angry, and do not sin" (Ps. 4:4).

The Fathers teach that anger in and of itself is not a sinful passion. Anger was instilled in human beings to be used for good. "Abhor what is evil. Cling to what is good" (Rom. 12:9), St. Paul teaches. In order to "abhor evil" one must have anger toward evil, toward all manner of sin and destructive behaviors, toward things that lead us away from God and into darkness.

Unfortunately, as with many good things the Lord has given us, we use anger with misguided intentions and out of passion rather than choice. I, being such a person, misunderstood and assumed the priest was in a state of anger, when in reality he was expressing anger over a particular issue and thus had the clarity of mind and peacefulness of heart to respond calmly and appropriately to the man's interruption.

Clothing the Lilies of the Field

IF YOU'RE ANYTHING LIKE ME, you worry, not only frequently but about as many and as varied things as the mind can possibly fret about. It seems placing my trust in God and keeping my trust in Him are not one and the same. Those few times when we fully see how much God takes care of us mean a great deal, not only because the constant worrying subsides, but because we are filled with enough courage to tell ourselves, "See, He really does care for you! You are just too blind to notice, so He has to show you in big ways to remind you He is always there caring for you."

The summer Fr. John was to be ordained a deacon, before we left Greece for Canada, he contacted an abbess and asked her if she could suggest a clerical store where he could buy vestments. To our surprise, she told him, "Just last week some Russian nuns came by. They were traveling around selling handmade vestments from their monastery. I wanted to help them out, so I bought some priest's vestments and a set of deacon's vestments as well. I think they will fit you."

Sure enough, when we visited the monastery, Fr. John tried the vestments on, and they fit perfectly.

"I tried talking Gerontissa out of purchasing deacon's vestments," the guest mistress told us as Gerontissa folded up the vestments to give to Fr. John. "I told her, 'Gerontissa, we don't even have a priest, let alone a deacon!' But she thought she should buy them anyway. I guess she was right!"

We were astonished, not only by the generosity shown to us, but by the way God had arranged everything. Despite the fact that I all too often fret and am filled with anxiety, that day I gave thanks to God that as He does for the lilies of the field (Matt. 6:28), He had provided for us.

The Apple Doesn't Fall Far from the Tree

BY GOD'S PROVIDENCE, a combination of factors led our mother to desire membership in the Orthodox Church, and to our great joy, she was baptized in 2010. Before that, she had been attending the only Orthodox parish in our province for over a year. Although she had acquired knowledge of various aspects of our faith, she wasn't fully aware of certain customs and practices.

We were visiting a monastery together, and I ran into the abbot and took his blessing. Since my mother had not yet met him, I went to get her to introduce them.

"Father, this is my mother, Chris," I said gesturing to my mother.

The abbot gave her his right hand, but since I had already taken his blessing, she hadn't seen the proper way to greet an abbot. So instead of kissing his hand, she shook it, and then (to my utter horror) held it between her two hands as she went on and on about how wonderful his sister and mother were, all the while patting his hand.

I stood there—every shade of red coloring my cheeks, I'm sure—discreetly puckering my lips and trying to illustrate with my own hand how she should kiss the abbot's hand. But she chattered on, oblivious to her daughter's red face and ridiculous sign language, while the abbot listened to her in silence. Finally, she said goodbye to the abbot and let go of his hand. As we walked away, I wrapped my arm around her shoulders and whispered, "Mum, you're supposed to *kiss* an abbot's hand—not *hold* it!"

Now it was my mother's turn to be painted red with embarrassment. "Oh, Connie! Why didn't you tell me?" she said, alarmed.

"I tried!" I said, laughing. "I was making faces at you, but you didn't notice."

By the time we got safely into the guest quarters, we were laughing our heads off. Since then it has become a beloved family story that everyone loves hearing now and again.

Similarly, my younger sister—in her characteristically simple and kind way—was oblivious to the Orthodox practice of monastic penance. Once while she was visiting a women's monastery she ate with the sisterhood in their trapeza. She noticed how a few times certain nuns would make full prostrations to everyone who was exiting the trapeza.

Wow! What humility! she silently reflected. *Look at these sisters bowing and blessing us!*

She thought this because she couldn't understand what they were saying in Greek, so she assumed they were blessing those passing by, when in fact—as she later learned—they were saying aloud what they had done wrong and asking the sisters to pray for them. Thus, they were not bowing simply out of their own personal love and humility, blessing the sisterhood, but completing a penance and asking forgiveness.

She and I laugh about this now as well—and the fact that we both have a propensity to make fools of ourselves in one way or another. But we no longer wonder from whom we inherited this "charming" characteristic.

Rejoice, You through Whom Creation Is Renewed

DURING THE YEARS my husband was a deacon in Greece, we spent every Sunday of the summer months at a monastery where he assisted the priest for the celebration of Divine Liturgy. We would also go for some liturgical feasts that fell during the week, such as the Feast of the Transfiguration. Our last summer living in Greece, we joined the sisters to celebrate their patronal feast, the Feast of the

Dormition of the Theotokos. That particular year, an icon of Panagia Paramythia (the All-holy Comforter) had been lent to the monastery as a blessing for the feast of the Mother of God on August 15.

The prototype of this icon is located at Vatopedi Monastery on Mount Athos and has an incredible history behind it. Tradition has it that the figure's hands and faces were in different positions originally, as it was an icon of the Directress, in which the Mother of God holds the infant Christ with one hand and directs our gaze to him with the other. However, on January 21, 807, the abbot of the monastery was praying privately when he heard a woman's voice warning him not to open the gate to the monastery. The voice informed him that pirates had already landed on the shores of the Holy Mountain and warned him to drive them away, for they would come to pillage the monastery.

Hearing this, the abbot turned toward the icon of the Mother of God the Directress, from whence he heard the woman's voice. Just as he turned, he saw the small hand of the Christ child reaching up to cover His Mother's mouth. He heard Christ tell His Mother not to watch over the sinful flock but to let them fall to the pirates. At this the Theotokos held the child's hand back and turned her head away to repeat the warning to the abbot.

On account of the Most Holy Lady's warning, the lives of the monks were spared that day, and the depiction of the Mother of God and Christ has remained in that position even until today: the Christ child's hand reaching up to His Mother's mouth and while she holds his hand away. Thus, the icon was given the new name of *Panagia Paramythia*, *paramythia* meaning "restrain," "comfort," or "calm down."

The icon that had been lent to the monastery was a hand-painted replica of this icon from Vatopedi Monastery. The nun who painted it lived in Jerusalem at the time and was almost completely blind. However, the likenesses of the Theotokos and Christ were so precise that it was hard to believe any hand could create such an exact copy, let alone a hand belonging to someone with very limited eyesight.

Being myself an iconographer, I examined the icon with interest. The original is covered in a rizo (a decorative silver encasing), but this one was full of brilliant color. I had the blessing of venerating it before and after the service and was told it would be returned to Jerusalem following the after-feast.

A week later, monks from the Holy Land came to reclaim the icon. As they were processing with it to the parking lot, just as they exited the gates of the monastery, I was told hundreds of birds swooped down all at once and bowed to the icon. Witnessing this miracle, the monks were so astonished that they decided they should contact the iconographer-nun to tell her about this divine occurrence. Once she heard the news of the miracle, she said, "It seems the Mother of God would like to stay there."

And that is how the brilliantly colored icon of Panagia Paramythia, painted by an almost completely blind nun in the Holy Land, came to reside permanently in a monastery in Greece, where my husband had the blessing of serving on numerous occasions.

Fool, Your Soul Is Demanded of You

JOHN AND I WERE STAYING at a monastery outside Thessaloniki (while he was still a layman) when we were invited to dinner at the home of a professor who lived relatively close to the monastery. He also invited some colleagues and the abbess to the dinner. Some of his colleagues were theology professors, others were psychologists; so some interesting conversations unfolded.

Over the course of the evening, one of the psychologists explained that he did not believe the human soul to be immortal (as the Orthodox Faith teaches). He stated that in his opinion, the soul dwelt in the brain, and thus once the brain was dead, so too would the soul be.

Different dinner guests offered alternative opinions, and a few explained the Orthodox position that while the human body can become ill, die, and decay, the human soul was created to be immortal. Thus, even after bodily death, the soul remains alive and is placed either in Hades or in Paradise until the Second Coming of Christ, when the body and soul are reunited for eternity—to dwell, body and soul, either in heaven or in hell. Even though the psychologist was reminded that Christ Himself taught that when the body is killed the soul does not die (Matt. 10:28), he reiterated his erroneous belief that the human soul is mortal.

When it came time to leave, John, the abbess, and I all got into the car to return to the monastery. Just as we were about to pull out of the driveway, however, the abbess decided to go back in the house. We waited for her, and once she rejoined us, we were off. It was dark by that time, so John was extra cautious driving on the highway.

All of a sudden we saw brake lights, the traffic slowed, and many pulled off the road and got out of their vehicles. We discovered that just minutes before, an accident had occurred. A car had collided with a motorcycle. The motorcycle driver was lying in the middle of the road, apparently conscious because we could see him raising his arm in the air, as if it were sore and he was stretching it.

As soon as we saw this, we began praying. The abbess took off the cross she was wearing and began blessing the people with it while she quietly prayed. We then saw an overturned car and another man lying on the ground. It appeared as though the man had been thrown from the car. We could see his leg had been torn off.

"His soul has departed," the abbess told us, blessing him three times.

Just then ambulances and police began arriving, so we moved out of the way. But John and I commented that it could have been us in that accident if Gerontissa hadn't gone back into the house when we were about to leave.

"Just think," she told us sorrowfully as we drove passed, "if, after saying such foolishness as that professor said—that the soul dies—you were to find yourself in this situation. Just as his bodily eyes closed, the eyes of his soul would open, and he would see what a mistake he made believing the soul dies!"

It was a very sobering experience, a vivid reminder that we never know when we'll hear the fearful words, "Fool! This night your soul will be required of you" (Luke 12:20). For we will be judged not only according to our works, but according to our right or wrong belief. May God preserve us all and prepare us before our bodily end!

A Few Good Stories

WHILE PLAYING AT THE MONASTERY with other children, a little boy dislocated his shoulder. His father set out immediately to take him to the hospital. However, on the way, the child claimed his arm was all better. Sure enough, at the hospital they could find nothing wrong with him. The child piped up and said, "It was Prodromos [the

Forerunner]! He fixed my arm! I saw him!" They couldn't deny the fact that the child's shoulder was perfectly fine. They were compelled to believe that the patron of the monastery where he had been playing had healed him.

A NUN AT THE HOLY MONASTERY of the Life-giving Spring in Aegina (founded by St. Nektarios of Pentapolis) told us a story about a woman who wanted to take some flowers from the grave of St. Nektarios as a blessing. But each time she reached for red flowers, she heard a voice say, "No, not those, they are the Lord's flowers." (I assume those particular flowers were brought in honor of the Lord.) This happened three times, until finally she took a few of the white flowers. She brought them home to her house as a keepsake from the saint, and the next day they turned from white to red. I guess the saint honored her desire to have red flowers.

A HERMIT FROM ATHOS who had left the Holy Mountain to relocate closer to Thessaloniki suddenly reposed. That night a godly priest dreamt that a woman in red told him, "Take Father So-and-so to Joanna to be buried."

The first time the priest had this dream, he ignored it, prudently guarding himself from putting his trust in dreams. Besides, he told us later, he didn't know who Joanna was. The second night, again the same woman in red told him to take the reposed monk to Joanna to be buried.

The next morning it occurred to the priest that he had had a student at the theology school who later became an abbess at a monastery near Thessaloniki; her name was Joanna. So he called her and asked if it would be possible for the hermit to be buried at her monastery. She considered it a great blessing, and the burial took place.

After this reunion with his former student, now an abbess, the priest frequently visited the monastery and introduced us there as well. As a result, we too got to know the abbess and had the blessing of frequently visiting her monastery, where the hermit is buried and prayed for—surely a blessing for both parties.

WHILE WE WERE VISITING a women's monastery on a Greek island, a nun told us a story about a young man who had sustained significant injuries in a car accident. However, the sister informed us, he was saved because he had once helped the monastery. There had been a large group of pilgrims visiting, and afterward he helped the sisters stack chairs. "His good work was rewarded," the nun told us. God sees all and rewards in kind.

LOOKING OUT THE WINDOW of a large women's monastery after Divine Liturgy, my friend saw a few nuns walking toward the woods with satchels on their backs. Inquiring who they were, she was told they were ascetics who lived in the wilderness and had come to the monastery to attend Liturgy and to receive some food.

Although we are much weaker in our times and far less ascetical than the early desert fathers and mothers, let it never be said that extreme Christian asceticism is extinct. Who knows how many St. Mary of Egypts are hidden in the wilderness?

THE THREE-MONTH-OLD BABY had cried during most of the baptismal service; he was hungry and tired. Having been immersed in the water, he quieted down for a little while. After he was dressed in his white baptismal clothes and back in his godmother's arms, he remained silent during the reading of the Holy Gospel.

After the priest finished reading, he held the Gospel out for the godmother to venerate, at which time she also leaned the baby toward the Gospel. I distinctly heard a kissing noise as I saw the baby's lips meet the Gospel book. But I thought I might have imagined it or at least had mistaken an unrelated noise for a kissing noise. I decided not to ask anyone if they saw or heard what I thought I did.

"Did you see the baby kiss the Gospel?" my brother asked me afterward.

"You noticed it too?" I asked, surprised.

"Yes! He leaned in and kissed the Gospel as the priest held it out!"

Perhaps when the baby, who had "put on Christ," kissed the Gospel of his own accord, it was a testament of his faith: "By You I have been upheld from birth; You are He who took me out of my mother's womb. / My praise *shall be* continually of You" (Ps. 70/71:6).

THERE WAS A YOUNG MAN who was very ill and hospitalized. The doctors informed his mother of how serious his condition was. She, not fully understanding the gravity of the situation, asked how soon he would be able to start studying for his final exams.

"Ma'am, it looks as though your son will not live, let alone take his final exams!" the doctor bluntly told her.

Despite the grim prognosis, the young man had great faith. He told his mother he would study and with the help of the 179 martyrs of Daou,* he believed he would not only pass his exams but be healed.

---

* The story of the 179 martyred fathers of Daou is told beginning on page 244.

Every day at noon, he would have his mother take him from the hospital and drive to the Holy Monastery of the Transfiguration in Pentli, where the martyrs had lived and suffered death in 1680. Although the monastery was closed for *mesimeri* (the afternoon siesta), he would study in the car, parked outside the gate. The sisters told me he would even go up to the gate and rest his head on it, praying for the holy martyred fathers to enlighten him.

As with many cases testified to in the Scriptures and in our Orthodox Tradition, the young man's strong faith and commitment bore fruit. He passed his exams, and his health was restored. If I remember correctly, he went on to study in America.

THERE WAS A BABY GIRL at our church in Thessaloniki that the whole parish was delighted to see every Sunday. Although she was only a few months old, she would begin to squeal, kick her chubby legs, and flail her arms with joy and excitement every time her father brought her up to venerate the icons before Holy Communion. She would continue this ritual of squealing and kicking until the priest exited the Royal Doors and she received the Immaculate Mysteries. This went on for months.

People were amazed. They would smile and whisper to each other. It was a beautiful thing to witness, because we all understood that the baby perceived the presence of God and expressed her delight in the only way a baby can.

MY MOTHER AND I made a pilgrimage to a women's monastery one summer. While the abbess spoke with a guest inside, we stood outside speaking with one of the sisters and a woman who was visiting with her husband and children. Somehow the conversation turned to the topic of temptation, and we were swapping stories of encountering temptations while traveling to monasteries. We all agreed that temptation is often heightened when we attempt to make pilgrimages.

"Gerontissa says that sometimes when the evil one is not able to make ground with us personally, he will cause problems in the monastery. Something will go wrong with a machine or one of the animals."

At that moment we heard the distinct sound of water pouring onto the ground. We turned to look at the children who had been quietly dipping their hands in the water of a nearby fountain. Just as our eyes fell on the children, we saw the marble fountain collapse onto the two-year-old. We all ran like mad and pulled the marble pieces off of him. Immediately we pulled his wet clothes off, and my mother, who is a nurse, began examining him, fully expecting to find a compound fracture. By the grace of God she found no fractures. She told the boy's mother she needed to take him to the hospital immediately to check for internal bleeding.

The abbess came rushing out with other nuns who wrapped the little guy in clean towels. "Glorify the Mother of God, because your child could have died but she protected him," she told the mother, crossing them as the family got into a vehicle to head to the hospital.

As they drove off, we began praying for his health and recovery. After hours spent at the emergency room, they returned with a perfectly healthy two-year-old, who, by the next morning, was doing his best to keep up with his older brother on the playground.

My mother was astonished—we all were—but with her experience in medicine, she couldn't stop saying, "It's a miracle! He could have died, but he's perfectly fine!"

"It's a miracle!" the abbess confirmed.

A Woman's Glory

THAT'S IT—*I'm cutting my hair off!* I vowed to myself after weeks of
thinking about shedding my long locks in favor of a short bob. All it
took to convince me was seeing a woman with short black hair after
the Akathist service at our parish one Friday night during Great Lent.
She had the hair I wanted.

I was standing in line waiting to venerate the icon of the Annunciation, decorated with flowers and prominently displayed in the
center of the church on an icon stand with a large burning candle next
to it. That night we participated in the reading of the third stasis of
the Akathist to the Mother of God. It is a custom in some Orthodox
churches (the Greek church in particular) to chant the service in
four parts on the first four Fridays of Great Lent, combined with the
Small Compline service. The Akathist is read in its entirety on the
fifth Friday of the Great Fast.

This particular night, we had the blessing of hearing the service
chanted by a renowned veteran chanter from the Danielite brotherhood of Katounakia on Mount Athos, Fr. Daniel. He was down
from the Holy Mountain and decided to attend the service at the
church of St. Anthony the Great, our parish. I was told he had been
nicknamed the "nightingale of the Holy Mountain" on account of
his beautiful voice.

That Friday night, we heard a voice that matched the majesty,
beauty, and solemnity of St. Romanos's words in the Akathist hymn
to the Most Holy Lady Theotokos: "New was the Creation which

the Creator showed to us His creatures, when He sprang forth from the seedless womb; and He preserved it incorrupt even as it was, that we, seeing this marvel, may praise her as we cry out" (Ikos 7). Those words are some of my absolute favorite words of the Akathist hymn, and that third Friday in Great Lent we heard a voice worthy of those words chant them.

After venerating the icon of the Annunciation, I noticed that a crowd had gathered at the back of the church, clearly waiting to greet the elder monk and take his blessing. I waited with them, not only for the elder but for my husband, who, having served as deacon, was divesting in the altar.

Having finished, my husband joined me, and we waited together with my brother for the elder to pass by. Our friend and chanter was escorting him down the main aisle in the church, and when they arrived at my husband, our friend introduced us to the elder. We took his blessing, and he held both our hands, one in each of his. Since we had been introduced as Americans, he told us about a trip he had taken to America to visit St. Anthony's Monastery in Arizona and about his impressions of the people and the state of the church there.

"People want to see our beards," he told my husband. "They want to see our *rassos* (cassocks). It's a symbol of piety. Some mock us, but it's okay. You with your beard . . . it's a confession of faith."

"And you," he said, turning toward me, "with your long hair! Saint Paul says a woman's glory is her hair."

At this, involuntary loud laughter erupted out of me. I think I may even have startled the patiently waiting crowd with my sudden and unexpected laughter. Of course they didn't know that just moments before I had made up my mind to chop off my long hair, but *I* did.

Fr. Daniel asked if we planned to return to America, and when we affirmed this, he told us, "Good, because saving just one soul, one soul, covers many sins," to which my husband responded, "And we have many sins."

Needless to say, I kept my hair long for a few years after meeting Fr. Daniel, and I have chuckled numerous times thinking back on our conversation with the holy elder. This was the greatest element of our life in Greece: the countless opportunities available to encounter living saints and receive spiritual words from them, even ones as seemingly insignificant as concerning the length of one's hair.

A Holy Monastery: A Silent Teacher

ON ONE OF MY FREQUENT TRIPS to a particular women's monastery in Greece, I couldn't help but be affected by the lessons a monastery imparts to the human soul. An Orthodox monastery may be a silent teacher, but what it teaches is so rich, so instructive.

As I had done countless times before, when I arrived I immediately went into the catholicon for Vespers. The sisters' chanting inspired me to chant with my whole soul, to strive to convey with my insignificant voice the spiritual depth of the divinely inspired hymns. Leaving the church I walked down to the monastery's graveyard, and the piercing silence made me want to be more silent and to communicate holy silence to others. Going into the monastery and observing the sisters interact with love and care and concern for one another, I wanted to be more charitable, more merciful, more helpful, and more sacrificial.

Attending the abbess's homily and listening to her wisdom impressed upon me the great and important work of reading, truly studying and seriously contemplating the Holy Scriptures, hymnography, and hagiography, and applying those holy words to my daily life.

As I left the monastery and walked down the road past the stone walls covered in vibrant green vines and brightly colored flowers, the evening light shining through the tree tops, the whole place exuded beauty and fragrance. The sweetness of grace hung in the air. I came upon a tortoise on the road. It was skittish and shy when I approached, but even that small, timid tortoise taught me a lesson. I wanted to become humble so that the tortoise wouldn't be fearful of my presence.

There is a story about a monk who was going along a path and saw a beautiful little flower. He gently touched it with his walking stick, saying, "Don't shout so loud!" as if its very presence were a loud testament to God's glory. The holy atmosphere of a monastery is like that. It speaks to the soul in such a way that for once, and possibly only once, the soul sees and perceives the glory of God in all things.

Like This Little Child

SITTING IN THE SHADE on one of the monastery's large verandas, guarded from the sun's hot rays, I was surrounded by tables filled with trays of dried flowers, herbs, and orange peels. To my right was a pile of paper bags, to my left were decorative, descriptive tags to place on the bags, and at my feet was a large basket into which I had poured the contents of a few trays.

I was bagging tea for the sisters to sell in their bookstore, and I was accompanied by the abbess's six-year-old goddaughter. She sat across from me and talked incessantly. I enjoyed her stories, descriptions, and the faux mature manner in which she explained that her younger brother was a handful.

"When I can't sleep, I say *Lord Jesus Christ have mercy on me* again and again until I finally fall asleep," she confided in me.

"Is that right?" I asked.

"Yes. I think I might want to be a nun when I grow up," she said, and within the same breath added, "or get married and have babies."

Her sweet innocence was endearing, and it reminded me of many of the children I have met at monasteries, whose little worlds are blessed to have the influence of the grace and beauty of Orthodox monasticism.

Children are so naturally guileless and pure that introducing them to an environment of prayer and good works, such as a monastery, impresses on their malleable hearts from a young age a genuine example of what it is to serve Christ through love.

If we strive to plant the seed of faith in our children's hearts and show them the love of Christ—not our own corrupted human love—then we will have taught them, not with empty words, but with heartfelt prayer and good works, what Christianity is. St. Porphyrios instructed, "Prefer prayer and speak to [our children] through prayer. Speak to God and God will speak to their hearts."[18] By following the godly-minded elder's advice, not only will we begin to mold our children into the strong Christians we hope them to become and remain, but we will also develop the ability in ourselves to be transformed by their naturally pure state and spiritual intuition.

An example of this was related to me by a friend. The mother of the family sent her children off to school on a Wednesday with corn dogs. In this particular family, their rule was to allow the children to abstain from meat on Wednesdays and Fridays. This day the mother had simply forgotten and had packed a lunch with meat for the children. To her surprise, they came home from school and said, "Mum, you gave us meat today!" When she opened their lunches, she saw that they had eaten the outside of the corndogs and had left the meat.

Similarly, I know a child whose father took him and his siblings to visit a monastery that belonged to a schismatic group. The father simply brought the children to the monastery to venerate the chapel's icons and to show the monastics love. The oldest child went with his brothers and sisters to kiss the icons in the church, and then went immediately to his father and said, "Dad, can I go outside now? It smells horrible; I don't want to stay in here." The father was shocked, not only because he couldn't smell anything himself, but because his son had never said anything like that to him before.

All we need to do is give our children the proper predispositions toward faith, prayer, and good works, and they will begin teaching us more than we could ever teach them. For example, I was put to shame by my friends' four-year-old daughter's commitment to and success at memorizing the dates of various saints' feast days. Her father and I were talking, and the name Arsenios was mentioned, at which point she interrupted us to ask when St. Arsenios's feast day was. "November tenth," we answered (the Arsenios we were talking about was named for St. Arsenios the Cappadocian). More jokingly than seriously, I asked her, "When do I celebrate my nameday?"

She stared off for a few seconds and finally said, "Twenty-one" (as in May 21). I was astonished and looked at her father for an explanation. He simply shrugged and said, "She looks at the calendar we have with icons and memorizes the dates of the saints' feast days."

I was intrigued, to say the least.

"When is Saint Makrina's feast day?" I asked, not fully expecting her to know.

"Twenty-two," she said after a long pause.

I couldn't believe it. I began an inquisition: "Saint Catherine?"

"Twenty-four," she said.

And so on we went until I started asking saints she didn't know, and then I began telling her the month for each number she provided. "Prophet Moses?"

"Four," she would say—always after a long pause.

"That's right, September fourth!" I said.

It was one of the most amazing things I had ever witnessed. Here was a four-year-old who before long could become a walking, talking *synaxarion*—telling us not only the dates of each saint's feast day, but something about their life as well.

If only we were as obedient and faithful as these little ones. I'm sure whole volumes of books could be filled with the wonderful works of faithful children—works that would put us adults to shame. These are just a few. I'm sure every Orthodox mother in the world has observed the seemingly innate spiritual depth of her child or children. May God make us worthy to imitate their shining examples.

He Condescended

IN A PRIVATE HOME in Pilaia (just outside Thessaloniki), Elder Gabriel of the Holy Mountain was offered hospitality as he was recovering from surgery. (This is the same Elder Gabriel my husband had met the year before while on pilgrimage to Athos with my brother and our friends.) Although the elder had not left the Holy Mountain for some twenty-three years, he was compelled to go to Thessaloniki for surgery. News of his visit spread, and thus every day hundreds of visitors came to the home seeking the elder's blessing. One of those visitors was Gerontissa Ioanna.

She went with the intention of receiving the elder's blessing, but was sorely troubled when she arrived and found that she would have to ascend many stairs to reach the room in which the elder was staying. On account of her severe arthritis, she was be unable to climb so many stairs. Dejected and saddened at the prospect of not being able to converse with this living saint, she thought her trip was in vain. But to her surprise and delight, someone informed her that when the elder learned she had come all the way to see him but could not make it up the stairs, he himself had decided to descend them to see her. What condescension! What love! The ill elder goes to the ill eldress!

After meeting her, the elder asked someone, "What monastery is that abbess from?"

Someone informed him where the abbess's monastery was, and the elder replied, "That is where we will attend Divine Liturgy on Sunday."

And so it was that I found myself standing in the monastery's crowded catholicon awaiting the arrival of Elder Gabriel the following Sunday. The abbess had requested that our priest serve Liturgy since the monastery did not have a priest assigned to it. And so, not only did our priest serve, but my husband, Fr. John, and my brother, Fr. Matthew, were asked to serve as well, as they were both deacons at the time.

We had been at this monastery for its patronal feast, when a great crowd attended the service, and yet the crowd on this day—all wanting to see a living saint from the Holy Mountain—far surpassed the crowd that had gathered a few months prior. The reputation of the holiness of this old, frail elder had spread like wildfire, and hundreds of people came seeking comfort from a man of God.

After the Divine Liturgy, a crowd waited in the reception hall to receive the elder's blessing. Those who could not fit into the hall waited outside. Once we had approached the elder and kissed his hand, my sister-in-law and I were invited into a smaller dining room to eat with the clergy. However, the elder did not accompany us on account of the great crowd; only after each and every individual had received his blessing did he come to eat.

Since we had finished our meal by that point, the sister who was tending the guests requested that I stay and help her. I had the great blessing of serving the elder as well as those who had accompanied him to the monastery. Once the abbess entered to speak with him as he ate, I excused myself, not thinking it appropriate to overhear the conversation of a meek eldress with an equally meek and holy elder. This story of a spiritual giant's humility, to condescend for the sake of a humble abbess, may be simple, but I find it profound in its simplicity and have kept it as a special memory as well as a great lesson of love.

Conforming to Christ

AFTER WE RETURNED to Canada from Greece, Fr. John was ordained to the holy priesthood. However, he was required to return to Thessaloniki for one month to defend his doctoral dissertation. During his time in Greece, he went to visit dear friends of ours (a priest and his family) who live and serve the Church in a village in the mountains. While there, Fr. John co-celebrated the Divine Liturgy.

During the service of Proskomidi, our friend, a more senior priest, noticed that Fr. John had turned the diskos toward himself to make cutting and preparing the prosfora loaf for use in the Divine Liturgy a little easier. Seeing this, the priest immediately came over and rebuked him heavily for his audacity. Of course, this shook Fr. John up a great deal, but once he settled down and finished the Proskomidi, the priest approached him again. "The whole purpose of the Christian life," he instructed Fr. John, "is conforming ourselves to Christ, not dragging Christ to us."

When Fr. John came home, he told me about this experience. I knew it must have had a very great impact on him for him to relay it to me, since he quite often prefers to ponder things in his heart rather than share every experience with his wife. Since that experience, he has employed this story as an example for the greater context of our Christian life: our sins and passions are the manifestation of us turning things toward ourselves in order to appease our will, our insatiable desires, and even at times our wicked intentions. But Christianity is about conforming to Christ, to His commandments, and taking the necessary steps toward turning ourselves away from the world, from the easy path that leads to the wide gate—from sin and the passions, in other words—and toward the straight and narrow path that leads to life (Matt. 7:14). May God direct our steps!

☒ FOUR ☒

Blessed Are Those Who Hunger and Thirst
after Righteousness
for they shall be filled

A Prayer Request for Archangel Michael

ON THE GREEK ISLAND of Thassos, far below the Holy Monastery of the Archangel Michael and just above the Aegean Sea, is a tiny cave. It is revered by the locals and nuns alike as a miraculous cave containing a spring of *agiasma** (holy water) with wonder-working properties attributed to the Archangel Michael. Unfortunately, I do not recall the details of how this spring was discovered.

While on pilgrimage to the monastery, my friends and I decided

---

* *Agiasma*: not to be confused with *agiasmos*, which is the water the priest blesses in the Lesser and Greater Blessing of Waters (which the faithful drink only after fasting). *Agiasma* is the water that comes from a sacred spring that works miracles of healing, like the famous Life-giving Spring of the Theotokos in Constantinople, which is well known for its miracles of healing.

to make the long trek down the path and over the large sea rocks to this special cave. When we finally arrived, a few of the nuns who were with us noticed a glass bottle floating in the water, gently knocking against a rock, just below the entrance to the cave. They opened it and discovered it contained incense with a piece of paper attached. Written on the paper was a request for the archangel's prayers.

I was amazed by this and couldn't quite wrap my head around how a bottle cast into the sea from who knows where could arrive as close as possible to the cave of the archangel. The sisters told me this kind of thing was common, however. Many people would throw in bottles from all over the place to request the prayers of Archangel Michael, and they would end up right there, virtually at the foot of the cave.

We took the incense with us and crawled into the cave. The cave was so small that we had to lie flat on our stomachs to get to the spring. There we were, lying on the cold, dirty ground with one sister holding a small censer emitting fragrance and smoke while another intoned a hymn in honor of the archangel. We each took a sip of the *agiasma* and made our way out of the cave.

During the whole trek back to the monastery, I marveled: at times the sheer supernatural element of the Orthodox Faith stuns me, and yet it is often treated as the most natural thing by those who have grown accustomed to the inner workings of the spiritual life. St. Dionysius says in his work *The Celestial Hierarchies* that the human spirit "naturally yearns for and seeks whatever contemplation of the supernatural may be attainable."[19] Although that day I had only witnessed a glass bottle containing incense and a prayer request sitting in the water just below the archangel's cave, it was enough for me to contemplate, in wonder, the marvelous ways in which the spiritual life co-exists with this earthly, temporal, and fleeting world.

Attending Services in Mind and Spirit

THE ORTHODOX CHURCH has designated two weeks in August for fasting in honor and remembrance of the bodily death (formally called the Dormition, the "falling asleep") of the Mother of God on August 15. During this fast period, it is customary for the faithful to pray the Supplicatory Canon to the Mother of God every evening. When we lived in Greece, all the parishes in Thessaloniki served the Supplicatory Canon combined with the Compline service.

This beautiful service of prayer and supplication to the Holy Lady Theotokos is very beneficial, but it is not always possible for busy families to make it to church each evening for two weeks, nor even to find the time to say the service at home together. Sometimes, even monastics are not able to attend services if their obediences (their monastic obligations of work, such as kitchen duty) don't allow for it. But there is a difference between physical church attendance and spiritual church attendance. While our goal is to participate fully in both, I picked up some tips from visiting monasteries that taught me how to become creative when we can't (for *good* reason) physically be present during church services.

When some monasteries have a great amount of work to do, most of the monastics are given a blessing from the abbess or abbot to continue working while a select few read the Hours, Vespers, Akathist, Paraklesis, and Compline services in the church each evening. Some monasteries even have a broadcasting system set up so that while the chanters do the services, the other sisters can hear them via radio. Wherever one is working, all one need do is turn on the radio to hear the services.

For work and prayer are not mutually exclusive, but, as Gerontissa Philareti used to say, "Work, when combined with the Jesus Prayer, becomes prayer." The same thing occurs when we engage in the services with our mind and heart even while our hands work.

During the two-week fasting period in August, however, I remember one monastery had the rule that all were required to finish their work before Vespers so they could attend the services. Throughout the whole Supplicatory Canon, the sisters would do continual prostrations, and oddly they didn't mind because they were pleased to have the opportunity to "have to" attend the services.

Particularly busy times of year prevent the sisters from attending evening services on account of all the work. Many times while visiting the monastery I have continued working with the sisters, choosing to listen to Vespers on the radio as well. And, in fact, that is where I realized what a great idea it is for us in the world to also "attend" services even when we are not able to on account of work, children, illness, or whatever the case may be.

There are so many resources in our times. If we miss the Akathist hymn to the Mother of God during Great Lent, we can listen to it on CD when we have the time. If we miss Vespers or Matins, there are liturgical CDs available for us to listen to, and YouTube is a great resource for "attending" services as well. Ancient Faith Radio broadcasts the Divine Liturgy from Christ the Savior Church in Chicago every Sunday at 9:30 AM Central. My mother listens to the Matins service each Sunday via a live-streaming video broadcast from St.

John's Russian Orthodox Cathedral in Mayfield, Pennsylvania, so that she can hear it in English before attending Liturgy at the local Greek church (the only church in the province).

If all else fails we can even record ourselves reading various services in our free time so we can listen to them while washing the dishes or running errands in the car. This is not to supplant attending services in our parish or even praying them privately at home; it is rather a means to attend services we would otherwise miss altogether. The point is to put our mind and heart in church even if our body can't be there.

During a lecture in my dogmatic theology course at Aristotle University, my professor told us the following story: He had visited a monastery with a friend, and they had attended Divine Liturgy there. At the end of the service, they greeted the elder of the monastery, and he asked my professor's friend, "Where were you during the service?"

The man replied he was in church, but the elder insisted he wasn't. My professor testified in his defense, "I was standing beside him the whole time, elder. We were both there."

"No, he was elsewhere, surveying the land he is thinking about buying. Isn't that right? You weren't in church, but out looking at the land you might buy," the elder responded.

The man was dumbfounded by the elder's prophetic words, for at that moment he realized his mind had been wandering during the service. While his body was in church, his heart and mind were not.

Christ said, "For where your treasure is, there your heart will be also" (Matt. 6:21). This is how we need to approach both attending and missing church services. Where is our heart? Where is our mind, attention, desire? My professor used to say, "It doesn't matter whether you sit or stand—all that matters is where your *nous* [mind] is!"

We must struggle to keep our attention on worship and prayer. If it strays, we shouldn't become distraught; we should simply call our mind back. Even if it strays a thousand times, the point is to struggle. Our thoughts have such strength that they can carry us away from church, and so conversely, our thoughts can also carry us to church even when our bodies are elsewhere.

This is why it is said in the *Gerontikon* that at the Second Coming of Christ, when the dead will arise, some who lived, died, and were buried in the world will arise on Mount Athos, while some monks who lived, died, and were buried on Athos will arise in the world—indicating where each noetically passed his time during life, revealing where the "treasure" and therefore heart of each was. Thus, if we want to attend services, we should attend services whether or not we are able to go to church.

Freedom from Cares

MY HUSBAND AND I moved to Greece under the impression that all the documents we had sent a month before had been accepted at Aristotle University and we would begin classes at the Modern Greek School in short order, taking the language exam at the end of the year and beginning graduate studies in one year's time.

When we arrived in Thessaloniki, we were dropped off at a hotel near the university by a friend of a friend of a friend and pointed in the direction of the theology department. First thing the next morning, we walked to the university to meet with the professor we had been introduced to the month before at a conference in a monastery outside Chicago. At that time, he had informed us that all we needed to do was e-mail his secretary copies of our degrees and a few other necessary documents, and everything would be arranged for our studies.

We managed to find the professor's office with the help of a student who spoke English. We were escorted in to see him, and he joyfully welcomed us with customary kisses, greetings, and well-wishes. The student who had helped us find his office served as our translator.

The first question the professor asked us was, "How long will you be visiting Greece?"

We were stunned; I nearly fell over from shock. It appeared as though he had forgotten the conversation we had had just one month prior and our subsequent arrangements.

"Until we finish our studies," we answered apprehensively, exchanging glances with one another. The English-speaking student translated what we had said for the professor. However, translators aren't needed for understanding facial expressions, so we understood by the professor's face that our allegedly simple arrangements had not been as organized as we had supposed—nor even, as it turned out, remembered.

He called for his secretary to check her e-mail, and sure enough, there were our documents in an as-yet-unopened e-mail message.

That was just the beginning of the multiple roadblocks we encountered in trying to move to Greece. There were complications that prohibited us from studying in that department, and every time it seemed a solution was found, another obstacle sprang up. We went to the university every day for a week or two, spending hours on end trying to find a way for us to stay and study.

But it was during this time of trial upon trial that I experienced the most radical feeling of freedom I have ever felt. Instead of allowing countless anxious thoughts and stress-filled emotions to wash over me—dictating how I reacted to all the uncertainty around us—I felt completely carefree for the first, and perhaps only, time in my life.

We had flown halfway around the world only to find out all the plans we thought were in place had amounted to nothing. Worse still, every time a new plan was hatched, it was just as quickly revealed to be flawed in some fundamental way. Yet there I was in the midst of this chaos, and for a fleeting moment I didn't care what happened to us, so long as we were struggling to follow God's will.

Circumstances can dictate a lot in our life; they can exhibit a great degree of control over us, but God is free and uncontainable, and so to be of God is to be free and uncontained. For one brief moment I felt free and uncontained, uninhibited by anything, because I had no cares; my only care was to be "of God." It was only for a moment, but for once in my life I had tasted true freedom.

A solution was eventually found (though not without its own difficulties and additional trials), and we remained in Thessaloniki for almost six years, studying and learning, being tempted and receiving blessings. I never forgot that brief but poignant moment of radical freedom which inspired these words:

Search the price of freedom,
Hidden deep within.
Learn the means to acquire it,
Denouncement of your sin.

Flee from dark enslavement;
Don't look back nor sigh.
Run with great conviction,
To raise your eyes on high.

An Unassuming Vision of an Unassuming Saint

WHILE WALKING THROUGH the monastery, taking in the beautiful buildings, the exotic plants, and the bright flowers, my friend was not expecting to come upon a saint—at least not one who had fallen asleep over fifty years ago.

My friend had visited this monastery because his life was at a crossroads. He and his wife were going through a difficult time, and he needed prayers and guidance. A few months before his pilgrimage to the monastery, he began reading Elder Joseph the Hesychast's letters compiled in the book *Monastic Wisdom*. He was quickly filled with admiration for the holy person of Elder Joseph: his words, his life, his letters. He found respite in the elder's grace-filled writings. And he also found something he wasn't looking for—the conviction he needed to take the leap into Orthodoxy.

It was a simple, unassuming, almost random statement he read that affected him. The elder had said something in passing about non-Orthodox. The jest was, "If you want to love Christ, come and love Him." Reading this line, he felt all his hesitancy, all his anxieties, all his fears melt away, chased away by a divine fire, a strong desire to go and find Christ.

Having felt for months that the Christ he thought he knew all his life didn't exist (at least not his construction of Him), and having arrived at the monastery in the middle of the night, he sensed an overwhelming longing to find the true Christ come over him. He traveled to the monastery hoping to find Christ somewhere among dedicated monastics, to discover who Christ really is rather than who he perceived Him to be. What he did not expect was to find Him in the physical person of the deceased Elder Joseph the Hesychast.

As he was walking past the monastery's catholicon, my friend saw an older monk dressed in full monastic garb walking by with his cane. He felt he was in the presence of a very holy person, and he said to the people he was walking with, "Hey, look who is coming!" He quickly looked at the ground, feeling unworthy to gawk, but meekly turned to see the monk again, longing to look on his holy countenance. Feeling as though he had been struck by lightning, my friend was surprised and dismayed to find the monk was no longer visible. He asked the company if they had seen the monk who just walked pass them, but no one had noticed him.

Later he would explain it like this: "Since I had seen a person as real and as alive as you and me, my mind couldn't comprehend how a person—flesh and blood—could just vanish into thin air. It was the strangest feeling I ever had, because I *saw* him. It wasn't like a vision from heaven you see in movies. There were no clouds, or music, or haze. He just humbly walked by.

"It wasn't even until later that I began to realize who I had seen; certain things indicated that the person I saw was not a member of the brotherhood. For one thing, it was mid-morning, while the monks are away at work, and he was fully dressed as monks do only for trapeza or church services. And for another he was walking on a patch of grass that had a 'Do not walk on the grass!' sign.

"I thought I could be deluded, though, thinking a holy man like that would allow my sinful eyes to gaze on him. So the first opportunity I had to discuss it with the monastery's abbot, I explained what I saw that day—all the while expecting him to respond with something like, 'Ignore it. It was probably just your imagination.'

"Instead he said, 'It very well could have been Elder Joseph the Hesychast, since, as you can see in his photo, he walks with a cane.'"

After this my friend had even greater admiration for the saint. He had gone to the monastery seeking guidance because, after reading Elder Joseph's letters, he felt that finding a trusted, experienced guide he could give complete obedience to would be his only true path to salvation. Elder Joseph not only helped him find a spiritual guide, but even physically put himself in his path, illustrating in a physical form what was a spiritual reality: that he was with my friend, helping him on his long and difficult path to know the true Christ. His appearance was like an assurance: Don't be dismayed; here is Christ, you have found Him, now embrace Him in Orthodoxy.

Not to Send Them Away Hungry

I WAS LOOKING AT AN ICON of the Chinese martyrs, placed in the shop window of the Orthodox bookstore nestled in the entrance to the courtyard of the Orthodox church in Seoul, just next to the iron gate leading into the compound. We were waiting for the bookstore to open after Divine Liturgy so we could peruse the icon collection.

The items in the bookstore made up the typical inventory one would find at many parish bookstores. This particular shop had a wonderful and varied collection of small wooden icons imported from Russia. Coming from North America—where prices seem to be double or triple the price range of many items found overseas—we were excited that these unique icons were being sold for only 2,000 won, the equivalent of two or three American dollars.

That summer, during her four-month break from university, my sister was staying at a women's monastery. So we decided to buy a small icon for each of the nuns as a sort of blessing from Orthodox Korea. We chose all female saints for the sisters and even wrote down all the saints' names so my husband (who can read a tiny bit of Slavonic) could tell me who the saint in each icon was as we looked each one up online to read their lives.

Having made a list, I knew exactly how many icons we had bought and even which saints were depicted. We made sure the icons numbered the same as the sisterhood so each could receive a present. I shipped these icons in a box with two letters inside, one for my sister and one for the abbess; in each letter I mentioned the exact number of icons in the box.

My sister told me the box arrived on August 15, the feast of the Dormition of the Theotokos. After the Divine Liturgy, when the sisterhood gathered for formal trapeza, the abbess took the opportunity to give an icon to each nun. One by one they each came up to receive the icon Gerontissa chose for them. However, the abbess being the gracious person she is (as my sister put it), she did not want to exclude the four visiting young ladies who were with them in the trapeza. She gave icons to them as well and kept one for herself. This would be a perfectly ordinary thing to do if there had been enough icons to go around, but there weren't! Every nun, the abbess, and each of the four visitors received an icon. That makes four more icons than I sent in the box, and because I had written to my sister telling her exactly how many icons I had sent, she noticed this small yet significant "multiplication of icons."

I asked once, twice, three times if my sister was sure every nun had received an icon, and she assured me once, twice, three times that she had counted the people in the room numerous times to verify that there was a one-to-one person-to-icon correspondence, despite there being four extra people. We marveled at the miracle and at the abbess's compassionate refusal to send away empty-handed anyone who might be hungering for a blessing.

Unending Podvig

WE HAVE FOUR PERIODS in the church year where we fast and prepare for one of the Great Feasts, four chances to refocus and make a conscious commitment to struggle. Sometimes we do well in these periods of preparation, sometimes we start out well and end poorly, and sometimes we get to the end and feel as though we haven't even started. That is how I felt one Pascha. After fasting for fifty days, I had arrived at the greatest celebration of the year, and I felt I couldn't fully participate in the feast because I hadn't done enough, hadn't prepared enough to warrant such a glorious celebration.

At the beginning of the Paschal Matins, I was reflecting on my disappointment, feeling as though I had arrived at the feast shamefully unprepared and unworthy. But listening to the hymns about meeting Christ with a pure heart and clean senses, I realized that the *podvig*, the spiritual struggle, doesn't end with the feast; it continues. Yes, while my heart wasn't pure and my senses were not clean *as of yet*, there was still hope.

"Let us cleanse our senses, that we shall behold Christ, shining brightly with the unapproachable light of the Resurrection," the chanters sang out. I heard them and thought, *I can continue the struggle and produce fruit worthy of Christ even while feasting. Sure, I was late. Sure, I should have done more in the fast, we can always do more, but I'm not going to let despondency creep in and take hold, especially not on the evening in which Christ banished death and arose from the grave, "giving us eternal life and great mercy."*

Bright Week, the week of feasting following Holy Pascha, is called "Renewal Week" in Greek. I think this word, *renewal*, is a perfect description. The days and weeks after the Feast of the Resurrection are days in which our struggle, our conviction, is renewed. The renewal we started in the fast period continues, and our hearts become more pure the more we struggle. The struggle doesn't end when the fast ends; it just takes on a more hopeful tone. We trudge along, singing about Christ's victory over death, all the while seeking participation in His victory, seeking renewal and resurrection.

Open to Me the Door of Repentance

ST. BASIL THE GREAT RELATES A STORY about a person being crushed on account of the great crowd that had gathered for a funeral in a local church in Caesarea. Before moving to Greece, I had no exposure to such crowds. Canada has a huge land mass for a small population, so I am used to a lot of space. For this reason I always shied away from attending church festivals (*panagiria*) in Greece. It was not until 2012 that I garnered enough courage to attend the whole Vespers service in St. Demetrios's honor at his basilica, where thousands of pilgrims come from all parts of the Balkans and sometimes farther.

This particular year was no different; the church was packed, and we patiently and prayerfully waited for the archbishop to open the relics of the saint (something that occurs only once a year). At that time my brother was a deacon, so he was serving inside the sanctuary. When it came time for the clergy to assist the archbishop in opening the reliquary in order to collect and distribute the miraculous myrrh that flows from the saint's holy relics, he was at an advantageous spot to see the process.

It seemed to me that it was taking a long time for the archbishop to open the reliquary, but since I had never stayed for this part of the service, I wasn't sure how long it was supposed to take. The chanting continued, and the mass of clergy remained around the reliquary, but people began whispering and wondering aloud what was going on. At some point the archbishop's voice came over the speakers, and I heard him say, "It seems as though the saint doesn't want us to open his reliquary."

My brother explained to me afterward that the archbishop was not able to open the main part of the sarcophagus that holds St. Demetrios's relics. However, he was able to open the top compartment into which myrrh from the relics flows from below. Thus, we soon saw priests going toward the doors with large bowls full of cotton dipped in the saint's myrrh. Seeing the priests, everyone began rushing toward the exits in a chaotic and rather terrifying manner so as to receive some cotton as a blessing and keepsake from the saint.

At that moment, I remembered the man killed at the funeral on account of the crowd, and I made my cross. Although on account of my height I didn't feel as oppressed by the crowd as I might have, I still had to look up at the high ceiling to keep myself from panicking. Here we had come to the church of the Great Martyr, and I could not even bring myself to remain in the crowd in order to receive the small swab of cotton with the saint's myrrh. As soon as I was able to escape through the bookstore exit, I took the chance rather than risk a panic attack in the wild crowd.

By the grace of God, and no doubt with the help of the saint, I somehow managed to find my brother and sister-in-law quickly in the massive crowd outside, and we proceeded down the hill toward the water, my brother sharing with me a piece of his myrrh-soaked cotton. We shared our astonishment that the saint's sarcophagus did not open and agreed we didn't believe it could have been a coincidence.

In the days after this, there was much talk of a technical problem with the locks on the saint's sarcophagus. Many believed this technical problem to be the reason the main part of the reliquary wouldn't open, but I couldn't help but laugh when I heard this. We are talking about fragrant, indescribable, inexplicable myrrh flowing from centuries-old dry, dead bones, and we are really going to believe it was happenstance that the reliquary wouldn't open? I couldn't and I don't believe that.

Although I do not know why the saint chose for his reliquary to remain closed that year, I do know we would be wise to take it as a sign indicating our need for repentance. As far as I know, in subsequent years the saint has allowed his reliquary to be opened and all of his myrrh distributed, but in my opinion in 2012 he withheld his blessing. May we be enlightened to know and correct the error of our ways so that we may never again be deprived of the blessing of Thessaloniki's patron saint!

Miraculous Leaven

"TELL ME," THE BLIND MONK Elder Isidoros said as I sat next to him on a small couch. We were in a small room, old icons lining the walls, and a crowd of people waited in the reception area downstairs to speak with him. "Do you make prosfora [bread to be used for Holy Communion] in your home?"

"For years I've wanted to, but I never have," I told him.

I was staying at the monastery when he arrived, and I waited for the crowd to die down a bit before I waited in line to speak with him.

The last time we met, he told me to identify myself by stating who my spiritual father was so he could remember me. I did so, and it didn't take him long to detect my accent. As soon as he recognized my voice, he said, "Okaaayyyy" in his usual playful way, and I understood that he remembered me, as he had previously scolded me for saying "okay" instead of the Greek equivalent, *entaxi*.

Watching his weary face now, I noted how tired he appeared, how quiet he seemed. He was wearing a black woolen vest over his cassock as well as a woolen hat that fastened under his chin, causing the gray hairs of his beard to stick out. This hat was reminiscent of a bonnet a small child would wear. Usually he was very jovial, but for the last month he had been traveling around Greece speaking with countless souls who had come to him seeking his prayers, spiritual words, comfort, and even miracles. He was tired and considerably subdued.

"Pay attention to what I'm about to say so that you'll understand," he said seriously. "Either on the Feast of the Cross, September 14, or on Holy Friday you'll put water and flour together in a container, and you'll take a flower from the *epitaphios*[*] or basil leaves and place them on top, not inside. You wait two days, and it will rise, and you will use this when you bake prosfora. Is that, or is that not, a miracle?"

---

[*] *Epitaphios*: an icon printed or embroidered on fabric, depicting Jesus Christ lying

"It is," I answered, smiling.

He put his hand inside his black cotton shoulder bag and began rummaging around in it. He took out a few clear plastic bags, one with a cross and a few with dried bay leaves, most likely having collected them from the service on Holy Saturday when the priest throws bay leaves to the faithful.

He laid the bags on his lap and he searchingly felt one of them between his fingers.

"Are these bay leaves?" he asked.

"Yes," I said.

"Take this," he said stretching out his hand toward me. I kissed his hand as I took the little bag, a blessing.

"Okay, so either on Holy Friday or on the Feast of the Cross you will do as I've told you," he reiterated.

It is customary for Orthodox Christians to use what is called *prozimi* when making prosfora. The way to make prozimi is as Elder Isidoros describes above. Although the prozimi is only flour and water, it rises of its own accord on these two feast days, Holy Friday and the Exaltation of the Honorable Cross (September 14), and serves as a leaven in the prosfora. Like many things in Orthodoxy, it is difficult to understand or explain, but it occurs all the same, and this "little leaven leavens the whole lump" (Gal. 5:9).

The Miracle-Working Icon of St. Seraphim

ORTHODOXY HAS BEEN ESTABLISHED in South Korea for over one hundred years. A party of Russian missionaries arrived and

on the burial stone after the Crucifixion.

served the very first Divine Liturgy on the peninsula on February 17, 1890, the After-feast of the Meeting of the Lord in the Temple (Old Style). So while initially they were under the Russian Church, during the Japanese occupation (1910–1945) the Korean church was under the jurisdiction of the Japanese Orthodox Church. However, during the Korean War the Orthodox faithful were scattered, and the one and only Orthodox church was destroyed.

Sometime later, while searching through the rubble of the destroyed church, a soldier found the epitaphios icon intact and in fairly good condition. This recovered icon now hangs on the wall in the Russian chapel of St. Maximos the Greek in Seoul. Also housed in this small chapel are the vestments of St. John of Kronstadt. They are kept behind glass in the narthex. I was told the saint had wished to serve the Orthodox faithful in Korea, but his health had deteriorated, making it impossible for him to travel the great distance, and so he sent his vestments in his stead as a blessing.

After the Korean War, a Greek priest came to minister to the Korean faithful, and they decided to go under the omophorion of the Ecumenical Patriarch. Currently there are ten Orthodox churches throughout the country, and the flock is composed of Korean faithful. Services are conducted in Korean by native priests, some of whom completed theological studies in Greece.

The Russian chapel of St. Maximos the Greek and St. Nicholas Cathedral are located in the same compound in Seoul in the district of Aeo-ga. We would split our time between the two churches while we lived there. Each had its own charm. The small chapel conducted services in Slavonic with a small but talented choir, and the young Korean priestmonk's peaceful and prayerful presence was very attractive, while the large fresco-covered cathedral, which predominantly used Byzantine melodies (though sung by a choir rather than chanters), had its own appeal. Though the churches were on different calendars, the congregations celebrated Great Feasts like Holy Week and Pascha together.

While the chapel of St. Maximos the Greek houses the vestments of St. John of Kronstadt and the miraculously preserved epitaphios, the Cathedral of St. Nicholas houses two miracle-working icons, both of which are from Russia. The first is a myrrh-streaming icon of the Mother of God the Directress. It was a gift from a tsaritsa to someone (I have since forgotten to whom it was given). The other miracle-working icon is of St. Seraphim of Sarov. We were told this latter icon is known for renewing itself, which means that the image becomes clearer of its own accord, not by means of cleaning solutions, but by the grace of the saint.

During the year we worked in Seoul, after the divine services we would wait in line with the rest of the Orthodox faithful to venerate these two miracle-working icons. The icon of the Mother of God was located next to the northern door of the temple, while St. Seraphim's icon was next to the southern door. The icon of St. Seraphim depicted him kneeling on a rock in front of a tree. But only the saint, the rock, and a portion of the tree were clearly visible. I suppose due to age or many years in an environment of smoke produced by candles and incense—likely a combination of both—it had darkened significantly. One Sunday, however, Matthew, Catherine (my brother and sister-in-law), John, and I all noticed a significant difference in the clarity of the image—or at least we thought we did.

Years later, Fr. John was ordained to the Holy Diaconate at a small chapel in rural Quebec dedicated to St. Seraphim of Sarov, during the chapel's patronal feast of the Opening of the Relics of St. Seraphim (August 1). At the time of the ordination, I had forgotten about the miracle-working icon. The memory came flooding back to me after the ordination while I was looking at an icon of St. Seraphim the parish had given us. I marveled all the more at the mercy of God, the blessings He bestows even on the unworthy, and I tearfully thanked the saint for allowing my husband to be ordained in his little church in Canada.

St. Seraphim, you who prayed for one thousand nights while kneeling on a rock, who perpetually felt the joy of Christ's Resurrection, and who work miracles even for us lowly ones, remember us sinners before the throne of the Almighty God. And pray for our Korean brothers and sisters to continue to preserve and uphold the faith of their fathers!

Out of Love

WHEN I WAS YOUNGER, I was easily enticed by idealism, unconsciously thinking any kind of compromise was beneath me. I did not realize I thought this way with regard to fasting until I visited a certain women's monastery. It was long enough ago that I no longer remember the exact details, but I remember speaking to the abbess about fasting, and I must have mentioned that I felt as though desserts—despite being "fast-friendly"*—weren't appropriate during a fasting period. And that is when she mentioned that fasting was about depriving our bodies of the nutrients in meat, dairy products,

---

* The phrase "fast-friendly" applies to foods that accord with the Orthodox fasting

and fish, but not about eating horrible-tasting food.

She explained that at the monastery they not only ate decently prepared food, but some desserts as well, because otherwise it would be too difficult for the sisters, especially the young ones, to manage. I wasn't fully convinced in that moment, but I quickly began to see the merit in what she was teaching me. When I read the following in the sayings of the desert fathers, I was more than convinced that the abbess spoke and acted out of great discernment, akin to that of St. Anthony the Great. This is what I read:

> A hunter in the desert saw Abba Anthony enjoying himself with the brethren and he was shocked. Wanting to show him that it was necessary sometimes to meet the needs of the brethren, the old man [Abba Anthony] said to him, "Put an arrow in your bow and shoot it." So he did. The old man then said, "Shoot another," and he did so. Then the old man said, "Shoot yet again," and the hunter replied, "If I bend my bow so much I will break it." Then the old man said to him, "It is the same with the work of God. If we stretch the brethren beyond measure they will soon break. Sometimes it is necessary to come down to meet their needs." When he heard these words the hunter was pierced by compunction and, greatly edified by the old man, he went away. As for the brethren, they went away strengthened.[20]

Years later, I was attending a theological lecture at Aristotle University when I heard the professor say, "When you fast out of love for God, you don't feel as though you're fasting at all." Although I can honestly say I have felt this way for perhaps one fleeting moment in

---

regulations, namely foods that do not contain meat, dairy products, or fish, and sometimes oil.

my life, I believe what the professor said to be true. It is a sentiment echoed in our hymnology. For instance, in the Matins service for Clean Monday we hear:

> All mortal life is but one day, so it is said,
> To those who labor with love.
> There are forty days in the Fast;
> Let us keep them all with joy.

Out of love and discernment, the abbess made sure the nuns had tasty fasting food and even fasting desserts so they wouldn't "break." Out of love and discernment, Abba Anthony would occasionally enjoy himself with the brethren to help lighten their load. The goal is the same in both cases: to encourage us to fast, to lead a Christian lifestyle, out of love, genuine love for God. A kind of love that when attained enlightens us to recognize that all hardship—all sacrifice—pales in comparison to the love between a soul and her Creator, God Almighty.

It's in the Little Things

WHILE IN GREECE, I attended a chanting class held at a monastery on the outskirts of Thessaloniki. At the end of every class, our teachers would offer us a sweet. Sometimes they would offer us more than one. If a girl in the class particularly liked a certain sweet offered that day, the sisters would encourage her to take a few for the road. While we were leaving the monastery after one class, a group of us were walking together, and one of the girls lamented that she had eaten too many sweets that night.

"What do you have to worry about? You're so skinny, those calories won't go anywhere on you!" one student teased.

"You know where those calories go?" the other asked seriously. "Straight to my *logismous* [thoughts], that's where!" Although we all laughed about the calories going to her thoughts, this little observation really struck me. *What a spiritual way to think!* I thought to myself. Great spiritual insight is often conveyed in the small things.

I've heard laypeople express their frustration with life in the world and the temptations that come as a result. Although monasticism appears to be the more difficult of the two paths, many times I have heard laypeople say how much easier it would be to struggle in an environment where everyone dresses the same way, eats the same food, and does obedience in common to the abbot or abbess. Fair enough; there is some merit in this complaint. In the world we are more distracted by secularism, less focused on the spiritual life, and find little to no support for leading an Orthodox Christian lifestyle.

However, where there's a will, there's a way. Perhaps leading a spiritual life requires a little creativity for us in the world, but it is definitely possible. It all comes down to our mindset and disposition; if we want to, we can become saints even in the middle of the city, as the newly canonized Saint Porphyrios used to say.

St. Paisios of the Holy Mountain teaches, "If someone neglects the little things the danger is that he'll start neglecting the greater, holier things. And then, without realizing it, rationalizing it all to himself—'This is nothing, that doesn't matter'—he can end up, God forbid, totally neglecting the things of God and becoming irreverent, arrogant, and atheistic."[21]

It's in the little ascetic practices that we will make progress in the spiritual life. Our times are so fraught with temptation and distractions. A prudent approach is for us to take baby steps toward a spiritual life and do what is within our strength. So, for example, although books about barefoot ascetics living off of dry bread may seem to have no relevance to us, there are things within our power that we can do to spiritualize the everyday elements of our life, to become micro-barefoot ascetics in a sense.

Perhaps we will eat a little of everything, but we do not need to *overeat*. This is within our grasp: to get up from the table before we are completely full. Some ascetics struggled to keep silent for hours on end. This is not an ascetical practice you usually see done in the world, but we can avoid gossiping and cursing. We can refrain from talking back to and shouting at people out of anger. These struggles are not small ascetic feats, but neither do they require us to live in an Orthodox monastic community in order to practice them.

My dear classmate was onto something when she perceived that eating too many sweets goes to her thoughts. Our body is not unrelated to our soul; nor is living in the world unrelated to spiritual exercises. May God help us to see with our spiritual eyes and make an effort even in little ways, so that by struggling and being victorious in the small battles, we might win the great battles and receive great spiritual spoils as a result.

Witnessing

IF ONE WERE TO ATTEMPT to count all the men and women who converted to the Orthodox Christian Faith as a result of an encounter they had with a living saint, I suppose it would be impossible to discover an accurate number. St. Katherine the Great Martyr, for instance, singlehandedly influenced two hundred soldiers and philosophers to believe in the True God. Countless citizens of Nicomedia came to believe in Jesus Christ on account of the witness of St. George the Great Martyr. And who knows how many Carthaginians were influenced by the Christian bravery and disdain for worldly goods shown by the African martyrs, St. Perpetua and her companions. There is an undeniable quality about holy people that draws others to them. Perhaps this is what is meant by the passage, "Let your light so shine before men, that they may see your good works and glorify your Father in heaven" (Matt. 5:16).

My husband, usually a very immovable sort—whom some may describe as being as excitable as the famous *Star Trek: The Next Generation* android, Data—was himself once so moved by the presence of a holy abbess that he could no longer go on denying the appeal of Orthodox Christianity.

We were visiting a monastery in the States. I was a catechumen, desperately hoping, praying, and impatiently waiting for my husband to share in my enthusiasm for the Apostolic Faith. An American abbess approached a group of us standing outside the monastery's trapeza. We all bowed to the ground and each kissed her hand. She greeted us and continued on her way.

With an astonished look on his face, John said, "Did you see that? It was as if she didn't walk, but glided above the ground!" I and those with us exchanged rather bewildered glances, since no one else in the company had seen this. I certainly noticed her sweet, meek appearance, but I did not observe her walking as though she were off the ground.

For whatever reason, this experience deeply affected John. While I can't say it catapulted him into Orthodoxy, it most certainly helped soften his heart to the mystical elements of the Orthodox Church. It was only a few months later that he began immersing himself in the life of the Church through fasting and prayer, having himself become a catechumen.

Having Only Made a Beginning

DURING THE LAST VISIT I made to one of my beloved monasteries in Greece, I spoke with Sr. Seraphima. Sr. Seraphima had become a nun at a young age and so, although she was only around forty years old, she was the third most senior sister in the monastery (seniority is based on years as a monastic, not on age). She was one of the most hardworking nuns I have ever met. In my opinion, she was everything I expected a true monastic to be. She worked hard and prayed hard, but more impressively, she loved properly.

Once, after a long day of physical labor, she came into the bakery around ten PM and sat down to eat some food the sisters had saved for her. "This is the first time I've sat down since I woke up at five AM. I ate lunch standing up," she told me. Imagine—seventeen hours on her feet! But that wasn't the amazing part. One of the sisters, who was scheduled to start the prozimi for baking the prosfora the next morning, wasn't able to do it, and so Sr. Seraphima volunteered. Now this is what astonished me. She had been working all day, and instead of returning to her cell to say her prayers and go to sleep, she said—*with enthusiasm*—"Tell me how to do it, and I'll do it."

I was quite seriously stunned, because here it was late at night, and *I* was exhausted from working all day, even without having done the physical labor she had. I couldn't have volunteered to help if my life depended on it, but she sacrificed for the sake of the sister who was unable to do it, for the sisterhood at large, and most especially for the love of Christ. I saw before my eyes what is meant by Christ's saying, "By this all will know that you are My disciples, if you have love for one another" (John 13:35).

So here I was speaking with Sr. Seraphima for what turned out to be the last time before returning to Canada.

"Constantina, you have learned a lot here, not only from living in Greece but also from visiting monasteries and speaking with Gerontissa. You have made a wonderful foundation for you and Fr. John to return and share the light of Orthodoxy in America." (As I've mentioned, Greeks would often say America in place of Canada.)

"But," she continued, "never think you know anything. Always tell yourself you've only just made a beginning. It will be easy for you to think you learned something here. But don't. Just tell yourself, 'I only just made a beginning.' And always call Gerontissa and your Geronda for advice. When you're not sure about something, call them and ask them questions."

I found a great deal of wisdom in her words. Forcing ourselves to have a humble mindset is most essential in leading a Christian life. Even if I have acquired all the wisdom in the world, it is all nothing if I don't have love, St. Paul says (1 Cor. 13), and true love is firmly rooted in humility.

Sr. Seraphima's abbess once told me, "Humility is the most important thing: for us to bow our heads in humility."

My dear nun's advice is a practical tool to keep my head from tipping too high upward in my pride. I did indeed learn a lot from studying in Greece, living there, and visiting many monasteries, but I have only just made a beginning. I still have so much to learn, and more specifically, to put into practice.

O Beloved Orthodoxy

JOHN AND I WOULD USUALLY do Vespers in English at home in our Greek apartment. However, we decided to attend the local parish for the Vespers service of Ss. Constantine and Helen (my nameday). There is no debating that God works in mysterious ways—that He orchestrates things to work for the good of those who love Him (Rom. 8:28).

During the Vespers service, I noticed two nuns whose monastic habits differed from the habit Greek nuns wear. I decided I would introduce myself, despite not knowing whether they spoke English. To my surprise, they not only spoke English but were from a monastery in the United States.

They informed me they had just arrived a day or so before; they were making a pilgrimage to Greece. A woman in our neighborhood who had brought them to the local parish for Vespers was offering them hospitality. She was the mother of a friend of the monastery back in the US. The lady they were staying with could not speak English, and neither nun spoke Greek; they had been getting by thus far with facial expressions and sign language. This fortunate communication challenge resulted in my becoming their translator for the length of their stay in Thessaloniki.

And so, a few days later, I found myself on a boat tour off the coast of the Athonite peninsula. It is forbidden for women to visit Mount Athos; however, they are permitted on boats a certain distance from the monastic peninsula. This allows for a long-distance view of the miraculous, ancient male monasteries of the famous Holy Mountain.

Having seen the towering monasteries, the monks working in the distance, and the fog-enclosed peak of Athos, we sat and took up conversation. While the boat sped back to the port in Ouranopoli, dolphins jumped alongside us intermittently, as if knowing one day someone would incorporate their presence into a story about a layperson who had the blessing of becoming a temporary tour guide for two revered American nuns.

"What is the number one thing you think Orthodox families should know in contemporary North America?" I asked as we gazed out on the blue water while waves crashed on either side of the boat.

"We need to teach our children to be proud of being Orthodox, to be proud of our Orthodox Faith," the senior nun emphasized. "They go to school with other children, and they find they are in the minority. But they should be proud to be Orthodox."

I silently nodded in agreement and pondered what she had said. She spoke from her experience, enlightened by years of conversations and relationships with Orthodox families living in the world.

My understanding and appreciation of her advice has deepened on my return to North America. I am constantly reminded that Orthodox Christians are in the minority, as my husband serves the only parish on the island and indeed in the entire province of Newfoundland and Labrador. The children in our parish tell me of their experiences at school. They ask me hordes of questions that demonstrate they understand they are different, that *Orthodoxy* is different.

I want them to know there is no shame in being Orthodox Christians. Orthodoxy is the Truth; it is power; it is everlasting. It is not, cannot be, diminished merely because we find ourselves as one in a million, isolated, and in the minority. Orthodoxy is always true, always good, always overcoming. It cannot be overcome; it cannot be conquered. We *should* be proud to be Orthodox—not lording our Faith over others, but treasuring the precious pearl we have been entrusted with. Joseph Vriennios, the spiritual father of St. Mark of Ephesus, wrote the following God-inspired words:

> Our Orthodox faith,
> Our wealth, and our glory,
> Our stock, our crown, our pride.
> We will never deny you, O beloved Orthodoxy,
> nor belie you, O time-honored reverence,
> nor walk away from you, O mother piety.
> We have been born in you, we live in you,
> and we will die in you.
> If time asks for it,
> We will sacrifice our lives ten thousand times for you.

May God make us worthy to fulfill such words in our everyday lives!

Drink of This, All of You: Keeping a Prayer Rule

IT IS A CUSTOM in the Orthodox Church for the faithful to keep a personal rule of prayer—some form of set prayers said daily, whether it is praying the Matins or Compline service, a set number of Jesus prayers, or making prostrations; it varies from person to person. Our rule is usually given to us by our priest or spiritual father. Sometimes the individual Christian chooses it, but it ought always to be taken on with a blessing. Our prayer rule is our unique and personal connection to Christ; similar to a medical prescription, our prayer rule is a spiritual prescription particular to our illness, to our needs. When we miss our prayer rule, especially if we miss it frequently, not only do we not become healthy, but we in fact become more ill, as the ever-memorable Abbess Makrina taught:

> Many times we neglect our prayer rules saying, "I'll do it tomorrow or the day after tomorrow," and they pile up. The soul weakens, just as the body weakens, when we don't give it the necessary calories and it begins to break down. . . . And we are darkened, because we imagine as insignificant and unimportant everything that we must be careful of. And the body begins to become fat while the soul collapses. And later we say: "My mind has become dim, I don't remember God, I am darkened; I'm not able to pray." It is because the soul is hungry, it is not being fed and nourished by the body; in this way the body is not given strength and the soul becomes ill.[22]

There was once a nun who was lax when it came to her prayer rule. Although she had dedicated her life to monasticism, she had forgotten her first love (Rev. 2:4) and neglected to complete her prayer rule every day. At the end of her life, as she lay dying on her bed, she struggled greatly, unable to take her last breath. Her fellow nuns observed this and asked the abbess why it was that their sister and co-struggler was not able to give up her spirit. After praying, the abbess discerned that this was a result of the nun's failure to keep her prayer rule faithfully. So the abbess advised the sisterhood to begin praying to make up for the prayers their dying sister ought to have completed. Once the sisterhood had fulfilled the necessary number of prayers on behalf of the negligent nun, she took her last breath, and her soul departed.

Many are the stories of monks, nuns, laypeople, even whole families, who keep an extensive prayer rule faithfully but do so never having asked a blessing from a discerning spiritual father. This too can have long-lasting, damaging effects on the soul. I know of one case in which a layperson, after speaking with a spiritual father and revealing his intense rule of prayer, was given a blessing to continue, and yet he suddenly found himself unable to say so much as the Our Father daily.

Similarly, according to the *Gerontikon*, there was once a monk who could do three thousand prostrations a day, because his effort was fueled by his self-will. But once he was given a blessing, he ceased to be able to do even a few prostrations. This is why we should always seek a blessing from our priest or spiritual father when it comes to spiritual practices and most especially such things as our personal rule of prayer.

When we keep a rule of prayer with a blessing, not only are we protected from spiritual delusion, but prayer does not become something we merely do when and if we feel like it. For this would make our spiritual life subject to our ever-changing and fickle will—the last thing we should put our trust in. When we have a blessing from our spiritual father, we approach our prayer rule the way we would a medical prescription. By taking the prescribed dosage on a daily basis, we gradually become healed of our particular spiritual ailments. However, this spiritual medication cannot have an effect if we do not make the effort to take it regularly.

Once when I had the opportunity to speak with Gerontissa Philareti about prayer, she told me, "We can sit down and say the

Jesus Prayer for hours every night, but if our mind is wandering all over the place, there is no profit in that. The purpose of a prayer rule is to offer God our attention morning and evening, to focus on Him.

"There is no such thing as a small or large prayer rule," the abbess went on. "There is just a personal rule of prayer. We need to make sure we keep it faithfully, every day, no matter what. We shouldn't try to take on too much. We should just do those prayers our spiritual father prescribes for us. If we take on too much, we'll end up not even being able to do that which was first given to us."

She went on to tell me a story about a nun she knew when she herself was a young novice. This nun had the obedience of doing three hundred prostrations daily as a part of her prayer rule. However, she had begun to become prideful when she observed the small number of prostrations some of the younger nuns did for their prayer rules. She began making comments such as, "I, a woman of fifty years of age, do three hundred prostrations a day, and these young twenty-somethings only do fifty!"

"That's what she said until Geronda heard of it, anyway!" the abbess told me.

Once the sisterhood's spiritual father saw the soul-destroying sin of pride rising up in this nun, he told her, "My sister, you will do three prostrations a day from now on."

"What do you mean, Geronda? I do three hundred!" she rejoined.

"Not anymore. From now on you'll only do three, and you'll learn humility," he told her. Gerontissa Philareti taught me not only that keeping our prayer rule consistently is of extreme importance (no matter the size), but also that above all else, we ought to keep it with humility. Gerontissa's simple words that evening opened my eyes to the reality that our prayer rule is like a medical prescription, but it's up to us whether we become healthy. If I took nothing else away from all my experiences, lessons, and conversations with enlightened, holy people, I take this: Nothing will benefit my soul like faithfully offering God my attention, my mind, heart, soul, and strength, through faithfully keeping my prayer rule.

✠ FIVE ✠

Blessed Are the Merciful
for they shall obtain mercy

"Just Don't You Do"

W E WERE SITTING on the balcony of our Thessaloniki apartment, eating supper with our dear friend the Romanian priestmonk, who was also studying at Aristotle University at that time. He had just returned from Romania for the fall school semester, and this was the first opportunity we had to tell him of Fr. John's ordination to the diaconate a few months prior and to hear about his monastery's feast day, in which the monks welcomed some thirty thousand pilgrims.

While we were catching up, I told him of a recent trip we took in which we attended Divine Liturgy at various parishes. Although I enjoyed meeting all the different people and participating in the divine services with them, I was admittedly surprised by some practices I observed among the faithful at one particular parish. I had not encountered such things previously, and I was expressing the uncertainty I felt about what I saw.

"Well, Con [he always called me by my nickname], I will tell you a story. There were some monks at a monastery in Romania who did not like some of the things their fellow monks were doing. So they decided to visit a holy elder to ask his advice. When they told the elder everything, he gave them a simple answer. It literally translates as, 'Just don't you do.' So, just don't you do either," he told me.

"You know, I've served in many parishes in Thessaloniki and have seen so many things that surprised me," he continued. "Not all priests are as careful and reverent as our priest, Fr. T. But we have to remember the elder's words, 'Just don't you do.'"

This spiritual word from our dear friend was tremendously helpful. First, it does not condone improper behaviors or practices, but neither does it condemn the individuals who, knowingly or unknowingly, do such things. For it is one thing to witness someone making a mistake, and it is quite another to pass judgment on the person for having done so. This friend's spiritual word was also great practical advice for avoiding judging others. This is something we can readily apply to a variety of situations in which we find ourselves confronted with thoughts condemning behaviors or actions we deem unfit. We can say to ourselves, *Never mind what they do; I just won't do it.*

Once while I was helping Sr. Xenia put her freshly made marmalade into jars, she told me that after our death, the Archangel Michael will cut the heads off those who pass judgment on others. For to judge is to condemn, and condemning someone is the opposite of having mercy. If we wish for the Lord to be merciful to us, we must also have mercy on others, and this means not judging, not condemning—even when we see people doing strange things or things we find inappropriate. Abba Dorotheos writes:

> The Lord Himself said: *"Be merciful, just as your heavenly Father also is merciful"* [Luke 6:36]. He did not say: *"Fast as your heavenly Father fasts,"* neither did He say: *"Give away your possessions as your heavenly Father is without possessions"*; but he did say: *"Be merciful as your heavenly Father is merciful."* This is because this virtue—above all—emulates God and is a characteristic of Him.[23]

So, we won't concern ourselves about the behaviors of others; we will be merciful, not only in our actions but in our thoughts. We will look inward instead and pray for Christ to have mercy on us and protect us from erroneous practices as well as from judgmental thoughts. We will pray for Him to make us merciful just as His Father is merciful.

The Promise of Mercy

WHEN YOU ENTER into the presence of a saint, you enter into sacred space. Things can seem to shift into slow motion as everyone's attention is pulled toward the holy hermit lying sick on a bed while hundreds of people pass by, asking his prayers, taking his blessing, receiving a word, and soaking in his Christlikeness.

We had only recently learned that Elder Gabriel, the disciple of St. Paisios of the Holy Mountain, had left Mount Athos for the first time in twenty-three years in order to undergo surgery in Thessaloniki. As I mentioned above, while recovering he received visitors every day for three hours. In the span of one month, some twenty thousand people visited him.

I first learned from my Byzantine chant classmates that he was in mainland Greece and staying at a house in Pilai. A few days later, my sister-in-law, a friend, and I decided to take a bus up to Pilai.

"Even if you didn't know where to go, you could always follow the crowd and you'd find the house," our friend said as we followed behind a few other people walking up the slightly inclined road to the hospitable family's home.

Once we arrived, we saw that although we arrived one hour before the scheduled time for the elder to receive people, a crowd of about fifty had already gathered. We all waited outside the gate. Soon we were allowed into the yard, where we took turns writing down our loved ones' names so the elder could pray for them.

Groups of twenty people were allowed into the elder's bedroom at a time. Four groups of twenty went before us, as children and the ill were given priority. At least two hundred people waited behind us. When the group before us were taken upstairs to the elder, our group was ushered into the basement of the house, where we venerated holy relics: a blanket that had belonged to St. Paisios, holy vestments worn by Venerable Elder Tikhon (the spiritual father of St. Paisios), as well as a small chair the saint owned.

I hadn't planned on going to this home to visit Elder Gabriel, because we were expecting to see him at Gerontissa Ioanna's monastery a few days later. However, after speaking with my friend (who had gone six consecutive days because, as she informed me, "I have a lot of people I need to go for"), I realized I shouldn't miss the opportunity to go on behalf of my own loved ones.

Standing in the basement waiting for the fourth group to leave, I grew anxious. *How can I tell him what I have to say in a quick but comprehensible way?* I must have asked myself this question a thousand times. *It doesn't matter, God is just going to have to help me say what I need to when I get the chance.*

"How fortunate I am that I came here!" a woman said as she was coming down the stairs. "What a blessing that we came here to see this elder."

Suddenly our group was being told to begin our ascent to the elder's room. We climbed the spiral staircase, my nervous anticipation escalating with each step. Finally we arrived at the last stair. As soon as we stepped into the room, it felt as if we hit a wall of fragrant grace, such was the presence of the holy monk.

He was lying on a small bed, holding a crucifix from Jerusalem (which contained earth from various holy sites) in his right hand. His white hair and beard looked slightly disheveled. Those in front of me each briefly knelt, kissed his hand, and rose up swiftly. Following suit, I knelt down, and he held my head and crossed it. I kissed his hand. Although I'm not a shy person, at that moment I just couldn't bring myself to say anything. I arose and stepped aside. As others followed, having their heads crossed, kissing his holy hand, and shedding a few grateful tears, we waited to the side.

"Okay, please exit now," one of the men assisting the elder said to our group.

Oh Lord, I didn't ask him to pray for my loved ones! What am I going to do? We have to leave now! How can I tell him? I silently fretted.

But just then, my friend took a coughing fit. As someone took her over to the kitchenette to give her a drink of water, I stood staring at the elder.

"Geronda," I said as I came close to him. But my nerves got the better of me, and I started crying. I was mortified. I had specifically prayed to St. John Maximovitch before I came, asking him to help me say what I needed to say *without* crying, and here I found myself overcome with emotion and unable to express myself.

My Panagia, what am I going to do? I can't stop crying! I thought. I only managed to utter two words: "Very sick . . ." This was not exactly the information I intended to share.

"Don't worry; don't worry; don't worry," the elder responded as he crossed my head three more times with his cross. "God will have mercy," he said.

He said "God will have *mercy*." Not "God will heal the illness," but "He will have *mercy*."

The elder had answered my prayers. I kissed his hand again and stepped back, still far too emotional. But it didn't matter. He was a saint; he understood my thoughts even though I couldn't verbalize them. His holy presence and prophetic words communicated grace, peace, and the promise of mercy.

Thank God saints still exist, and that we—even in the midst of darkness—are benefited by their holy prayers and spiritual gifts!

More Blessed to Give Than to Receive

ALMSGIVING COMES in many forms. My husband and I have been at the receiving end of almsgiving far more than I would have thought possible. This is because almsgiving isn't merely pulling change out of one's pocket when passing by an unshaven man sitting with an outstretched open hand. There are numerous ways to give alms and to do good works and acts of mercy. We've learned this through experiencing and witnessing the goodwill and good works of others.

A lady who lived in our neighborhood in Thessaloniki was truly a good neighbor and, judging from her works, a great Christian. She was always on the go, giving food away to neighbors, opening her door and heart to the lonely and depressed, and taking the time to visit the sick in hospitals. She was a real shining example for everyone. She was a Christian who loved and helped all people with neither prejudice nor preference, always striving to hide her good works.

Someone else I knew well, who struggled to some extent to make ends meet for his own family, would give cash to people he knew needed help. Once while I was visiting with him in his iconography shop, a woman known to him came in to say hello. She appeared to be in need of financial help. He tried to be discreet, but I noticed he slipped her a fair amount of money when he shook her hand. Based on the fact that she didn't react to the hidden gift concealed in the handshake, I figured this was a normal, if not a frequent, occurrence.

Another friend of ours loved tending to the many little chapels in the areas surrounding her home. In Greece, it is common for some chapels to be left open so the faithful can come in, venerate, light candles, and pray. This friend of ours had the habit of buying supplies for these chapels, making sure the oil lamps—which remained alight all day and all night, burning in front of the holy icons—were filled with oil and had a ready supply of wicks.

After she had been doing this for quite a few years and far too late at night for her own safety, her spiritual father told her she didn't have a blessing to continue this good work by herself, as some of the chapels were quite secluded. This is how we came to know about her almsgiving, because she took us along with her once when we were visiting. I loved this practice and thought it was a great idea. Tending to the needs of local churches is a wonderful way to offer alms.

Sometimes we think of almsgiving in narrow terms. In reality, there are so many ways for us to give our money and our time, which can equal or exceed the value of money. St. Paisios the Athonite would say even if we don't have money, we can give away a good Christian book. There is always something we can give, either materially or otherwise. We just need to be creative and remember that it's more blessed to give than to receive.

A nun once told me that her sisterhood always served a meal to visitors after Divine Liturgy on Sundays. During a rough patch, when the sisters were struggling more than usual to make ends meet, they decided to cut back and offer only coffee and sweets to Sunday visitors.

"It wasn't blessed, though," the sister said with a frown. "It became very obvious that it wasn't blessed, so we went back to serving a meal after Divine Liturgy."

This made me curious. I wondered what had happened to make it apparent to the sisters that they shouldn't cut back on their hospitality. But I held my tongue and refrained from probing for more information. It didn't matter; she was telling me the sisterhood had learned from experience that it is more blessed to give than to receive, even when it feels as though giving is beyond our means.

Giving money to those who need it, offering a dish of home-cooked food to a busy or struggling family, caring for and visiting the sick, taking time to sit and chat with the lonely, and tending to the needs and expenses of Orthodox temples, small and large, are all wonderful ways to offer our money, time, care, and love to others and by extension to Christ Himself: "Assuredly, I say to you, inasmuch as you did *it* to one of the least of these My brethren, you did *it* to Me" (Matt. 25:40).

Leaving Home and Going to the Land God Showed Us

THE DIVINE PSALMIST SAYS, "Listen, O daughter, / Consider and incline your ear; / Forget your own people also, and your father's house" (Ps. 44/45:10). In moving to Greece, we did just that. We left all those comforts behind, moved halfway around the world, and subjected ourselves to whatever that foreign country would throw at us. From the moment we encountered Orthodoxy, all we wanted was to learn the Orthodox Faith. We went to Greece to study and learn as much as possible about living as Orthodox Christians.

Now I'll be honest: I had a romantic view of Greece. Despite the sound advice of others, I basically thought everyone walked around two feet off the ground, raptured in a state of prayer. A venerable Greek nun I met in Canada even advised me before we left, "Don't look anywhere in Greece! Don't listen to anyone! Things aren't the way they used to be." But I couldn't help myself. Every crazy person I encountered on the street I took to be a fool for Christ. I believed every housewife had noetic prayer. I considered every priest to have attained illumination, and I expected to just soak it all in while studying Modern Greek (a language I only knew the alphabet of before moving there). I thought this way, that is, until the first time I attempted to receive Holy Communion alongside a large crowd of Greek women.

We were at our neighborhood church, located literally steps from our apartment building. It was a large, beautiful church, newly built and covered in vibrant frescoes. I followed along with the service as best I could despite not knowing Ancient Greek (the liturgical language used in Greek churches). I had a sense of where we were in the service only because of physical cues: the epistle reading, the priest processing with the Holy Gifts, and so forth.

When the priest came out of the altar with the chalice, I knew it was time for Holy Communion, so I left my seat and attempted to get in line. Only there was no line. Instead, all the women huddled in the front of the church, blocking the path to Holy Communion. I naively assumed they too were waiting to commune, so I patiently waited my turn.

Once the priest went back into the altar, however, I understood I had missed my chance to receive Holy Communion. I realized then that the women had been waiting to receive antidoron (blessed bread). It never occurred to me to ask whether or not they planned to receive Holy Communion, but even if it had occurred to me, I wouldn't have been able to ask, since I had not yet learned the language. Watching them crowd around the priest to receive antidoron, all of my unfounded high opinions of the average Greek just flew out the church's blue and red stained-glass windows.

I should never have been so quick to judge others. Yes, even thinking highly of a person is judging them; it's forming a judgment on their character without cause. Needless to say, although I was very upset, my figurative feet touched down on Greek soil for the first time, and I began taking in with sobriety what Greece had to offer.

We made countless pilgrimages to holy monasteries, crawled into holy caves, walked through forests to reach holy springs, and each time we marveled that we walked on holy ground. We have been to places where saints, both old and new, living and reposed, have dwelt. We have kissed fragrant relics and taken the blessing of more than one living saint. We have attended services in churches older than almost anything one can find in North America. We have listened to contemporary homilies that made us think we were hearing St. John Chrysostom preach against the activities in the hippodrome.

We strove to take in all the blessings Greece offered, knowing we would (and believe me, *do*) long for those days after returning home to Canada. But we also strove to take them in because we knew that being able to share all the blessings we received is as important as being grateful for them.

Having said all that, actually settling down in Greece was about as difficult as writing about the good aspects of Greece is easy. Our years spent there were anything but trouble-free, but they were also filled with the benefits that come from suffering. I once confessed at a talk I was giving that although I had written one book (and now two) on the blessings of our time in Greece, I could have written five about our difficulties.

We moved away from home, forgot our people, our language, our "father's house," all because we wanted to inherit the mindset of Orthodoxy. I don't know if we have attained it. But we certainly hope our continually renewed attempt will one day bear fruit, and that we will be successful, with God's help, in offering to our people the beauty we received from that Orthodox country, Greece.

Let Him Call for the Elders of the Church

"YOU KNOW HOW my back was always killing me," my friend Katerina began as we sat at her table drinking coffee and enjoying a sweet she had made that morning.

"Well, once when I was stretching my back because I was in a lot of pain, a friend saw me and asked why I was stretching like that. I told her I had a lot of pain in my back. She said she had the same problem and would do similar stretches, trying to relieve the pain. She had gone to a doctor about it, and he told her she had a herniated disc in her neck.

"'You must have the same thing,' she told me. 'The doctor said there wasn't anything I could do about it.' So I didn't think much about it again.

"Awhile later I went to visit Elder Isidoros—the blind monk from Philotheou Monastery—while he was in the city. I went for one reason only, to ask him to pray over my hands in hopes I would stop being so clumsy. You know what I'm like: I drop everything!" she told me.

"I said, 'Geronda please cross my hands with the holy relics so that I will stop dropping things.'

"He reached up and touched the back of my neck and asked, 'Here?'

"I guided his hands down to mine and said, 'No Geronda, my hands.'

"And again he placed the small box of relics on the back of my neck and said, 'No, here,' and crossed my neck.

"I sighed and thought, 'Great, I'm going to keep on dropping things!'

"I got up to leave, and once I was outside the room, I began to feel like I was missing something, like I had forgotten something. It was really strange—I couldn't put my finger on it, but I felt as though something was different, something about me was missing.

"A few days passed, and then it dawned on me: the chronic back pain I'd had for years was gone. And I remembered, the elder crossed my neck—not where I felt pain, but where my friend told me the source of pain was."

In the first century, St. James the Brother of Our Lord counseled Christians who were ill to seek out the prayers of holy elders, since "the prayer of faith will save the sick" (James 5:15). Here we are two thousand years later, and the sick are still healed by faith, prayer, and anointing with oil by holy elders—sometimes without their even asking for it.

Following the Path of St. Paul

LIVING IN A FAMOUS BIBLICAL CITY like Thessaloniki—a city St. Paul not only wrote two epistles to but preached and prayed in, reprimanded and wept over—it is surprisingly easy to take for granted all the sites worthy of pilgrimage. One fall, however, I made up my mind to make a *tama** to St. Paul: I promised to visit three sites the apostle was known to have visited while in Greece. The first one I went to was the Areopagus in Athens. The Acropolis is a central attraction in Athens, but just next to it is a less celebrated but perhaps even more significant historical site, the Areopagus.

In ancient times a number of myths circulated about gods being

---

* A vow or promise made to God or to a saint.

judged on the site of the Areopagus for crimes they had committed. In classical times, the Areopagus acted as a court of appeal, a judicial council before which the city-state's inhabitants came for rulings in civil matters. In the Apostle Paul's time, the Areopagus was a place in which many speeches were given and where, St. Luke the Evangelist tells us, Athenians and foreigners alike passed their time, looking only to talk about and hear "some new thing" (Acts 17:21). It was there at the Areopagus that St. Paul was invited to speak about the strange new doctrine (Acts 17:19), that is about the Christ and His Gospel, before an attentive crowd.

While speaking to the crowd that had gathered, the apostle rightly observed that there were a large number of pagan altars throughout Greece in honor of various Greek gods. He told them that some days before, he had come upon an altar dedicated to an unknown god. He explained that they worshipped that which they did not know or understand; for, as he told them, the altar to the unknown god was in fact dedicated to the One and only True God. He then expounded on creation and the purpose of man's life, teaching the crowd that God does not dwell in stone or gold (in pagan idols, in other words) and has no need of the sacrifices offered by men. But rather, St. Paul advised the attentive crowd, we "should seek the Lord . . . for in Him we live and move and have our being, as also some of your own poets have said, 'For we are also His offspring'" (Acts 17:27–28).

When, however, St. Paul revealed to them that the True God had risen from the dead, the arrogant crowd began to mock him, for they were so highly educated that it was difficult for them to humble themselves to receive and understand the Gospel of Christ. Considering his words to be foolishness, they scornfully drove him away. St. Dionysius the Areopagite, a woman named Damaris, and a few others were the only ones in the crowd who initially accepted the apostle's good message.

Now that I've reminded you of the Areopagus's history, let me tell you about the setting. Today the Areopagus is a large rock-covered hill that sits in the northwest shadow of the Acropolis. It overlooks the site of the ancient market (the *agora*) as well as the tenth-century Church of the Apostles. If you look out straight across the city, your eyes will doubtless fall on the Church of St. George, which is situated on top of the tallest hill in Athens, directly across from the Acropolis.

Despite the fact that there are modern stairs that lead to the top of the Areopagus, I climbed up the original stairs chiseled into the stone, for I wanted to honor the apostle as best I could and walk in his footsteps as much as possible (if only in a literal sense). Although it was a hot, sunny day, the wind up there made for a naturally air-conditioned site. So I sat on the smooth stone, and looking out over the city, I prayed on my prayer rope, "Through the prayers of the Apostle Paul, Lord Jesus Christ, have mercy on me." It was so wonderful to consciously take in the history and spiritual significance of such a place.

Having completed the first section of my three-part pilgrimage in the apostle's honor, I descended the steps. My next stop included the two sites associated with St. Paul in Thessaloniki.

The Holy Monastery of Vlatadon is situated in the old part of the city of Thessaloniki, where houses are small and cobblestone pedestrian streets are preserved. In this monastery's catholicon, to the right of the Holy Altar, there is a *proskinitari** dedicated to St. Paul. It

---

* *Proskinitari*: often translated as "shrine" in English, it is a stand (usually intricately

is believed that St. Paul preached the good news of Jesus Christ to the Jews on that very spot. I walked up the hill to this monastery one evening to venerate the icon and ask for St. Paul's prayers and blessing.

Not far from this monastery, just a little eastward but still on top of the hill, a massive church has recently been built in St. Paul's honor. It is said there was a spring close to the site of this church in St. Paul's times. Tradition says that when the Jews drove St. Paul out of Thessaloniki (Acts 17:5), he came to this spring and wept over the city. The site of the spring is now on private property, and so I couldn't go traipsing about searching for the exact location, but I did attend Vespers at the church named for him just beside this area. The church is magnificent, and the large balcony surrounding it overlooks the whole city (as does the Holy Monastery of Vlatadon).

I had fulfilled my promise by completing my three-part pilgrimage in honor of the apostle, and I gave glory to God that the prayer request that promoted the *tama* I made had been granted before I even set out on my spiritual journey. Even if I were to attempt to rightly praise the Apostle Paul, my words would prove to be feeble when compared with the grace and eloquent words with which St. John Chrysostom praises him, so I'll simply quote him instead:

> Paul, more than anyone else, has shown us what man really is, and in what our nobility consists, and of what virtue this particular animal is capable. Each day he aimed ever higher; each day he rose up with greater ardor and faced with new eagerness the dangers that threatened him. He summed up his attitude in the words: *'I forget what is behind me and push on to what lies ahead.'* When he saw death imminent, he bade others share his joy: *'Rejoice and be glad with me!'* And when

carved) where an icon of the saint or saints is placed.

danger, injustice and abuse threatened, he said: *'I am content with weakness, mistreatment and persecution.'* These he called the weapons of righteousness, thus telling us that he derived immense profit from them. . . . The most important thing of all to him, however, was that he knew himself to be loved by Christ. Enjoying this love, he considered himself happier than anyone else; were he without it, it would be no satisfaction to be the friend of principalities and powers. He preferred to be thus loved and be the least of all, or even to be among the damned, than to be without that love.[24]

St. Paul justly received what he gave—with all manner of sacrifice he reaped all manner of virtues. May we struggle to compete with St. Paul's zeal and love for the Lord, that we too might learn to say, "I have been crucified with Christ; it is no longer I who live, but Christ lives in me" (Gal. 2:20).

The Quickest Way to Lose Grace

"ONE OF THE QUICKEST WAYS to lose grace is to judge your fellow human being," the hieromonk told a small group of us after a baptismal service.

"Elder Ephraim of Katounakia saw a monk's soul fall from grace for a simple judgmental thought. There was a brother who would walk around his chapel before services and bang a *talanton* [the long wooden plank used in monasteries to call people to prayer by hammering a rhythm on it]. However, he lived in an isolated area, alone. A monk judged him for this. He had the thought, 'What is he doing? There is no one around to call to prayer.' And immediately Elder Ephraim saw grace depart from the monk who passed judgment.

"Justify others. Condemn yourself. Say, 'I'm acting like this, feeling this way because of my passions. If I didn't have passions I wouldn't act like this, react like this.'

"Don't even pass judgment in your mind," he continued. "Fight thoughts: push them out, don't let them stay in your head, don't argue with them. If they are strong, confess them right away. When judgmental thoughts come, if you immediately condemn yourself, 'I'm like this because of my passions,' then immediately grace will come to your aid, if you fight back with humility and self-condemnation.

"It helps to remember King David's words: 'I was brought low'— humbled, in other words—'and the Lord saved me.' Be compassionate and loving toward others, just as the Lord was and is compassionate and loving toward you."

And with those words we left with the weighty knowledge that one of the easiest sins to slip into results in one of the quickest departures of grace.

Discarding the Thorns

I WAS AND STILL AM overjoyed that my first book, *The Scent of Holiness: Lessons from a Women's Monastery,* has had such a positive reception. Many people have told me how much they liked it, and how inspirational they found many of the stories. It means a great deal to me that people have benefitted from my book.

My two primary goals for the book were to inspire people to struggle to live for Christ, and to encourage people to visit monasteries, to look at our precious monastics as lighthouses, shining out in prayer, guiding us safely to shore. I'm very thankful my simple effort in recording my experiences has had a positive effect.

However, I also feel a great responsibility to share with you, dear reader, that visiting monasteries is not without struggle and temptation. Although I would encourage everyone to visit monasteries, I stress the need to do so with a healthy dose of prudence and humble-mindedness even more.

Monastics are struggling Christians, just like us. They stumble; they sin, and get back up again and struggle. Like us, they squabble, they disagree, they get frustrated. Some are good monks and nuns, some are bad monks and nuns. However, we are not the judge of who is "good" or who is "bad." The point is for us not to be scandalized and to avoid judging others—no matter what they say or do. And this is the temptation of visiting a monastery.

Putting aside for the moment the fact that temptation sometimes gets the better of us when we visit there, monasteries are like foreign countries: just as our own country has its own laws, customs, and language, so does a monastery. And this takes some getting used to. Books like my own depict the "nice parts" of monasticism, the highlights. Of course, I made it clear in *The Scent of Holiness* that monastics work hard and have temptations, but I would also like to emphasize that for every one incredible experience I had and recorded, I had three difficult experiences I fought to discard.

I believe it is all about perspective. If we can take in the words, ways, and actions of those around us and grind the experience through the mill of a humble mind and heart, we can separate the good from the bad in every experience. So, we take the good out of the situation or conversation and leave the bad, forget it even. And by *bad* I don't necessarily mean bad things said and done by others, but rather our own poor reactions or skepticism. I mean the feeling we sometimes get inside when something rubs us the wrong way. If we earnestly seek to take something positive out of every encounter and conversation, we can always learn a valuable lesson about ourselves, about others, even about God.

And that's speaking about the more difficult things we may encounter in a monastery. It is also a possibility that we'll visit monasteries and not feel as uplifted as we had hoped to. We may go and think, "Well, that was *okay*, but I certainly didn't experience anything or meet anyone of the caliber I've read about in books." Many people (monastics in particular) are good at hiding their spiritual stature, but the fact that we don't see it doesn't mean it's not there. This is true of entire monastic communities, not just the individuals who make them up.

It takes time to develop relationships, so it shouldn't surprise us if we don't find a kindred spirit in a monk or nun the first time we visit their monastery. The point is to visit: go for the sake of the monastery's saint or patron, to receive a blessing, to pray and give alms if we are able. We should visit monasteries solely for the reason that our soul will receive benefit whether or not we even lay eyes on a monastic. Over time we will begin to perceive the wealth of grace contained in a monastery—that is, if we don't perceive it immediately.

What I'm trying to say is, as St. Basil the Great says, you may need to go through the thorns to get the rose. Discard the thorns but keep the rose. Don't be discouraged if you've had negative or even neutral experiences at Orthodox monasteries. I have had plenty of those; I just didn't write a book about them. I wrote a book about the roses.

"Orthodox Christians Are **So** *Watchful"*

I USED TO LISTEN to a radio program on Voice of Russia World Service called Christian Message from Moscow. Each episode is unique and interesting. Sometimes they are narrations of Russian saints' lives; other times they are stories of laypeople living their Orthodox faith in the world.

One episode in particular—I don't remember the name of it now—made an impact on me in a real way. It was about a faithful nurse who worked at a local hospital and lived with a few older nuns, whom she took care of. She was very close to her spiritual father, and he had given her the obedience of reading the Psalter in its entirety every single day as a portion of her prayer rule.

As described in the program, she once bought an electric kettle—which was a rarity in those days—and she decided to bring it to the hospital to use in the lunch room. However, not long after she purchased it, a young nurse forgot to unplug it when she was finished. As a result it burned, was ruined, and had to be discarded. When the Psalter-reading nurse found out, she was very upset and criticized the young nurse severely for her negligence, pointing out that she had to be stupid to have left the kettle plugged in.

About a week later, she was at a friend's home when she noticed a lot of firetrucks driving by. She thought little of it, but when she returned home she found the firefighters surrounding her home. She realized at that moment it was, in fact, her own home that had caught fire. The old nuns were being taken out of the house and brought to safety just as she was arriving. She was horrified at the scene she saw before her. It turned out, a fireman informed her, that the fire had started in the kindling box. Someone had negligently put some smoldering coal into the kindling box, and it caused the fire. That someone was her.

Well, it didn't take her long to realize what had happened. She quickly understood that because she had criticized the young nurse for leaving the electric kettle plugged in, God allowed her to act in a similar negligent manner so as to teach her the severity of the sin of judging and criticizing.

It was perhaps a month or so after I heard this program that I read about a man in the news who accidentally forgot his child in his car on a very hot day, and the child died of heatstroke. This was the first time I had ever heard of such a thing, and I was horrified.

I lived in Greece at the time, in an apartment with a door that closed the kitchen off from the rest of the apartment. We did not have a toaster, so I had the custom of toasting my bread in our small oven. As I made myself breakfast, I thought about the news story. *Surely this would not happen to an* Orthodox Christian! *We're so watchful. With all our fasting, we're always paying attention to whether or not we can eat this or that, do this or that—we're always on alert. Orthodox Christians are so watchful, this kind of thing could never happen!* Lost in my own thoughts, I closed the kitchen door and returned to the living room.

After about thirty minutes, I started to smell something burning, and I remembered my toast. I ran into the smoke-filled kitchen and flung open the oven door. Not only was the bread burnt to a crisp, but even the plastic outside the oven had begun to blacken and bubble. I couldn't believe I had almost caused a fire! I quickly opened all the windows and balcony doors to try to get rid of the smoke before my husband returned. But it was no use; the apartment still reeked of smoke by the time he arrived, and I was forced to tell him I had almost caused a fire.

It was then that I realized the similarities between myself and the nurse. She had criticized overtly, I covertly. And so I confessed, "I judged the man whose baby died in the hot car. I was thinking to myself, *Orthodox Christians are so watchful*, the whole time, and this is why it happened."

He laughed at me and from then on, even to this day, he occasionally taunts me, "Orthodox Christians are *so* watchful." But despite his light-hearted teasing, as you can tell by my decision to include this story in this collection, I have never forgotten the value of the lesson I learned that day: If we judge someone, God will allow us to fall into a similar sin, or at best temptation, to humble us.

Saint Nektarios: A Flowing Spring of Divine Gifts

THE GREEK ISLAND of Aegina is located south of Piraeus, and like many Greek islands, it is home to a great saint, St. Nektarios of Pentapolis (in fact, it is home to several saints, but I'll stay on topic). St. Nektarios lived at the turn of the twentieth century. After being exiled to Greece from his bishopric in Alexandria, living as a poor preacher, and subsequently heading the Razaro School of Theology in Athens, he retired to live near his spiritual daughters at their monastery in Aegina.

St. Nektarios is a great saint of our times and is called "wonderworker" because, like St. John Maximovitch, he is known for his great works of healing. Also like St. John, after exhumation his body was found to be incorrupt, but after some time it dissolved so that his relics could be distributed throughout the world (as he revealed to one of his spiritual daughters, a nun, who was dismayed by this event).

Just as in life, so in death St. Nektarios pours out healing on all who cry to him for help in faith and love. Many times my husband and I called on him for his intercession, and he helped us. We visited his holy monastery in Aegina and venerated his holy relics four times in the almost six years we lived in Greece. The first three visits each preceded a trial in our lives. But the fourth and final time we went to Aegina was after a joyful event, Fr. John's ordination to the diaconate.

On one of those pilgrimages, we went to the monastery with our priest, his presvytera, and our church community. During this trip we were treated to a talk by one of the sisters. We sat outside on a patio where water and sweets were laid out for us, and she told us, "The saint appeared to one of the sisters after his death and said: 'No one can come to my monastery unless I first invite them.' And so, since you are all here today, that means the saint is here welcoming you himself." And that is how we felt each and every time we visited his holy monastery.

Those who have been to Aegina and to St. Nektarios's monastery can attest to the fact that his grace is palpable there. Not only is the monastery awash with fragrance and grace, but the whole island seems to give off a spiritual warmth. Although his presence is strong throughout the monastery and even the whole island, it seemed to me to be strongest in the tiny chapel he was buried in. The marble sarcophagus is still there, and it is said that many times pilgrims put their ears to it and can hear the sound of the saint's feet shuffling. Like many saints—such as Ss. Gerasimos and Spyridon of Kefalonia—they say St. Nektarios is busy helping people, and that is what you hear: him running about helping those in need.

During our pilgrimages, I would always sit for some time praying in this little chapel. Once, after praying, I made my way to the saint's cell, which is directly behind this chapel. Just outside the door of the cell, I noticed for the first time the jasmine tree. Small white flowers covered the tree, and a few hanging low from the branch attracted me to smell their beautiful aroma. I thought of how amazing it is that such a small flower could be so fragrant.

As I was thinking this, I looked down and saw another jasmine flower that had fallen from the tree. I picked it up and smelled it. It too, though "dead," was fragrant, and I immediately thought of St. Nektarios. Like the little flower that still gave off a sweet scent, so the saint's body, though dead, was a source of grace: "Though thou hast reposed, Yet thou livest to eternity, and lo thy body is a source of grace, Thus clearly showing forth our Savior's victory over death" (Paraklesis to St. Nektarios, Ode 5). I asked one of the sisters for a blessing to keep that "dead" jasmine flower, and she told me, "The saint planted that jasmine tree with his own hands."

Because of our deep devotion to St. Nektarios, my husband and I decided to name our home chapel after him. While still in Greece I painted icons of St. Nektarios, the Directress, and Christ the High Priest. Once we moved into a house in Newfoundland, we established a domestic chapel in his honor. My father built icon stands, and we continue to furnish our small chapel as best we can. Fr. John serves Matins and Vespers every day in this chapel. Although we don't know if this will be our forever home, someday I'd like to plant a jasmine tree outside the chapel in honor of the saint. It won't be a Greek church with intricate frescoes and top-of-the-line liturgical furniture, but after hearing the following story from a nun at his monastery, I know the saint won't mind.

The sister told us that a Russian priest wanted to build a church in the saint's honor. He wanted to build it out of the same kind of materials they use to build churches in Greece (usually stone). However, he was only able to find someone to build the church out of wood, the usual material used to construct churches in Russia. The priest was distressed by this because he wanted to honor the Greek saint with a "Greek" church. One night the saint appeared to the priest and told him, "Why are you upset? When I am in Russia I am Russian, and I want my church built out of wood." Perhaps when in Newfoundland, St. Nektarios considers himself a Newfoundlander.

> Thou art truly a flowing spring of divine gifts for us,
> Gushing forth with spiritual nectar which doth dispel the grief
> And grievous bitterness of all our failings and passions,
> And doth grant the sweetness of grace, O beloved of God.
> (Paraclesis of St. Nektarios, Ode 3)

Skin-Deep Judgments

HER LONG, STYLISH DYED HAIR, perfectly manicured nails, long eyelashes, and skillfully applied make-up surprised me the first few times I saw her in church. She was pious, attentive, and prayerful. These latter qualities made me perplexed as to why she seemed to try so hard to make her outward appearance beautiful when her inner person shone with beauty. The more I got to know her, the more perplexed I became.

She impressed me so much with her depth of knowledge and enthusiasm for the faith. But still, that nagging question wouldn't be silenced: Why? Why, if she was so spiritual, would she spend so much time on her appearance? These are the thoughts—the honest, if cruel, thoughts—of a judgmental person.

Driving back home from the baptism of our mutual friend's baby, we were story-swapping, telling each other various details of our lives and journeys in the Orthodox Faith. She told us about a pilgrimage she had taken to the Holy Land. They had visited St. Savva's Monastery in Palestine. This monastery, like Mount Athos, is closed to women visitors. While the men in the group went into the monastery compound, the women were escorted to an area where they were offered water and a sweet.

She told me that day she was wearing no make-up except on her eyes. But she was wearing large sunglasses so that her make-up wouldn't be noticeable. Despite this, a monk from St. Savva's approached her and with pain in his voice said, "My child, why do you paint your face? Don't you know it's a sin to obstruct the image of God?" Hearing the monk's words, she was surprised and speechless. He continued, "I will pray for you not to paint your face." This simple conversation had a great and lasting impact on her.

Finishing her story, she looked at me in the rear-view mirror (I was sitting in the backseat) and said, "Constantina, will you pray for me to stop wearing make-up?"

Now it was my turn to be surprised, and I quickly answered, "Yes."

She repeated herself, "Will you pray for me to stop wearing make-up?" And again I said yes.

What a lesson I learned that day! Who am I *ever* to ask that dreadful, damaging three-letter question: W-H-Y? Who am I to look on someone and form any kind of judgment about their appearance, any kind of judgment about their internal state? Her struggle is her struggle; we each have our own.

Having her look me straight in the eyes and appeal for me to pray for her cut me to the quick. I had rashly judged her, and there she was asking for my prayers. I hope, through *her* prayers, I will struggle against that judgmental and condemning involuntary question that arises in my heart when I see something or someone I don't understand. We never know what someone is working through and where they are on their spiritual journey. We make judgments based on what we see, but they are only skin-deep judgments. If only we knew people's hearts, their struggles, we would pray instead of entertaining the judgmental "whys" that come to us—that come to me most of all.

Abba Dorotheos writes:

> Should we not tremble hearing what happened to that great father who, when he heard that a certain brother had committed fornication, said: *'Oh he did badly'*. Do you not know what a terrible thing is said about him in the Sayings of the Fathers? It is said that the holy angel brought the soul of the sinner to him and said: *'Look. This is the person that you have judged, he is dead. Where do you command that he should be put, in the Kingdom or in Hell?'* What could be more terrible than this burden?[25]

Simplicity in Christ's Name

"GERONDA, DO YOU KNOW the Akathist hymn to the Mother of God?" I asked Elder Isidoros while a group of us were working together at the monastery.

"No, I know *Kyrie Isou Xriste eleison me* [Lord Jesus Christ have mercy on me]," he answered forthrightly.

I winced when I heard his response. *I'm such an idiot*, I thought. I bowed my head and felt a little ashamed of my question. I asked him that question thinking that since many monastics (and even some faithful laity) have the Akathist hymn memorized, he might have wanted to pray it with us while we worked.

While I was initially worried that I might have embarrassed him by my probing question, I marveled at his simplicity and natural humility. He knew the most important prayer—supplication for God's mercy while professing the Divine Incarnation of the Word of God in the person of Jesus Christ. Learning that prayer well would be sufficient.

"The prayer, *Lord Jesus Christ have mercy on me*, is a confession of faith," my professor of dogmatic theology once told a classroom full of students. "It is a confession that God became Man—the Person of God the Word, that is Christ Jesus, became Incarnate. With this prayer we ask for His mercy. Mercy, according to patristic theology, is nothing other than the compassion of God, which is expressed as the Kingdom of God." And so, when we say this simple but theologically profound prayer, we are in fact supplicating Christ to grant us His Kingdom—truly the one thing needed.

An Unknown Ascetic in the World

I DON'T REMEMBER the first time I saw Evgenia at our parish in Thessaloniki. But I do remember what a great impact her appearance had on me.

She was a strikingly thin old woman with hair as white as snow and eyes as bright and blue as the morning sky. She was short and stooped, and walked very slowly. No matter the season or weather, she always wore the same long, greyish-blue coat that tied at the waist and her blue patterned head scarf. Her hair would stick out from underneath the scarf, as would quite a few white hairs on her chin, and she was forever dragging a canvas bag around with her. Her general appearance, combined with the fact that she didn't seem to own any other clothing than the one outfit I have just described, gave the impression that she was very poor.

Every time she communed, her eyes seemed to shine even more brightly than usual. And each time she walked back from Holy Communion, if our eyes met, I felt an overwhelmingly strong feeling of familiarity, as if she reminded me of someone I knew, but I couldn't put my finger on whom. At some point it dawned on me that in those moments she looked just like a very old and holy elder I had once met. Christ dwells more intensely in those that occupy higher spiritual states, and so I assume it might have been His likeness I was catching a glimpse of when I looked at Evgenia's bright face, the same likeness that shone forth in the holy elder I had met.

I was irresistibly drawn to her and wished on many occasions to speak with her. But even after months of living in Greece, I didn't feel comfortable striking up a conversation in Greek with this revered mother. So weeks passed, months, a year, until the last Sunday I saw her. Funny, the things that remain in our memory.

I had worn a blouse to church that day that had a tie on the side. Instead of pulling it into a bow, I tied it and let the tails hang freely, because I thought it looked better that way. As I was standing in line for Holy Communion, Evgenia leaned over someone in a pew and tugged the hanging tail of the tie. I understood her gesture. I smiled and promptly pulled it into a bow. I felt as though she had lovingly rebuked my vanity. I didn't realize at the time it was the last time I would see her.

On "Soul Saturday"—the day before Judgment Sunday—in 2009, the whole parish was grieved to learn that on her way to church that morning, while she was crossing a busy road, Evgenia had been struck by a motorcycle. Old and frail and badly injured, she lay on the ground; the only thing the young man driving the motorcycle could make out was that she was requesting the priest and presvytera of the nearby church—our church.

Our priest and presvytera visited Evgenia in the hospital as soon as they heard the news. But Father was not able to locate any of her relatives, because she had lived a very quiet, secluded life, so that not even those who lived near her knew much about her or her past.

Father explained to us the next day that Evgenia was in the hospital, and she would need full-time assistance while there. He just matter-of-factly stated, "We need to cover the costs. I want everyone to help pay for expenses, and I want the women to make a schedule so that Evgenia has someone by her side at all times." And that is what the parish did. Everyone pitched in to help. I also wanted to visit her in the hospital, but my limited language skills prohibited me from doing much. Thank God for the good will of others, though, for she was well looked after.

For weeks different parishioners visited her in the hospital, as did Father and Presvytera, making sure all her needs were taken care of. And naturally the doctors began taking notice of such a great display of Christian love. One doctor told our priest, "I didn't think Christians still existed. But I have seen true Christians and a true priest." How much good God brings out of bad circumstances!

But it was only a matter of time before the little holy old lady was no longer able to fight off death. A few days before we celebrated the Sunday of the Life-Giving and Precious Cross, Evgenia gave up her spirit. She was buried that Monday, the day after we celebrate Christ's victory over death by suffering death.

Father said when he and Presvytera went to Evgenia's apartment after her death, he was surprised to see all the plants she had every-where—plants and icons.

"She must have loved nature," he said. "She lived in the city and couldn't have a garden, so she brought a garden into her home."

Father didn't find a stove in her apartment; it would seem she didn't eat cooked food. And for a bed she had a mat on the floor. It turns out she was as ascetical in practice as she was in appearance. She lived unknown to the world, denying herself the pleasures of this life, opting instead to store up treasures in heaven.

Father served a memorial for her on her fortieth day, and afterward we had the customary memorial food and drink of kolyva and cognac in the church hall. Father invited people to tell stories about Evgenia.

We learned that on account of her appearance, many had assumed she was poor and had offered her money. A doctor in our parish shared that once when she refused his money he asked her to let him at least buy her groceries, and she said, "No, it's okay, I have an onion at home." At this we all laughed. Another time Father offered her money, and she laughed and said, "Father, I have more money than you do!" And it turned out she really did. She was a widow and a retired nurse. She had a large house outside the city as well as a spacious apartment in the center of Thessaloniki. She donated the house to Father's institute, and it became a hostel for traveling monastics and theology students. The rest of her money she donated to the Church.

When she was hit by the motorcycle, Father was quick to address any bad thoughts anyone might be having. He told us not to be scandalized that at the end of her life she suffered and died in such a way. He said we mustn't think that a bad death indicates a bad life. Rather, God knows what each soul needs, and suffering a tragedy at the end of a pious life isn't a commentary on one's quality of life, but rather on the ineffable ways of God. Looking back, we can see all the good that came of Evgenia's tragic death, so it really wasn't tragic at all. Our parishioners were given the opportunity to practice acts of mercy, and those who witnessed such acts saw the light of Christ in those moments.

Abba Mark once asked Abba Arsenios, "Why do some good people, when they die, their soul separates from their body with much grief and bodily torture?"

And Abba Arsenios responded, "So as to go there pure, after they are 'salted' here with the salt of hardship and become even more worthy."

I believe Evgenia departed this temporal life more pure and more worthy by suffering what she did. And God—all-good that He is— made sure that even more good works were brought about on account of this holy, unknown ascetic living in the midst of the world, who had entirely abandoned herself to God. Please remember the handmaid of God Evgenia in your holy prayers, and may she remember us in hers!

✠ SIX ✠

Blessed Are the Pure in Heart
for they shall see God

The Pure in Heart Watch and Pray

GROWING UP IN A SMALL VILLAGE, far from big cities, in a pious environment with a priest for a father, a certain young boy's heart had been safeguarded from a great deal of sin and passion. One day, as he described to my husband, he was tending to his family's sheepfold out in the fields when he heard a group of people nearby playing a kind of music he had never heard, and for the first time in his young life he felt a passion rise up in himself he had hitherto never experienced. Just think of how pure this young boy must have been to distinctly remember the first time he experienced this passion (he was around thirteen years old). This is a perfect example of how easily and frequently sin and passion can enter our heart through the senses.

St. Nikodemus tells us that the senses are the doors and windows through which either life or death enters the nous and, in turn, the heart. Life, he explains, enters when our senses are well governed, whereas death enters when we partake of sinful passions that harm the soul.[26] Whatever enters man's heart comes in first through the senses and then enters the nous.

Impure music, for example, has the ability, after entering the nous, to go down into the heart, at which point it is easy for a man to sin in his heart (Matt. 5:28). If the sinful image seen by the eyes or the sinful sound heard by the ears remains in the nous, it clouds it, making it ill, and the disease—if left untreated—spreads and infects the heart. For this reason, the Fathers have taught us above all to guard and cleanse the nous. Christ said, "First remove the plank from your own eye" (Matt. 7:5)—in other words, purify your nous.

In the case of this young man, it was easy for him to safeguard his nous and heart because he lived in a pure environment. Thus, the first time he encountered a strong passion, he could actively rebut it. However, contemporary man lives in an environment full of many unclean sights and sounds, and quite likely he has grown accustomed to the passive state in which he allows all manner of impurity to enter through his senses. But "he who does not want any impure passions of the senses to enter his soul must drape his senses with [spiritual] nets. What are these nets?" St. Nikodemus asks us. They are "memory of death, for one; our account before Christ on the day of judgment; the memory of eternal suffering."[27]

I know for some, the exercise of keeping the memory of death and eternal suffering in the forefront of our mind may seem morbid. But I think St. Nikodemus is simply saying that when we actively remember that this life is temporal, as the Psalmist says ("*As for* man, his days *are* like grass; / As a flower of the field, so he flourishes," Ps. 102/103:15), we will struggle to guard and protect our soul, which will live on, while the body will die and decay.

We go to great measures to preserve the good quality of so many material possessions. Many women, for example, are mortified if their expensive purse is laid on the ground. Why? Because it is valuable and worthy of care so that it will last and keep its beautiful form. Some women even keep their leather purses in special bags when they are not being used so as to protect their quality. And yet, what measures do we take to keep our nous and heart from becoming unclean? Isn't it true that we leave the doors and windows of our senses wide open, never paying attention to what enters?

We need first to become aware of the fact that our nous and heart become defiled by the things we watch, listen to, look at, and read about, and then we need to take the necessary measures to limit the infiltration of sinful sights and sounds by means of prayer and watchfulness. For Christ taught us, "A good man out of the good treasure of his heart brings forth good; and an evil man out of the evil treasure of his heart brings forth evil" (Luke 6:45). If we guard our senses and occupy our nous with prayer, our heart will not only have the evil expelled—that is, become purified of the passions—it will become an abode for the Holy Trinity, a dwelling-place, a room for God "to lay *His* head" (Luke 9:58). It will, in other words, store up good things. We must watch and pray lest we encounter temptations and unwittingly welcome them into our heart.

Visiting the Monastery Founded by St. Porphyrios

MY HUSBAND AND I had gone to Athens for some meetings, a preliminary step in the process of his ordination. An abbess from one of the monasteries we often visited had put us in contact with Helen, a woman living in the suburbs of Athens. She agreed to host us, and as it turned out, she was quite keen to take us around Athens and the surrounding areas to all sorts of monasteries and churches. It was a wonderful opportunity for us to see many places we might not have had the chance to see otherwise. On our last evening in Athens, she took us to the Holy Hesychastarion* of the Transfiguration of the Savior, the women's monastery founded by the newly canonized St. Porphyrios of Kafsokalyvia.

I have loved and admired St. Porphyrios for years and wanted to visit this monastery from the time I read his biography. On our way to teach English in South Korea, my husband and I had a seven-hour layover in the Toronto airport, so we took the subway into the city to stop by the Apostle Paul Bookstore in the Greek village. Since my spiritual father had suggested I read books on contemporary elders, when I saw *Wounded by Love: Life and Words of Elder Porphyrios* I grabbed it. We bought as many books as we could carry with us to Korea that day.

I began reading *Wounded by Love* on our flight from Toronto to Japan, and I couldn't put it down. I didn't sleep a wink on our eighteen-hour flight. Needless to say, St. Porphyrios's life and words inspired me. However, I never thought I would actually get the chance to visit the holy places he traversed. But one never knows where life will lead.

We arrived at the saint's monastery in the early evening to an overflowing parking lot. We were perplexed to see so many people there at such an hour on a Friday night.

---

* A *hesychastarion* is a monastery like all others, only it is not under the jurisdiction of the local bishop but rather directly under the Ecumenical Patriarch.

"What's going on here?" Helen asked a man who was buckling his toddler into a car seat.

"One of the sisters reposed, and they just served her funeral," he responded.

We walked through the open gate to the monastery, crossed the courtyard, and went into the church. A nun turned the lights on for us so we and a few other latecomers could venerate the icons.

I looked up at the many arches running alongside the nave, the large ceilings and the scaffolding obstructing my view of the *iconostasis*.

"I think this is the largest church I've been in next to Agia Sophia in Constantinople," I whispered to Helen. The walls, like all the other buildings in the monastery, were pure white, awaiting colorful iconographic frescoes to cover their nakedness.

We each took turns venerating the icons lying on the wooden icon-stands in the middle of the church and made our way out of the church and into the sisterhood's trapeza. People and movement were everywhere. Groups of men, women, and children were sitting at the many tables lining the room. Clusters of small, white Greek coffee cups, cookies, and cookie crumbs spotted the tabletops. This was not a formal meal; it was *kerisma*—a treat offered to pilgrims on behalf of the sisterhood.

Despite the chatter of the crowd, my attention was pulled toward the bright, new, colorful frescoes decorating the walls. I was especially drawn to a painting of St. Porphyrios, not exactly iconographic style, but not exactly a portrait either.

"If you want, you can become holy in the middle of the city," St. Porphyrios was known to say. What a beautiful, if often unheard, truth. He himself became holy in the middle of Athens. And here I was standing in the monastery he planted, prayed in, and guided to help grow.

"I want to introduce you to Sr. G.," Helen said, interrupting my thoughts and pointing to an older nun standing across the room.

"Should we tell her you're going to become a priest?" she asked John as we made our way over.

"Yeah, I guess we could ask for her prayers," he shrugged.

The sister was finishing up a conversation with some pilgrims as we approached. Helen bowed to kiss her hand (a customary greeting to monastics in Greece), but before she could introduce us, the sister looked at us and said, "Don't worry, everything will work out!"

Looking at me, she gestured toward my husband. "And you chose a good *papa** too," she said, smiling. She then turned and walked away.

Helen stared at us. "Did you hear that? I didn't even say anything!" she said. "She knew it all on her own. And she said not to worry, it'll all work out!"

The sister's clairvoyant words had provoked great excitement in Helen. I think the only thing they produced in us was shock, at least initially. I couldn't quite wrap my mind around the fact that Helen hadn't told Sr. G. anything about us, even though I knew she hadn't. We were there with her the whole time. She hadn't even said a word to indicate our identity, much less our future plans.

Later I found out that this sister is nicknamed the "mouthpiece of St. Porphyrios" because, like her spiritual father before her, she has the gift of clairvoyance and prophecy. And just as the sister said, so it happened—everything worked out.

After this prophetic encounter, we made our way upstairs to the

---

* *Papa*: an informal Greek title for a priest.

saint's cell, which appears to be preserved in the exact state in which it was left at the time of his repose. The room was not very large. I remember his bed was covered in a white blanket. Icons stood on the bed, leaning against the wall. A large portrait of the saint was in the middle; his priest's stole was laid out over the white blanket. We knelt and venerated it.

Although there was a strong feeling of blessedness throughout the monastery, here in the intimate quarters of the saint, the feeling was palpable. Here he lived, prayed, wept, loved; he admonished, advised, and guided countless souls. Here he was sanctified. As we proceeded to the door of his cell, I stopped and kissed the doorframe in a place I imagined the holy saint's hand once touched. At that time we called him "elder," but now we boldly call upon him as a glorified saint. May we have his blessing!

> The most-holy temple of the Comforter
> And the beloved of the All-Pure Theotokos,
> Let us praise Porphyrios from our heart,
> For he loves and heals all, he protects
> And intercedes that we be granted *theosis*.
> Therefore, we cry out:
> Rejoice, O Father Porphyrios!
> (Kontakion of the Saint)

For They Shall See

IT WAS LATE AT NIGHT, and the sisters were still hard at work in one of the workrooms outside the monastery gates, when suddenly they received a phone call.

"Sister Arsenia, I want you and the sisters to pack up immediately and come inside the monastery," the Gerontissa Philareti's voice was heard to say on the line.

"*Evlogison* [bless], Gerontissa! We haven't finished yet. We're almost done, another fifteen minutes and we'll be ready to leave."

"No, I want you to come into the monastery right away."

"May it be blessed," Sr. Arsenia responded.

"Sisters, Gerontissa wants us to stop our work and go into the monastery immediately," she informed the others.

All the sisters quickly got ready, locked up, and left.

They had just made it inside the monastery when the electricity went out. If they had waited until they were done with their work, they would not have been able to see anything on their way back.

It pays to be obedient, because even when it is blind obedience (when we obey while not understanding the reason), so long as our guide is able to see we'll arrive safely at our destination.

Personal Life and Theological Views

I HAD GONE TO THE UNIVERSITY to speak with my professor about a paper I was writing. Often his office was full of students, coming and going, asking him questions or asking his opinion on this or that matter. This day was no different. Once we were alone, he began to tell me about a conference he had recently attended with a professor I know from a different university. He told me they had had an interesting theological conversation. He said, "He holds some wrong theological beliefs. Tell me, has he perhaps made some mistake in his personal life?"

At first I didn't know why he would ask something that didn't appear to have any relevance to their theological conversation, but I told him what I knew about the professor's personal life.

"Ah, see, that makes sense! A person will not make a mistake in theology if they do not first make a mistake in their moral life," he told me. "If we stray from the commandments of Christ in our moral life, than we may stray from correct dogmatic beliefs."

Keeping in mind what my professor said that day, I began noticing this same sentiment reiterated in books I've read. For instance, when Elder Joseph the Hesychast left the zealots* and accepted the stance of the Athonite monasteries concerning the calendar issue (that adherence to the New Calendar did not mean those churches that adopted the New Calendar were without grace), some of the zealots believed he had become deluded. In fact, one of the zealots openly and harshly spoke out against him and his brotherhood. Years later, when this zealot saw the fruit of Elder Joseph's holy life and teachings—the repopulation of the Holy Mountain—he realized he had been wrong, and Elder Joseph was right to side with the monasteries on the calendar issue.

The zealot had initially erred in his judgment because his life was not in complete accordance with Christ's commandments. "When we are knowledgeable but lack humility [a moral sin], 'knowledge puffs us up' . . . But people who are enlightened by God don't make dogmatic mistakes."[28]

I suppose this is because, as the Scriptures tell us, sin separates us from God (Is. 59:2), while keeping His commandments results in

---

* Zealots: a group of Athonite fathers who believed that any church following the Gregorian or "New" Calendar was devoid of saving grace.

divine enlightenment and protection by the Holy Spirit (John 14:17). This is why my professor believed the other professor had erred in his theological views. This is also a reminder of how careful we must be. It's not enough for us to hold intellectually to the true Faith; we must live well morally in order to safeguard our faith. We must avoid being led astray in our personal lives so we won't be led astray in our spiritual lives.

She Who Is Full of Grace

A DEAR FRIEND OF MINE, who later became a nun, was visiting a monastery dedicated to the Most Holy Lady Theotokos. She was staying in the guesthouse, which had an internal door leading to the monastery's chapel. That night she awoke to say her prayer rule and decided to go into the church to pray. She opened the door and saw a nun making prostrations in front of the iconostasis; she assumed one of the nuns had come over from the monastic cells (located on the other side of the monastery grounds) to pray there. So she discreetly left the chapel so as not to disturb the praying nun.

The next day my friend approached the guest-mistress and explained that she didn't realize the nuns used the chapel at night to say their prayers. The guest-mistress assured her the woman she saw could not have been a nun from the sisterhood, as they all stayed in their cells to pray. The guesthouse chapel was locked from the inside, and only one or two sisters had keys.

Since the monastery is dedicated to the Most Holy Virgin Mary, the sisters thought it might have been possible that it was in fact the Mother of God—the patron of the monastery—that my friend saw.

The guest-mistress said it was not the only time the Holy Lady had been seen by visitors to the monastery. Another woman—a close friend of the monastery—was washing dishes in the monastery's kitchen once when she saw a tall lady in red out in the field, walking across the monastery grounds in the snow, in the middle of winter.

In the life of St. John Chrysostom, it says he was once taken into heaven, and he asked to see the Most Holy Lady Theotokos. But he was informed she was not in heaven, but rather ministering on earth. This is confirmed in these stories. Who can fathom the grace contained in such holy places as this monastery, that the Most Holy Theotokos not only visits but allows herself to be seen praying in and caring for the monastery?

Faith that Moves Mountains

WHEN I SHOWED some of the sisters a copy of *The Scent of Holiness*, they were very encouraging and happy for me, if a little embarrassed and shy that a few stories featured them. Rather quickly, though, they began their good-natured teasing.

"Constantina, you know I love you, but I'm not going to talk to you anymore because I'm afraid you'll write another book," one sister joked.

When I asked another sister how her recent pilgrimage went, she teased, "What, are you taking down an interview now?"

We all got a few laughs in, but quite a few would also tell me, "Oh, you should have put this story in your book!" Or, "I have a story for you. Make notes and include this in your next book!"

So, at the behest of a few of my dear sisters, I will tell you a wonderful little story about an ill woman of great faith.

A monastery was celebrating a feast day somewhere, and a special miracle-working icon of the Mother of God was being brought as a blessing for the feast. A certain woman, although she greatly desired to be in attendance, was bedridden on account of the cancer she had in her stomach. So, like many in Greece, she watched the events on a church television station.

When the icon arrived at the monastery, the cameras displayed the procession and all the faithful who flocked to greet the Lady Theotokos. As the icon passed through the crowd, many crossed themselves, just as the woman would have done if she had been able to be there in person. Despite her being stuck at home, her strong conviction in the Mother of God's power to heal the sick was in no way diminished; she went up to the television and crossed her stomach in front of the televised image of the icon.

And of course, it should be no marvel whatsoever that she was healed of her cancer, for Christ Himself tells us if only we have faith the size of a mustard seed, we will move mountains. This lady's faith in the Mother of God was so great it cured her cancer.

Out of the Darkness I Called You

MY HUSBAND, an ordained Orthodox priest, was raised an atheist. Yes, I'll let that sink in for a moment. That revelation catches most people by surprise.

By *atheist* I mean the word in its literal definition: that his upbringing was devoid of a belief in God. This is not to say he was raised in a family devoid of love and morality. On the contrary, he himself credits his wonderful parents with raising him "in a home of boundless love," as he stated in his own ordination homily: "I must thank God for the family environment within which I was raised. Under the watchful eye of conscientious parents who encouraged me to learn God-pleasing virtues, and who sought to shield me from soul-destroying vices," he preached on the Sunday of St. Mary of Egypt, just after his ordination to the priesthood.

Despite this loving environment, however, the concept of God was not something he ever once remembers so much as contemplating. He did not attend church, not even on Christmas or Easter. His mind, like those of many Canadian boys, was drawn to hockey: playing it, reading about it, collecting paraphernalia, and later, coaching it. It was not until he began studying philosophy during his undergraduate years that the more substantial, meaning-of-life type of ideas began to occupy his hitherto typical thoughts.

If you ask him—as his wife has done on numerous occasions—what author, what idea, what line of text began to open his eyes to a whole new world, he will tell you, "It wasn't one thing; it was a bunch of stuff." He'll say it was a mixture of Aristotle's description of the Unmoved Mover; the German philosopher Kant's assertion of the possible existence of the *noumenal*; the idea of repentance as described in Dante's *Divine Comedy*. It was, in other words, "out of obscurity and out of darkness" (Is. 29:18) that God granted him, "blind from birth" (John 9:1), the eyes to see: the eyes to see *Him*.

At the same time that John was being called "into His marvelous light" (1 Peter 2:9), my own brother and his wife were undergoing a similar change in mindset, also through the study of philosophy at the same university. It would take one year before John formally met them. Nevertheless, the unique simultaneous spiritual transformation taking place was nothing short of miraculous.

My once-atheist husband went on to convert to traditional Anglicanism. He, along with my brother and sister-in-law, other friends of a similar mind, and myself (once I moved to the same city to study at the same university), began reading the Church Fathers. We were atypical university students who drank beer on Friday nights and read fathers like St. John Chrysostom out loud, sometimes even at outdoor pubs. We all thought we had found what we were looking for. And to an extent we had. We had found Christ; we had found a traditional form of Christianity. This provided a wonderful foundation for us.

After his undergraduate studies, John began his Master of Arts at Durham University. His Master's thesis was on the concept of "image" in St. Augustine and St. Dionysius the Areopagite. (This was before he was Orthodox.) He went on from there to do his PhD in homiletics at Aristotle University, and as I said, become a priest. And yet, he was the last of our small gang to embrace Orthodoxy. In fact, when my brother Matthew first decided to become Orthodox after reading Fr. Seraphim Rose, John began his own personal study in pursuit of convincing Matthew that "jumping ship" was unnecessary.

However, once he read the work of St. Gregory Palamas, he was confronted with a piercing truth: that he was reading the unbroken theology and tradition he had discovered in St. John Chrysostom all those years before. Once again, his eyes adjusted to the new rays of light shining before him: Orthodoxy had preserved that which we loved, honored, and cherished in the early Church. Orthodoxy was everything good in Anglicanism and so much more. What else could he do but fall down in worship?

In his Epistle to the Romans, St. Paul quotes the Prophet Isaiah: "I was found by those who did not seek Me; / I was made manifest to those who did not ask for Me" (Rom. 10:20). In so many ways this could be said of my husband, whose youthful mind never once wandered to the contemplation of God. And yet, to see him now, preaching, with his long hair and beard, his colorful vestments, and his large Byzantine cross, you would never mistake him for anything other than a Christian, hopelessly devoted to his Savior Christ.

A Consoling Gift: A Gift of Prayer

GERONTISSA TOLD ME a story about a widow whose son had died suddenly. The mother was grief stricken and continually prayed to the Mother of God. One day she noticed she had begun saying the Jesus Prayer unceasingly and without effort, not only orally but noetically, almost as though the prayer prayed itself. She said it so frequently and intently that an ineffable fragrance began to fill her house.

She visited Gerontissa and confided in her about this new spiritual environment she found herself in. The abbess informed her it was a consoling gift from the Mother of God to help her with her grief over losing her son. Who knows how long it would or did last, if indeed it ever left. But what an impression it made on me: a laywoman living in the midst of the world, yet full of fragrant, unceasing prayer.

I have often been told that prayer of the heart is a gift, when the spiritual heart dwells in a perpetual state of prayer and concentration on Christ even while the intellect is occupied with other matters. It is not something one easily acquires. My understanding is that although it is not necessarily disconnected from our personal struggle for holiness, it is also not something we receive merely in exchange for something we've done. It is a free gift of God. But to think it is possible, to think this woman was given a pure gift from the Mother of God as solace for great sorrow, is itself a great consolation!

Yet another example of this indescribable gift happened to a woman I know personally. While on pilgrimage to the Holy Land and after being "baptized" in the Jordan River (a practice many Orthodox pilgrims do as a blessing, not as something sacramental), she experienced an extraordinary state of prayer. Her mind and heart were also unceasingly occupied with the Jesus Prayer. This state of prayer lasted only for a time, however. Once she left the Holy Land, her intense prayer left too. But it made a deep impact on her. I suppose it's like tasting the fruit of Paradise—once you've tasted it you intensely long to taste of it once more.

Even if prayer of the heart is not something we can or will receive in exchange for our meager spiritual striving, it is worth the struggle. What is sweeter than to have our whole being in constant and continual communication with God Almighty? All we need to do is prepare ourselves for this state of prayer by saying the Jesus Prayer as often and as intently as possible, struggling to keep a humble heart and mind, and keeping ourselves pure in thought and action. The rest is up to God's great mercy, which, as we have seen in the above stories, He liberally pours out.

She Thought He Was the Gardener

IT WAS THE EVE of the Feast of the Entrance of the Theotokos into the Temple, and I was staying at the monastery helping the sisters make a batch of incense. After a long day of work rolling, cutting, and coating incense in magnesium, we headed into the warm catholicon for the all-night vigil that began around ten PM. First the sisters would chant the Vespers service, then Matins, and afterward Divine Liturgy. It usually lasted three to four hours.

While I always enjoyed sitting near the woodstove on the left side of the nave, it was not long before the warmth would make my tired eyelids heavy with sleep. Nevertheless, this winter's night I chose the heat of the woodstove.

The chanting was beautiful and serene, as always, but to my surprise, when the sisters began chanting the katavasia of the feast I heard the familiar rhythmic knocking on the talanton, the ringing out of the *symandron*,* followed by the joyful clanging of the bells in the bell tower. For the first time in the Nativity Fast, the sisters chanted, "Christ is born, glorify Him. Christ is come from heaven, receive ye Him. Christ is on earth, be ye elevated. Sing to the Lord, all the earth; and ye nations, praise Him with joy; for He hath been glorified."

In celebration of this joyous event, the sisters loudly announced to all the birds, the trees, and the mountains surrounding the monastery the same joyful proclamation an angel had announced to simple shepherds keeping watch at night some two thousand years before: "For there is born to you this day in the city of David a Savior, who is Christ the Lord" (Luke 2:11).

Not unlike many other all-night vigils I attended at monasteries

---

* Symandron: a shaped metal piece that is hung outside a monastery church and is hit rhythmically with a metal instrument before the services to call the faithful to prayer.

in Greece, this vigil left me both quietly joyful and falling asleep
from time to time. Near the end of Divine Liturgy, not long before
it was time to take Holy Communion, I turned around to see a tall,
beautiful, familiar-looking nun leaning against a stasidi. I thought to
myself, *I know this nun. But from where? From another monastery? Maybe from
one of the monasteries in Panorama? No, I don't think so. But who could she be? I
know her face.*

I tried not to stare too long but I kept turning to look at her.
Although only candlelight and oil lamps illuminated the nave, she was
not all that far from me, and I could see her clearly. Yet, I could not
for the life of me remember where I knew her from. All of a sudden
she began approaching to venerate the icons the way we do before
the priest exists the Royal Doors with the Holy Chalice.

What is she doing? She can't go before Gerontissa! I thought. And suddenly
it clicked, and I realized she was Gerontissa. How could I not have
recognized her?

I cannot definitively explain why I could not recognize her that
night, but it put me in mind of St. Mary Magdalene and how she
mistook Christ for the gardener:

> [S]he turned around and saw Jesus standing *there,* and did not know
> that it was Jesus. Jesus said to her, "Woman, why are you weeping?
> Whom are you seeking?"
>
> She, supposing Him to be the gardener, said to Him, "Sir, if
> You have carried Him away, tell me where You have laid Him,
> and I will take Him away."
>
> Jesus said to her, "Mary!"
>
> She turned and said to Him, "Rabboni!" (which is to say,
> Teacher). (John 20:14–16)

We were all created in the image of God, but since the Fall, it is only through the grace of God—combined with man's ascetic struggle—that we can become "in His likeness," as we were meant to be, and as the first-created man was fashioned. Metropolitan Hierotheos of Nafpaktos wrote, "When, through personal struggle and mainly by the grace of God, he attains the likeness [of God], then he is an actual person."[29] Namely, when a person has become transformed by grace, then he becomes a true person: in both the image and the likeness of God.

Although this "likeness" does not refer to the outward appearance of a person, but rather to the state of her heart and soul, still it cannot be denied that one is purified, illumined, and experiences *theosis* in mind, soul, spirit, *and* body. This is why saints' relics are venerated, since they are vessels of holiness, eternally connected and attached to the holy souls that dwelt within their carnal bodies. The new martyr Fr. Daniel Sysoev taught, "The tie between the Christian's body and soul cannot be destroyed. . . . It is for that reason that we pray before the relics of saints. . . . until the Savior's redemptive work of Redemption had been accomplished, that tie did not exist."[30]

Why didn't St. Mary Magdalene recognize Christ, her Teacher, her *Rabboni?* Because He was transfigured; He was the same person but manifesting a new likeness. Perhaps the same could be said about Gerontissa that night in the church during the vigil for the Feast of the Entrance of the Theotokos into the Temple. Maybe, just maybe, the spiritual transformation she experiences internally as a true ascetic was revealed through her physical appearance, if only fleetingly. And when did I recognize her? I recognized her as she approached to partake of the Body and Blood of Christ, just as Christ was recognized by Luke and Cleopas "in the breaking of bread" (Luke 24:35).

Alternatively, the heat of the woodstove, the long hours of work, and the fact that it was the middle of the night could have had a role in my eyes playing tricks on me. Nevertheless, it's nice to muse about seeing an abbess's spiritual transformation in front of your very own eyes.

Holy Icons as Vehicles of Grace

WE SAT IN A LECTURE HALL full of students. Some were enrolled in the theology department, but most were visitors, there to take in the professor's profound and engaging lectures. The class was on iconology (the theology of icons). Never confining his lectures to books alone, our professor would demonstrate to us through personal stories of his encounters with holy monastics that the things we learned about in our theology courses were true realities—things such as the power and grace of a holy icon.

When he had just finished his PhD in Germany, he explained to us, and was feeling confident about his knowledge of holy icons, he visited his father's good friend, a blind monk. He made small talk for a bit but quickly got to his point.

"Geronda, although you're blind, you venerate icons. Do you know and understand what you are venerating?" the young graduate asked the monk.

"Of course I do!" the blind monk responded.

"Is that so? Well then, would you mind if I gave you a little quiz?" he asked the monk.

"Not at all," came the response.

There was a shelf of icons just above where they were seated. So our professor—the graduate student—took down an icon of St. Katherine the Great Martyr and gave it to the blind monk to venerate.

Making his cross and bowing low to the ground, the monk kissed the icon.

"So, Geronda, which saint did you venerate?"

"St. Barbara the Great Martyr," he answered.

"Geronda, I'm sorry, but it's not St. Barbara," the graduate student said. "Perhaps you would like to venerate the icon again and see if you're making a mistake."

"I know the grace of St. Katherine. It is different from that of St. Barbara. *You're* making the mistake. Perhaps you should read the name again," the monk answered resolutely.

Looking down at the icon, the young graduate student couldn't believe his eyes. There written on the icon was the name *Saint Barbara*. The likeness of the saint was that of St. Barbara. How could he have mistaken her for St. Katherine? Sure, some icons show their resemblance, but this was shocking!

"Geronda, I'm sorry. I was mistaken. The icon *is* of St. Barbara," he said.

"The grace of each saint is distinct. I can tell which saint I am venerating by the saint's particular grace," the monk informed him.

After sharing this story with us the professor said, "I, who have eyes to see, did not see. While the monk who was blind saw what was for me invisible."

"And Jesus said, 'For judgment I have come into this world, that those who do not see may see, and that those who see may be made blind'" (John 9:39).

Not All That Glitters Is Gold

ONCE WHILE I WAS STAYING at a monastery, helping the sisterhood prepare for their feast day, an old lady dressed in black and claiming to be a nun arrived seeking hospitality. She came into the catholicon, where I was helping the sisters, and asked to speak with the abbess. There was definitely something about her presence that made me uncomfortable, but I tried not to pay attention to my feelings lest I pass judgment on someone because of something as fickle and untrustworthy as my fleeting emotions.

One of the sisters I was with took her to see Gerontissa. Apparently it was evident from Gerontissa's conversation with the woman that she was not what she presented herself to be. When she returned to the church after speaking with the abbess, the nuns informed me that we ought to keep an eye on her.

"Not everyone who wears monastic garb is a monastic," one of the sisters leaned in to whisper to me. This statement further enhanced my unease, but despite these feelings, I obeyed and occasionally passed by where she was sitting in the church, since she was not visible from where I stood near the door to greet pilgrims.

Although I was extremely uncomfortable in her presence and even slightly afraid when the sisters would leave me alone in the church with her, I struggled to occupy my mind with the Jesus Prayer and not dwell on the fact that something must be wrong if the sisters asked me to keep an eye on this poor soul.

It is an unfortunate reality that in Greece some come to monasteries on feast days under the pretense of being pious pilgrims, but instead they attempt to take advantage of the crowds and the occupied monastics by stealing holy relics and other such expensive and irreplaceable items belonging to the monastery. Even in the city, we had firsthand experience of people going around dressed as monks and nuns collecting money for their own purposes. Watchfulness was required.

I was told afterward that the woman began her conversation with Gerontissa by stating, "I am in a much higher spiritual state than you are!" She claimed to have acquired many spiritual gifts, including the gift of clairvoyance—that is, the ability to see without physical barriers (far distances, inner thoughts, and the spiritual or emotional states of those around her). The manner in which she spoke to Gerontissa revealed her spiritual delusion, and as it turned out, Gerontissa informed the nuns that God had enlightened her to see that the woman dressed as and claiming to be a nun did not have the light of tonsure within her. It would seem that not only was the woman falsely presenting herself as a nun, but she was in fact in a state of spiritual delusion.

Concerning this kind of delusion St. Ignatius Brianchaninov writes:

> All of us are subject to spiritual deception. Awareness of this fact is the greatest protection against it. Likewise, the greatest spiritual deception of all is to consider oneself free from it. We are all deceived, all deluded; we all find ourselves in a condition of falsehood. . . . With tears let us cry out to the Lord Jesus to bring us out of prison. . . . "For this cause did our Lord Jesus Christ descend to us," says the venerable Symeon the New Theologian, "because he wanted to rescue us from captivity and from most wicked spiritual deception."[31]

We can only hope and pray the lady masquerading as a monastic received healing, and that we all may be rescued and protected from the trap of spiritual deception.

Someone once asked Elder Epiphanios of Athens, "Elder, have you ever seen a vision?" and he responded, "No, my child, neither have I seen a vision, nor do I ever want to see one. All that I want to see are my own sins." The pure of heart see God; those of us with impure hearts should seek only to see our sins, since it is this sure path that will lead us to the gift of true clairvoyance.

A Miracle of Elder Joseph of Vatopedi

ELDER JOSEPH OF VATOPEDI Monastery was a monk from Cyprus who went to the Holy Mountain on a spiritual pilgrimage in search of an unerring guide, a true father and teacher of noetic prayer. He found what he was seeking in the person of Elder Joseph the Hesychast and Cave-dweller, who, only after much prayer, agreed to accept the young monk into his brotherhood. After years of disciple-ship to his holy elder, Elder Joseph (the disciple) eventually became the spiritual elder of the Holy Monastery of Vatopedi.

A friend of ours from Thessaloniki was having troubles and decided to write a letter to the elder. As he had corresponded with him in the past, he felt requesting the elder's prayers and counsel would be of great consolation in this time of need.

Not long after he sent his letter, he received a response from the elder. The elder's consoling letter addressed the concerns our friend had laid out in his correspondence. Shortly after this event, our friend got word that Elder Joseph had reposed. He was surprised by this news and asked when the elder fell asleep. When he was informed that the elder reposed on July 2 (2009), he was shocked. The letter he wrote to the elder was not even sent before July 2.

You may have seen a famous photograph of this elder after his repose; it is widely circulated on the Internet. The photo shows the elder dressed in his monastic robes with a large smile spread across his peaceful face. "Death is swallowed up in victory" (1 Cor. 15:54).

Spiritual Vision

ON ONE OF OUR TRIPS TO THE WOMEN'S MONASTERY we often visited outside Thessaloniki, Fr. John and I were accompanied by a friend of ours who served as a priest on the island of Crete. After Vespers one evening, we sat with some sisters drinking tea while the priest spoke to us about his experiences serving the Church on Crete.

"A group of us had gone to visit a well-known elder who was said to be clairvoyant, and he certainly was," the priest told us. "Four of us were there, and to each he revealed something personal. 'You need to watch out for this and this,' he told me. 'And you need to confess this and that,' he told another. 'You must have gone to confession and received absolution recently, because I see nothing in you,' he told another member of our company. 'And you should know,' he said to the other priest with us, 'Your prayer is not acceptable to God because you neglect to read the Thanksgiving prayers for Holy Communion after you serve the Divine Liturgy.'

"The two most essential things I took away from that experience are how important it is for us to always say the post-Communion prayers, and how powerful the sacrament of confession is," the priest finished.

That the clairvoyant elder could see nothing in the man who had confessed thoroughly is a testament to what St. John the Theologian says in his first epistle, "If we confess our sins, He is faithful and just to forgive us *our* sins and to cleanse us from all unrighteousness" (1 John 1:9). The elder's admonishment to the priest was also something we should take heed of; we must pay to God what is God's (Mark 12:17), and that includes giving thanks for having been found worthy—unworthy as we are—to partake of the all-immaculate and blameless Mysteries of Christ.

Let us take note of these two important lessons: to hasten to offer thanksgiving, and to firmly (and regularly) confess our sins, so that not only clairvoyant elders but Christ Himself will see nothing in us when we go before Him on the fearful day of Judgment.

Our Neighborhood "Slipper Lady"

THERE WAS A WOMAN who lived in our neighborhood in Thessaloniki who was different. In an older time, one might have even called her "touched." I saw her in church, without fail, at every single service I attended at our local parish. In fact, the very first time Fr. John and I went to that church when we first moved to Greece, she came up to me and shook my hand, welcoming me. She also said some things to me, but I hadn't yet learned the language, so I stared back at her blankly.

She constantly walked around the church in slippers during the service, sometimes exiting the church and re-entering, other times just walking in circles inside the church. I noticed she would do this in particular during the cherubic hymn, when, according to Tradition, angels descend and participate with the clergy and faithful in the Divine Liturgy. The chanters would be chanting, "Let us who mystically represent the cherubim and chant the thrice-holy hymn to the Life-creating Trinity," and she would pick up her pace, walking from the back of the church to the front, again and again. Other times during the Vespers service she would walk to the front of the church, and before the chanters could say the Our Father, she would loudly proclaim it.

From the moment I met her, I wondered if she might be a holy fool. However, as I've already said, I took most anyone for a holy fool in Greece if they seemed odd in the slightest way, so this wasn't something out of the ordinary for me. But there was something different about her.

The concept of foolishness for Christ's sake is somewhat difficult to comprehend, but our Orthodox Tradition is full of people who take on—in full health of mind and soul—the ascetic practice of foolishness for Christ's sake. These people are often referred to as "holy fools" or "fools for Christ's sake." In the book *The Law of God*, Fr. Seraphim Slobodskoy writes:

> One form of the ascetic Christian life is called foolishness for the sake of Christ. The fool-for-Christ . . . [takes] on an unusual style of life, appearing as someone bereft of his mental faculties, thus bringing upon himself the ridicule of others. In addition he [exposes] the evil in the world through metaphorical and symbolic words and actions. He [takes] this ascetic endeavor upon himself in order to humble himself and to also more effectively influence

others, since most people respond to the usual ordinary sermon with indifference.[32]

I had a deep affection for this woman and always made sure to greet her every time I saw her. If we were out in the town, I would say hello. If we were in church, I would silently bow to her. She would always respond in kind. That is, until after I inquired about her.

I was upstairs visiting with our dear neighbor Olga when I asked about the lady I considered to be a holy fool.

"Oh, you mean the one in the slippers?" she asked.

"Yeah," I said.

"Let me tell you, many people just think she's crazy, but she's not. Just a few weeks back she came up to me and started telling me all sorts of things about my family, things she couldn't know, things I hadn't even told my friends."

"I knew it!" I said. "I thought she was a fool for Christ!"

After that conversation I was perfectly convinced she was a holy fool, and I secretly hoped she would reveal her gift to me too.

Unfortunately, the opposite happened. The very next time I saw the slipper lady, I greeted her as I always did, but instead of smiling and saying hello she curtly nodded. And that was it—she never again treated me with the warmth she once had. Now, perhaps my husband would tell you I jump to conclusions, but I believe she grew cold toward me because I was convinced of her hidden spiritual gifts. Before my conversation with my neighbor, she was just another strange person I thought might be one of a hundred holy fools in the city. After our conversation, I felt I had proof of her spiritual state, and I believe she perceived this.

I think of Christ and how He would often tell those He healed to "tell no one about this." When I was young, I used to think He said this in jest, out of a false humility, but it was a means to teach *us* humility, as if to say, "I am humble and meek; be like Me." Holy fools are like Him; they are saints in disguise, living ascetically, praying wholeheartedly, and seeing with the eyes of their souls. They do not want their true spiritual state to be revealed because then people will treat them with respect and honor, when all they seek is for God to know their good works and reward them secretly. Such was, I believe, our neighborhood slipper lady.

"We've Been Expecting You"

DIONYSIA, ALTHOUGH her own health was not very good, began visiting an ailing neighbor to keep her company. She would read aloud to her, since it was difficult for the neighbor to read herself. At some point, Dionysia suggested if they were going to spend so much time reading together, it was best to read the Holy Scriptures. Thus, over time the neighbor began to soften and to desire to enter more fully into the Faith. Along with reading the Scriptures to her, Dionysia also began to share stories from the lives of the saints.

For reasons only God knows, this neighbor began to see and converse with certain saints Dionysia had told her about. After some time, she decided to invite a priest to bless her home. So Dionysia went to her priest and told him about her neighbor, how they read the Scriptures together and spoke about the lives of the saints, and how subsequently various saints had begun appearing to her neighbor. She told him the neighbor wished for him to visit her so he could bless her home. The priest made it known that he thought it was unlikely saints were appearing to this shut-in, but he agreed to visit her and do a house blessing.

When he arrived at the house, he knocked and waited for the woman to open the door. When she finally did, standing behind her was the unmistakable person of St. Raphael of Mytilene. The priest stood frozen in astonishment.

"Father, come in, we've been expecting you," the saint said to him. From that point on, the priest was no longer unbelieving, but believing (John 20:27). He saw with his own eyes that Dionysia's good works produced in her neighbor not only the desire to turn back to the Church, but the ability to see spiritual realities—something, truly, only the pure of heart have the ability to do.

Words without Disdain

SITTING WITH GERONTISSA while she sewed up a hole in a garment, I told her, "Through your prayers, the temptation I told you about the last time I was here has left. I don't feel that way anymore."

"Yeah, it happened because you judged a lot," she replied without lifting her eyes from her work.

Although her words surprised me, like a burn that initially produces a stinging pain and is followed by intense pain afterward, I only later realized how much her poignant words had wounded my ego. For about three days the wound stung. Each day the pain seemed to get worse. At first it hurt because I didn't want to see myself in that light; I didn't want to accept the fact that I am a judgmental person. Then it hurt because my thoughts started telling me that Gerontissa had a bad opinion of me. By the third day, my thoughts were trying to convince me that Gerontissa didn't like me at all and had said what she said with the intention of hurting my feelings. With each passing destructive thought, the wound became more infected.

Thankfully, these spiritual growing pains aren't all bad, and the Lord gives us some help and guidance even in the midst of them.

By the grace of God, by the third day I was able to sit down with my friend Sr. Sarah. Not only did we enjoy a slice of fasting chocolate cake and delicious French coffee (the Greek name for what we in North America know simply as coffee), but we talked. We talked and talked, and as usual she helped me immensely; all my bad thoughts got corrected. This wasn't a coincidence; it was God's mercy to help me through this particular trial.

"Sometimes it's difficult when God reveals who we are. You know, I just think, *Is this who I really am? Is this what I'm really like?*" I confided in her.

"I know, and I'm like, *No, please, I don't want to know myself. Ignorance is bliss!*" she comically responded. "That's why God *slowly* lets us see who we really are."

Before I even broached the topic of my troubling thoughts against Gerontissa, she was already rescuing me from them: "You know, sometimes Gerontissa or one of the sisters will say something to help you. It might be difficult to receive, but it's for your benefit. When Gerontissa says something, it's only to help us and never out of *empatheia*."

"What's empatheia?" I asked her.

"*Empatheia* is a difficult word because it has no relation to 'empathy' in English. It's more like disdain or contempt. Truly spiritual people don't have this when they correct others; the correction proceeds solely out of a desire to help the person. But sometimes we feel like when so-and-so corrects us, they do so out of disdain—as though they don't like us and so they are just pointing out our faults with hostility toward us."

She paused, adjusted her coffee cup, then continued, "When we have empatheia toward someone, it's like we dislike them for no real reason. We just feel contempt for them. This can often lead to not wanting to talk to that person. So, for example, if we need to tell that person something, because we dislike him or her, we will put someone else in the middle, we'll ask someone, 'Can you tell so-and-so . . .' so that we don't have to engage them in conversation. This is the kind of thing that comes from empatheia toward someone."

"Oh, Sister, this helps me so much!" I broke in. "Earlier this week Gerontissa said something to me that really stung. I wasn't offended immediately. But as the days passed, I began to feel more and more upset about it. First, I thought, *Why am I like this? Why do I do and think destructive things?* I felt devastated. I even started thinking maybe Gerontissa just doesn't like me. I thought maybe she said what she did to hurt my feelings."

"No, Gerontissa doesn't have empatheia!" she said, shaking her head. "But when we listen to our thoughts that tell us she does, then we can't receive things properly."

Through Gerontissa's statement, God administered the painful but necessary medicine for my passions. Through my conversation with Sr. Sarah, I feel He bandaged the wound.

"Rebuke a wise *man*, and he will love you," the Scriptures say (Prov. 9:8). It turns out I'm not that wise, since Gerontissa's simple rebuke "you judged a lot" was met with destructive thoughts rather than gratitude. But the spiritual life is a process. I can't expect to avoid obstacles while trying to lead a spiritual life, and most often the greatest obstacles we have to overcome proceed from our ourselves, as St. John Chrysostom says: "None can harm him who does not injure himself."

The truth is, when I judge others I harm myself, and so the wound was already there—self-inflicted, in fact. Gerontissa's minor rebuke merely brought the pain of the existing wound to mind:

> A man can be harmed by another only through the causes of the passions which lie within himself. It is for this reason that God, the Creator of all and the Doctor of men's souls, who alone has accurate knowledge of the soul's wounds . . . tells us to root out the causes of evil within us. (St. John Cassian, *On the Eight Vices: On Dejection*)

I hope and pray that through Gerontissa's prayers I may begin the process of rooting out the passions in me that cause so much harm to myself, not to mention the harm they cause others. It took a sighted person not only to guide me, but to show me in what manner I am blind.

✠ SEVEN ✠

Blessed Are the Peacemakers
for they shall be called sons of God

Perfecting Holiness in the Fear of God

WHERE DID YOU SEE THAT?" our Serbian iconography teacher shouted more than asked, his hand gesturing toward a photocopy of St. Theophanes the Cretan's icon of Christ taped to a student's easel.

"We've said a thousand times, you need to follow the prototype!" At this the student stood up and waited behind her chair for Dragan to sit down. Taking a paintbrush coated in the base color, he began painting over the mistake with broad strokes.

"After you're finished, will you come help me?" the student next to her asked.

"I need help too, teacher," another woman said.

"I'm going over to help the stupid one next," Dragan responded. Silence.

"Ah! No one claims to be the stupid one, eh?" he smirked.

"You know," he said while dabbing paint onto the board, "St. Basil the Great was once surrounded by a crowd, and he said, 'I'm going to speak to the sinful woman next.' A woman in the crowd responded, 'And who told you I was sinful?'"

"Everyone wants my help, but no one admits to being the stupid one," he said, smiling widely. Pausing his painting, he turned to observe our amused reactions.

While we each worked away on our own icons—some painting icons of Christ, others painting angels or saints—he would go from student to student, correcting, admonishing, and occasionally teasing.

"There goes the Canadian making fun of us in her barbarian language!" he would say when he overheard me speaking English.

This was a characteristic scene during our iconography class, held for two hours once a week at St. Mena's Church in Thessaloniki. Dragan offered this and another class once a week free of charge; both were primarily full of adult women. He gave freely, teaching not only the art of painting icons, but the art of the Orthodox Faith as well.

"I've seen better, and I've seen worse," he would say if he thought the student had done well. This was his nicest compliment. Only a few times did we hear him say, "Some here have painted their first icon better than I painted mine," but he never made it perfectly clear whom he was speaking about.

Once when a student knelt on the ground to fix something at the bottom of her icon, he said, "That is how we should paint icons, on bended knee."

"Metropolitan Augoustinos Kantiotes says our Church is being fought against today. He says it is fought against today more than all other times. And Christians are sleeping," he would passionately tell us as he ran his paintbrush down the curve of an angel wing.

Opening the glass door and stepping into his eight-by-eight-foot store and workshop, we would often hear Metropolitan Augoustinos of Florina's loud and expressive voice thundering from a speaker. And like that of the ever-memorable bishop, Dragan's character was simultaneously rough and gentle.

Our teacher yelled and became excited, especially when speaking about theology and modern innovations, but he was a spiritual gem. As irate as he appeared on the outside, he was golden on the inside. We all loved and respected him. And he was as serious about correct faith as he was about correct icon-painting—as strict about upholding the Orthodox Faith as he was about maintaining the traditions of iconography handed down to us by master iconographers.

He wasn't quiet or outwardly meek or soft-spoken. He was a lion regarding the respect and care we must show icons and a lamb regarding his personal virtue and good works. He was, in my opinion, "perfecting holiness in the fear of God" (2 Cor. 7:1).

Inspirational Words on the Feast of St. Basil

WE HAD VISITED the monastery on January 1, which is not only the secular new year but the feast of St. Basil the Great; we had come for the *vasilopita* (a sweet bread with a coin hidden inside).

The custom of cutting the vasilopita is an old and dear one in various Orthodox countries. In Greece, before we cut the vasilopita, we first pray St. Basil's apolytikion: "Your proclamation has gone out into all the earth, which was divinely taught by hearing your voice, expounding the nature of creatures, ennobling the manners of men. O holy father of a royal priesthood, entreat Christ God that our souls may be saved."

After this, the priest or the man or woman of the house (in this case the abbess) crosses the cake with a knife three times, saying, "In the name of the Father, the Son, and the Holy Spirit," and "Through the prayers of St. Basil the Great." The first piece is cut for Christ, the second for the Mother of God, the third for St. Basil, and sometimes the fourth piece is cut for the saint of the monastery or parish. The rest of the cake is cut in as many pieces are there are people present. Whoever discovers the coin in his or her piece is considered blessed for the year. This particular year, as in past years, the coin was in Gerontissa's piece.

After we had received our piece of vasilopita, the abbess addressed us with the following words: "The more I think about it, my wish for the New Year is for everyone to experience divine illumination, for us to truly see ourselves and to truly see the blessings of God. Divine illumination for us to see our sins . . ." She paused, reflecting. "It's difficult to see ourselves, our 'old man.' And sometimes, we see him so . . . *alive,* and we have to cast him down: 'Back off! Don't think like that! Don't act like that!' We need to see ourselves, our sins. And at the same time bad things can happen: unemployment, illness, difficulties . . . many view these things as bad. But we, as children of God—as we wish to be called—look at these things as blessings. We should consider these things blessings. Everything that happens to us happens for our own good." Again she paused, looking down. "Yes, these things I wish . . . for us to have the eyes to see our sins as well as the blessings of God."

May her words enter our hearts and become manifest in our actions!

Our Foundation Is Jesus Christ

WHILE ON A PILGRIMAGE to Athos, a friend of ours met a young monk who had a foreign accent.

"Where are you from?" our friend inquired.

"I'm from Athos," he responded.

"No, I mean where do you come from?" our friend tried to clarify.

"Oh, I'm from so-and-so monastery," the foreign monk responded.

"Where are you from originally?" our friend tried once again.

"Here."

"I mean, where were you born?"

"On the Holy Mountain," the monk answered resolutely.

By this point our friend caught on that this monk—like the monks of old—was unwilling to divulge his past, because he saw his monastic life as a new life, his current existence as separate from his "old man." This impressed our friend, and so he shared this exchange with us, expressing his surprise that there were still monastics who thought as this young monk did.

I remember the first time I was asked what Orthodox jurisdiction my husband and I belonged to. I was confused. "I'm just an Orthodox Christian," I told the American priest.

"That's a good answer. Ideally we would all see ourselves this way, but I was just curious what your background is," he responded.

"When we lived in Korea, we went to the Korean Orthodox Church. Now that we live in Greece we go to the Greek Orthodox

Church," I told him.

"The only Orthodox church in our province is Greek," my husband interjected. "When we lived in Canada, that is the church we attended, so I guess you could say our background is in the Greek Church."

Many urban areas in North America have several Orthodox churches of various jurisdictions. But for us, our one and only Orthodox church in New Brunswick was a blessing. All the Orthodox in the surrounding area went to the small Greek church in St. John. Thus, we became Orthodox in a pan-Orthodox setting and never identified as Greek or Russian, only as Orthodox. Canadian Orthodox was the closest label I would have given myself.

To be honest, there were so few converts in our parish (apart from my family, there were a handful) that we didn't even identify as converts. I know now, after returning to North America having been exposed to various Orthodox parishes, that this is unusual. But in all honesty, I still do not consider myself a convert. I am an Orthodox Christian. My life started the day I became Orthodox. Do I relate more to Blessed Augustine, St. Justin Martyr, or St. Vladimir of Kiev than to other saints because they were converts? No. In fact, I never even learned the Greek word for convert, because in Greece no one ever labeled us as converts.

Friends of ours who grew up nominally in the Church and who at some point began taking their Orthodox Faith seriously considered us to have had a common experience: originally we were not "of the Church" (as they say in Greek), and then, by the grace of God, we were enlightened to change our lives. This is what *metanoia*, repentance, means: to turn away from sin and turn back to God. Every day of our lives we need to convert, to repent, to turn to

God. How we came to the Faith, how long we've lived the Faith, or whether we are members of an ethnic group is beside the point. The Christian life is not about where we've been but where we're going. Christ doesn't relate to us as who we *were* but who we *are* and who we are *becoming*.

There is merit in the young monk self-identifying only as Athonite. It is not to disparage his past, his culture, or his language, but to demonstrate that our culture is Christianity, our language is a common one of faith and love, and our citizenship belongs to the Kingdom of heaven. We are Orthodox Christians—brothers and sisters in Christ—and although we celebrate and honor the particular local expression of our Faith, ultimately we are one in Christ. Above all else, our Faith unifies us, as the great apostle said: There can be no discussion of whether we are "of Paul" or "of Apollos" (1 Cor. 3:4), for we are all of Christ, and He is our foundation.

In Praise of Thessaloniki

I WOULD DO A GREAT DISSERVICE to the great saint and co-protector (together with St. Demetrios) of Thessaloniki if I were to write this whole book and not mention our father among the saints, Gregory Palamas, Archbishop of Thessaloniki.

You can hardly go two paces in that Byzantine city without being reminded of the various local saints and historical faith of the Thessalonians. But two places in particular always occupied a special place in my heart: the church of Hagia Sophia, where St. Gregory preached against the Barlaamite heresy, and the Cathedral of St. Gregory Palamas, in which his relics reside in a side chapel covered in icons depicting his life. Any time I was downtown, I made a point to venerate his holy, fragrant relics.

In a city like Thessaloniki, the cloud of witnesses feel more like companions, such is the intimacy of their presence. In many respects, life there is a living continuation of the Scriptures, and the many churches, sites of martyrdom or imprisonment of saints, and holy relics are enough to make you forget the modern world and enter into the spiritual world.

Practically every night you can attend a vigil in the city. The vigil service according to the Greek Typicon begins with Small Vespers, followed by Compline, Great Vespers, Matins, Hours, Liturgy, and finally the Ninth Hour. These vigils can last up to five, six, or more hours. They usually end well after midnight.

I remember one we went to in the heart of town for the feast of St. Gregory Palamas (November 14). During the Matins service, when the life of the saint is read from the Great Horologion, one of the chanters proceeded to the middle of the church to read a long version of St. Gregory's life. Looking at this young man in his long, black chanter's robe, standing before the royal doors with only vigil lamps and a lone candle stand illuminating the passage he read aloud, it was easy to be confused as to whether it was the first or twenty-first century, whether we were on earth or in heaven. Coming out of a vigil like that, you felt as though the whole city was more sanctified, as if the stones and stars themselves had participated in our celebration of the Bloodless Sacrifice.

O Thessaloniki, the city Apostle Paul wrote to, preached in, wept over; the city St. Demetrios fought for and continues to protect even after his martyric death; the city St. Gregory Palamas guided, instructed, reprimanded, and loved! Through the prayers of the great hesychast and of all saints of Thessaloniki, may you always be blessed.

An Orthodox Moment

THERE ARE TIMES IN LIFE when certain experiences, thoughts, and feelings are thoroughly entrenched in the mindset of the Orthodox Church, but this only becomes apparent in reflection after one becomes Orthodox. Things happen that aren't necessarily big enough to be called miracles, but neither are they simple coincidences. Rather, they somehow exist between these two: moments and experiences that manifest God's providence and grace, guiding us to adopt the mindset of the Orthodox Faith even before we understand it. I like to call these Orthodox moments.

The strongest Orthodox moment I remember experiencing before I became Orthodox was after a parish council meeting at our Anglican church. Always inclining toward Anglo-Catholicism, I had had an argument with some members over whether or not we could—as a means of opening up to the local community—hold some special events on the feast of the Virgin Mary (our patron) and pray the Angelus.* Naturally, the more Protestant-inclined members explained why that was not appropriate. Being the stubborn and fiery person I can be, I was quite upset driving home, and I thought, *Maybe Christians aren't supposed to agree on matters of the faith; maybe everyone is just left to make up their own minds.* No sooner had this thought passed through my mind than I found myself reciting the psalm, "Behold, how good and how

---

* Angelus (from the Latin word for *angel*): a short medieval prayer recited to the Virgin Mary.

pleasant *it is* / For brethren to dwell together in unity!" (Ps. 132/133:1).

This Orthodox moment corrected my thought. Christians are supposed to be of oneness of mind, to agree and "dwell together in unity." This realization didn't change the situation at my parish, but it was a moment that cleared up a misconception on my part. Later, when I became Orthodox, I understood more fully how important it is for Christians to agree on matters concerning the Faith.

Many years later, I experienced another Orthodox moment on the day of Fr. John's ordination to the subdiaconate. We had traveled to Hamilton, Ontario, with our bishop to celebrate the patronal feast day of the Church of All Saints of North America.

When a person is being ordained a subdeacon, the bishop hands the candidate the book of the epistles. Opening to a randomly selected passage, the candidate reads the first thing his eyes fall upon until the bishop signals for him to stop. Fr. John opened to 2 Corinthians 13 and read the following aloud:

> . . . since you seek a proof of Christ speaking in me, who is not weak toward you, but mighty in you. For though He was crucified in weakness, yet He lives by the power of God. For we also are weak in Him, but we shall live with Him by the power of God toward you.
>
> Examine yourselves *as to* whether you are in the faith. Test yourselves. Do you not know yourselves, that Jesus Christ is in you?—unless indeed you are disqualified. But I trust that you will know that we are not disqualified.
>
> Now I pray to God that you do no evil, not that we should appear approved, but that you should do what is honorable, though we may seem disqualified. For we can do nothing against the truth, but for the truth. For we are glad when we are weak and you are strong. (vv. 3–9)

It was a beautiful passage, a moving passage. But the Orthodox moment came later that evening, when we retired to the room we were staying in, hosted by a wonderful family.

Every day I read a chapter of the Scriptures before I go to sleep; I read consecutively through the books of the New Testament. That night my appointed chapter was none other than 2 Corinthians 13. Here again I experienced an Orthodox moment and glorified God for the small ways in which He reveals the mindset of the Church, His purpose and presence in our lives—the ways He reveals that we are truly meant to be united in Him.

Who Can Fathom the Ways of the Saints?

A FAMILY WAS STANDING outside the locked gates of a secluded monastery in the mountains, unsure of when or if the gate would be open to visitors. They stood contemplating whether to wait longer or to leave. Suddenly from around the side of the monastery came a tall monk. He approached them and said, "I know the sisters well. They will come and open the gate in an hour. Do not leave, wait here." He turned and left them, walking around the monastery walls once again. Thus the family waited.

When the gate finally opened, a sister welcomed the family into the monastery. She asked if they had been waiting long, and they said they had, but they didn't leave because the monk told them a nun would come in an hour to open the gate.

The sister was surprised by this and said they hadn't had any monks visiting that day. "What did he look like?" she asked.

"Well, he was very tall and had blue eyes," they responded.

The nun was convinced it was St. Raphael of Mytilene, who was both tall and blue-eyed. He was tonsured at that very monastery when it was a men's monastery.

SIMILARLY, AT ANOTHER women's monastery, a family of non-Orthodox pilgrims were admiring the grounds when they saw two monks walking in the yard together. Naturally, they wondered who they might be.

Finding a nun, they asked, "Do the monks live here as well, or were they just visiting?"

The sister explained to them that their monastery housed nuns only and that no monks lived in or near the monastery.

"But we've just now seen two monks walking together," they said.

The nun was surprised by this, since there were no monks or clergy visiting that day, so she mentioned this to the abbess.

The abbess believed the family had seen Ss. Raphael and Nicholas of Mytilene, the saints for whom a chapel at the monastery is dedicated.

Who knows the reasons behind such encounters and the benefits bestowed on those chosen to encounter saints in this life.

The Counsel of the Godly

EACH JUNE, our Byzantine chant teachers from a monastery just outside Thessaloniki would take our classes (first, second, and third year) on a field trip of sorts. It always involved a road trip in which we visited various monasteries in and around a different city each year. Lunches, drinks, and snacks would be packed, cameras would be in hand, and a few girls would even bring along their guitars and lyrics to some Greek folk and spiritual songs. It was always a load of fun. Often we would spend the night at the monastery the night before so we could be up and on the road early the next day.

Having spent the night in the monastery's guesthouse one year, we awoke early so we could get on the road and make it to our destinations on time. When we gathered to have a quick breakfast, our teachers informed us that Abbess Agathi of St. Stephen's Monastery in Meteora had reposed the night before; thus her funeral would be that day. We immediately went to the abbess to receive her blessing before she and some sisters left for Meteora to attend the ever-memorable abbess's funeral. Many abbesses, abbots, priests, and laypeople from all over Greece headed to Meteora that day.

We set out on our trip soon afterward. Arriving at the last monastery on our trip, we found that the abbess of this monastery had also gone to Meteora for the funeral and wasn't there to greet us. Since the third-year class had prepared to chant the Vespers service at the monastery, they went ahead and did a wonderful job. Afterward a nun took us into the guest dining room to offer us refreshments.

It is customary for an abbess or an older nun to address a crowd like this; on these trips we always had someone speak with us at each monastery we visited. But since the abbess was away, leaving behind the nuns that made up the small sisterhood, one of our chanting teachers asked the guest-mistress to give us a word. She did not feel she had anything worthwhile to say, but since our teacher kept pressing her, she finally bowed her head and said, "May it be blessed."

She sat down on the bench lining the wall at the end of the room and took a long prayer rope out of her pocket. She pulled the rope between her fingers a few times while she pensively looked at the floor. Then she began to speak.

"In the first psalm the Prophet David tells us, 'Blessed is the man that walketh not in the counsel of the ungodly, nor standeth in the way of sinners, nor sitteth in the seat of the pestilent.' This is what you girls are like. By going to the monastery, by being with the sisters and struggling, you are blessed. There are so many girls, so many young people out in the world who never know the comfort offered by a monastery, who never know what you experience by visiting monasteries and learning from the sisters."

She said a few other things, but it was difficult to hear her because she spoke quietly, and this in turn made it difficult for me to understand what she was saying in Greek. However, what I did hear was enough to ponder for a long time. Although this happened over five years ago, each time I read that psalm I think of her words and the sisters—our teachers—who gave us so much. They didn't only sacrifice two hours each week to teach us how to read Byzantine notation and to chant; they taught us so much more.

The guest-mistress's words also stirred thoughts in me regarding my chanting classmates. Just being with the other girls from class was so different from what I was used to. Although we were almost all in university or older, there was an innocence and a goodness in them I couldn't help but marvel at. On many occasions my sister-in-law (who also lived and studied in Thessaloniki) and I would discuss how impressed we were by the girls' natural virtue. It was a wonderful environment to be in and learn together. A great deal of giggling took place, but so did learning and spiritual instruction, which the sisters always offered us while we ate our treat at the end of class each week.

They would read a small passage from St. Porphyrios or from the *Gerontikon*. Sometimes they would read us something their previous abbess (who had reposed some years earlier) had written, or share with us something their current abbess had said in trapeza that day. Once Sr. Evsevia read us a story from the *Evergetinos* about a monk who was always displeased with his brotherhood and the monastery he was living in. He went from one to the next, to the next, always dissatisfied with the other fathers.

Finally, he arrived at the conclusion that neither the monastery nor the brotherhood was at fault, but that he himself needed to endure temptation in the place he found himself. So he wrote on a piece of paper: "In the name of our Savior the Lord Jesus Christ, I will be patient in all things," and resolved to remain in his monastery no matter what. Whenever he became upset with the other fathers, he took this piece of paper out of his pocket, unfolded it, and quietly read it to himself. Folding it back up and placing it in his pocket, he would exhibit patience.

Seeing this go on for some time, some of the fathers began to suspect the monk was reading a magic spell written on this piece of paper, and they went to the abbot to confess their suspicion. He in turn went to the monk and demanded to see the paper. When he read what was written thereon, he told the fathers, "This father does well."

All of us were moved and impressed by this story, and one of our classmates brought a number of small pieces of decorated cardstock to class the next week. On each she had written the monk's helpful words in a beautiful script. She gave one to each of us so that we too could remember to be patient in the face of all the trials and tribulations life throws at us.

On special occasions, the abbess would stop by our classroom to greet us. We would all stand up and approach her for her blessing one by one, and she would tell us some beautifully insightful, spiritual words that would always make my heart burn. It wasn't just the words—which I didn't always understand— that had this effect; it was her persona. It was her tone of voice, her gentle movements, and her visible humility that often left me as affected as her holy words.

Truly we were blessed to be a part of that environment, to learn and be instructed not only regarding Byzantine chant but regarding the art of salvation. When I reflect on that trip in which the humble nun shared those simple but profound words with us, I often think, *Blessed are we who walked in the counsel of the godly, who stood in the way of the righteous, and sat in the seat of the reverent.*

Reunion with a Holy Elder

I LEARNED THAT THE BLIND MONK, Elder Isidoros of Philotheou Monastery, was passing by Thessaloniki. Thinking it would be the last time I would get to see him, since we were moving back to Canada, I hurried to visit him, this time with my husband, brother, and sister-in-law. Quite a crowd had come to seek his prayers and counsel. While waiting for our chance to speak with him, we must have seen fifty or more people go in looking sorrowful, perplexed, apprehensive, even anxious, but they all came out with quite a different look.

Witnessing this again and again, I became convinced that you can tell if a person is holy by the impact he has on those around him. If the joy and peace on people's faces after speaking with the elder were any indication of holiness, then he surely has attained an elevated spiritual state. All who entered to speak with him exited looking as though they had not only left their problems behind but had been given comfort and joy in exchange.

When it was finally our turn, I excitedly rushed in to greet the elder. He was sitting on a wooden bench with his characteristic black cotton bag beside him.

Walking toward him, I called out the customary monastic greeting, "*Evlogeite* [bless], Geronda!"

I took his blessing by kissing his hand and sat down beside him. Before I could even introduce anyone, he was shoving a small rug at me. "Smell that. That belonged to a holy elder. He used to pray on it," he told me.

"It smells wonderful," I told him. Taking his hand in mine, I began telling him who was with me.

My sister-in-law sat down on his other side, and I told him who she was. He held his other hand out to her. I introduced my brother as well and my husband (although they had met some years before on the Holy Mountain).

"We just came to receive your blessing," I told him. "Here are my brother and sister-in-law. They are Orthodox, and our mother and sister are Orthodox as well. The only person who isn't is our father. You must pray for him to become Orthodox."

"He will be baptized," the elder said definitely.

"I hope so!" we echoed one another. Again we asked his prayers for our families, and he told us also to pray for them.

He rummaged through his bag and handed us some spiritual treasures to smell: the rug, relics of Elder Joseph the Hesychast, an undershirt belonging to a holy ascetic from Athos.

"Smell that! Smell that! What do you think?" he asked us enthusiastically. "Aren't they fragrant? Do you smell the fragrance?"

"Yes, Geronda, they smell very nice!" we responded. But he himself gave off such an extraordinary sweet fragrance that the scent on the holy objects he offered us to venerate seemed to pale in comparison.

We asked him for a spiritual word, and he told us, "Say *Lord—Jesus—Christ—have—mercy—on—me!*" he loudly proclaimed in his deep voice, slowly, enunciating each word. "And, *Most Holy Theotokos save us!*" he added.

After our discussion, he asked us to escort him out of the reception room, since we were the last ones waiting to see him. My sister-in-law and I guided him as we walked toward the door, but halfway across the room he stopped and began to slowly chant in a deep, loud voice, "Glory to the Consubstantial and Life-creating Trinity, always, now and ever and unto the ages of ages. Amen."

We all exchanged broad smiles with one another, surprised by this sudden burst of jovial song. And then he began, "Christ is risen from the dead." He started swinging our hands in his as though inviting us to chant with him. All of us joined him in spontaneously chanting "Christ is Risen" in the middle of November: "By death hath He trampled down death. And on those in the tomb, He hath bestowed life."

It was a beautiful moment, a treasured memory. We all became like little children in his presence. He communicated such genuine joy and love for the Lord. It softened our hearts in such a way that we were deeply affected by his faith, his hope, and his love. We, like all the other visitors, left our meeting with the elder filled with joy and peace, as though we were resurrected by being in the mere presence of such a holy person.

As we came out of the room together, the abbess of the monastery was standing speaking to some women.

"Constantina, what were you singing in there?" she asked.

"Christ is risen," I answered.

"Elder Isidoros with the 'Christ is risen' everyday," she smiled, waving her hand in the air.

Hearing the words of the elder that day concerning my father, I buried them with hope in my heart, truly believing his words would prove to be prophetic. However, I must confess I was still rather shocked—I think we all were—when the elder's prophecy came to fruition just over two years later. Our father was baptized on the Feast of the Theophany of the Lord by his son, my brother, Fr. Matthew (who by that time was an ordained priest).

We must never doubt the miracles of God and His will for "all men to be saved" (1 Tim. 2:4). After our father's baptism, we told him of the elder's words, and he laughed, he too having no doubt that the blind elder saw the wonders of God that would come to pass in the not-so-distant future.

He Who Comes in the Name of the Lord

ACQUIRING A SPIRITUAL FATHER requires prayer and discernment, a humble disposition, and an openness to the will of God, because a spiritual father "becomes the means of leading the life of men out of hell (by the negative effect of their passions), and into pure Christian life and spiritual freedom."[33] Thus, it is a precious treasure when one's spiritual father not only preaches Christ but lives like Christ, as Monk Isaiah wrote to Nun Theodora: "The Holy Spirit is for everyone; but in those who are pure of the passions, who are chaste and live in stillness and silence, He reveals special powers."[34]

The greatest spiritual guides are those whose manner of life teaches as much or more than their words and advice. If a spiritual guide does not live the commandments of Christ, if he has not experienced temptation, if he does not actively struggle to overcome his passions, then how will he teach others to do likewise? On this point Archimandrite Zacharias of Essex says, "If the word that the spiritual father says is not seasoned with grace, nor proceeds from a heart that is warmed by the love of Christ, it becomes like the work of psychologists or counselors—a 'half-blind' worldly activity. The word of the spiritual father must bear the seal of grace, the seasoning of grace."[35]

I was once visiting a women's monastery when it was announced that the spiritual father of the sisterhood would be arriving shortly. We all went to the courtyard to await his arrival. The nuns were abuzz with excitement, running from here to there in anticipation, getting ready to greet their beloved father and teacher.

Once he was close to the monastery, the church bells began to peal a joyous greeting for the sisterhood's spiritual elder with the honor and respect due to a person of great importance. The sisters opened wide the gates and allowed the car to drive right into the monastery (their elder was old and sickly and couldn't walk very far).

They had set out a chair for him in the shade of the garden beside the small chapel. He was led to his seat and offered some water while we all—nuns and visitors—gathered around him. Once the sisterhood had all taken his blessing (which took some time on account of the large number of nuns), we, the visitors, approached to receive his blessing. He smiled sweetly at us and passed on good wishes. He briefly addressed all present, but it was difficult for us to hear him on account of the crowd. His humble disposition and kind demeanor made an impact on me, but the sisters' joy and overwhelming love at having their spiritual father among them was more impressive still, contagious even.

The sisters' excitement and love for their holy elder was a beautiful testament to the great importance of spiritual fatherhood. For it is the spiritual father who gives "spiritual rebirth, who introduce[s us] to the life in Christ, and who guides [us] on the path of salvation. Our rebirth in Christ . . . makes us members in the community of our church and offers us the ability to live a life in Christ."[36]

Truly, what a great thing it is to follow our spiritual father on the path to salvation. "Let's not search for foretellers or foreseers," St. John Climacus advises us, "but above all for those who have humble mindedness in all things, and those who can deal with our spiritual illnesses" (*The Ladder of Divine Ascent*, Paulist Press, p. 88).

Catching Possession

ALTHOUGH IT WAS RELATIVELY early in the evening, it was already dark out, as it was winter. Our dear friend was taking us to some churches in Athens when she suggested we drive a little way up Mount Lykavittos. The church of St. George sits on the peak of the tallest hill in Athens, even higher than the Acropolis, which is directly across from it. The buildings on the two hills are like two pillars of history: one ancient, having long ago fallen out of use, and one modern (nineteenth century), offering services to crowds of Christians.

About halfway up the mountain is another church. I don't recall the name of it now, but it's nestled nicely into the side of the mountain. Our friend parked the car and then froze.

"Wait!" she said with urgency. "It's Wednesday. The priest here does exorcisms on Wednesdays. Maybe we shouldn't go up to venerate. If he is casting out demons, perhaps one will enter me if it doesn't have a place to go. Can that happen?" she asked us with trepidation.

I smiled and tilted my head. "I don't think it is very likely, so long as you confess and commune regularly. They would have to have some reason to enter you. I think you would have had to do something to give them the authority to enter," I said, not positive of my answer, but not in full agreement with her innocent fear either.

We walked up the many stairs leading to the church. Secretly, I was slightly apprehensive I would hear something of the exorcism, but I kept that fear to myself.

We arrived in front of the church, where there was an icon outside with an oil lamp. We decided that venerating that icon was enough, and so we didn't enter the church so as not to disturb the priest and the people—and truthfully, so as not to be disturbed.

On our way down the stairs back to the car, I thought about my friend's fear of having the demon leave someone and enter her, and this brought St. Parthenius to mind. I had first read about him a few years before, and his humility in dealing with a possessed man had stayed with me. Of St. Parthenius, St. Nikolai Velimirovitch writes in *The Prologue of Ohrid*:

> Through prayer, he healed every manner of illness and he was particularly powerful over evil spirits. On one occasion when he wanted to cast out an evil spirit from an insane man, the evil spirit begged him not to do so. Parthenius said to him: "I will give you

another man into whom you can enter and in him, you can dwell." The evil spirit asked him: "Who is this man?" "I am that man," replied the saint, "enter and dwell in me!" Upon hearing this, the evil spirit fled as though burned by fire crying out: "How can I enter into the house of God!"

Once, when my brother and I were young, having heard the Gospel passage about the Gadarene swine read in church that morning, we asked our father if it was possible for an evil spirit to enter just anyone. He told us, "If you are a house of God, then you can't house anything else."

We shouldn't fear evil spirits and whether or not they may dwell in us; we should fear whether or not we have made ourselves, and keep ourselves, houses of God. Of course we shouldn't be too secure in our opinion of how much God dwells in us, but if we have any fear at all, it should only be that we have not made ourselves worthy for Him to make His abode in us. Along with the humble example of our dear St. Parthenius, we should remember Christ said, "If anyone loves Me, he will keep My word; and My Father will love him, and We will come to him and make Our home with him" (John 14:23), and "There is no fear in love; but perfect love casts out fear" (1 John 4:18).

We drove away from the church and back down the mountain, on to the next church our friend wanted us to see, hopefully a little more at peace than when we approached.

The Love of a Father

ONE EVENING Mr. Demetri shared a wonderful story with us about his father. He told us when he was a child, he and some friends found a place outside the village where they liked to go and play. This particular day his mother had told him to be sure to return in time for supper, but the time got away from him. Before he knew it, he saw his father, a priest, approach. Rather than call to his son, he merely stood watching, not saying a word. A word was not necessary, because since his father had come all the way to fetch him, he knew without a doubt his mother would be upset with him.

The father and son walked home together in silence. When they approached the house, Demetri could see his mother coming out to look up the street, at which point his father took him by the ear. He did not squeeze his ear, but merely held it, giving the impression that he was treating the child harshly.

"When he took me by the ear, he did it so gently, just to give my mother the impression he was punishing me, that I began to cry. It was not because he was hurting me, or even because my mother was upset. Tears ran down my face out of love, on account of the gentle mercy my father showed me.

"Of course, my mother's anger was also appeased, because it appeared as though I understood I was in trouble," he added with a laugh.

The apostle of love, St. John the Theologian, tells us, "Behold what manner of love the Father has bestowed on us, that we should be called children of God!" (1 John 3:1). The fatherly love communicated to the young Demetri has remained in his heart all these years and is a powerful image for us well. God, with His fatherly love, does so much for us, and we, like small children humbled by the love shown to us, would be justified in shedding countless tears of wonder and thanksgiving.

Twilight in the Monastery, Midnight in the World

IN AN ANCIENT MANUSCRIPT narrating the life and martyrdom of St. Fevronia of Nisibis, it is said that a laywoman named Heria went to the monastery seeking counsel from the renowned Nun Fevronia. Heria's thirst and love for God compelled her to tearfully petition Abbess Bryene, Nun Fevronia's aunt, to allow her an audience with the spiritually wise nun. The abbess conceded to her request, as the manuscript describes:

> A certain young maiden named Heria . . . sought to gain an audience with Mother Fevronia, who had become well known in the region as "a lily blossoming forth in the vales of God." Hence, in desiring to quench her pious thirst for the faith, Heria went to Bryene with tears beseeching her: "I appeal to you by God Who made all of creation, do not reject me because I am an unclean pagan and the sport of demons. Deny me not the opportunity to speak and learn from the nuns the paths of salvation, and to know of those good things laid in store for Christians. Rescue me from the vanity of this world and from the defilement of idolatry . . . let me now partake of new life through the words of my sister Fevronia."

I know what it is to yearn for the opportunity to "speak and learn from the nuns the paths of salvation," for it is not only through the words of God-illumined abbesses that we are given new life. Many nuns and monks, in their own way, convey depths of spiritual wisdom in their words and deeds. This is just one of many reasons it is so vital for Orthodox Christians to make pilgrimages to monasteries.

In her autobiography, Abbess Thaisia, a spiritual daughter of St. John of Kronstadt, describes an intense temptation she encountered in the monastery. Weighed down by despairing thoughts, she began to consider it better to return to the world than to stay in the monastery. Filled with grief, confusion, and fear on account of her despairing thoughts, she would constantly cry and pray for God to help her, to support her, even to prevent her from going insane.

In the midst of this trial, she went for a walk and fell into a kind of spiritual sleep, or drowsiness as she describes it. Suddenly she heard the sound of the city's cathedral clock striking twelve. Unsure of how so much time could have passed so quickly, she looked toward the bell tower of the city, where everything lay in darkness. Then she heard a voice say, "You see, although it is beginning to get dark at the convent, it is still twilight, evening; while in the world it was midnight long ago".[37] At once she regained consciousness and understood, relieved that God had delivered her from the temptation to return to the world.

As one who visits monasteries as a laywoman, like Heria, I also approach seeking refuge from the vanity of the world, knowing all too well that "in the world it was midnight long ago." I am eternally grateful that I am able to escape to the twilight now and again and "partake of new life" through hearing the words and being in the presence of holy monastics.

Forgive Me, Teacher

WE IN THE MARITIME PROVINCES of Canada often use the phrase "Oh, I'm sorry" interchangeably with "Excuse me." The first time I became aware that phrase was merely culturally instilled in me was when I moved to South Korea. I would constantly say "I'm sorry" when attempting to squeeze through a crowd in the subway station. But when I observed others squeezing through crowds, I noticed they merely kept silent—reminding me that this Maritimer's "I'm sorry" was a simple replacement for "Excuse me." It had become a commonplace saying without much conviction.

Conversely, the phrase "Forgive me" is an intentional saying in monastic circles, and it is anything but an empty statement thrown about. The Greek word *evlogison* is in fact used interchangeably with the imperative "Bless," while also serving as a form of the phrase "Forgive me."

It was in reading about the life and teachings of Elder Iakovos Tsalikis, while working in Korea, that I first became aware of the monastic practice of saying "Forgive me." This holy, humble elder who lived and struggled on the island of Evia not only would interject this phrase when advising his spiritual children, but he would even ask forgiveness from his worldly minded and conniving monastic brothers when they would unjustly accuse him. Reading his biography, his example made such an impact on me that "Forgive me" was one of the first phrases I tried to learn in Korean.

At the school where I taught, the children were assigned English names to go with the whole English culture the school wanted to immerse them in. They called me Connie Teacher, but one day I told them I had chosen a Korean name for myself. I told them it was *Yongseo Songsaengnim*, which is literally "Forgive teacher," though I intended it to be "Forgive me teacher." When I told the children my Korean name, they howled with laughter; one boy clutched his hands together as though he were begging for forgiveness, which made the other children laugh all the harder. I was just playing with them, but

Elder Iakovos's example had made me take the act of intentionally asking for forgiveness to heart.

Despite knowing about this monastic practice, I found it disarming the first time a nun sincerely said out of the blue, "Forgive us." In fact, I was completely taken off guard.

Returning from a pilgrimage a group of us had taken with some sisters, as we were parting company, Sr. Silouani said, "Forgive us if we've done or said anything to hurt or scandalize you."

Immediately my mind began racing. *Did I act offended by something she said? Did I look bothered by something that happened? Did something upset me? No! Then why did she say that to me?*

As my train of thought testifies, I cannot even receive a simple apology without my mind playing an internal game of twenty questions. But the sisters' example taught me that an intentional attempt at reconciliation—even in cases in which offense was unintentional—is not only a self-humbling act, it is a core element of our Christian Faith.

There is no denying the emphasis Christ places on forgiveness. He tells us, "Therefore if you bring your gift to the altar, and there remember that your brother has something against you, leave your gift there before the altar, and go your way. First be reconciled to your brother, and then come and offer your gift" (Matt. 5:23–24). The Lord prompts us to *seek* forgiveness before approaching Holy Communion. This, of course, does not exclude the prerequisite of also offering forgiveness, but the emphasis is on the former.

The monastic practice of repetitively saying "Forgive me" is deeply rooted in Christ's admonition to reconcile with a brother or sister who "has something against you." They take this command so seriously that they ask forgiveness proactively just in case they have offended or scandalized someone. St. John Chrysostom says in his Homilies on Matthew (16, 12):

> Let the initiated hear this, as many as draw near in enmity: and let the uninitiated hear too: yea, for the saying has some relation to them also. For they too offer a gift and a sacrifice: prayer, I mean, and almsgiving. . . . So that if it be but a prayer, which you are offering in such a frame of mind, it were better to leave your prayer, and become reconciled to your brother, and then to offer your prayer. For to this end were all things done: to this end even God became man, and took order for all those works, that He might set us at one.

To seek and offer forgiveness is truly blessed, for it is at the heart of being a peacemaker. The reward is not only to be called sons of God, but—as St. John Chrysostom says—to be united as one. I guess I can't rightly choose my Korean name to be "Forgive me" if I don't in fact live this commandment.

Set a Watch Before My Mouth

SR. SARAH AND SR. THEKLA, having become novices around the same time, had a special bond. Not only did they share books and stories, work together, and were even tonsured together, they had a unique pact. From the very beginning of their monastic lives, they agreed they would never, under any circumstances, indicate to each other that they had gotten into an argument, were upset with, or had been offended by, a member of their monastic community. This decision to safeguard the bond of peace within the sisterhood was a very wise one.

"See, if I had a problem with a certain sister, if for some reason I got upset with her and went and vented to Sr. Thekla, then she might also find herself becoming embittered or disliking the other sister. You know, the way a person sometimes dislikes those whom their friends dislike. We never wanted this to happen, so we agreed that we would never say anything bad about another sister, ever."

This simple commitment brings with it immeasurable protection. Many times we allow ourselves to vent. We convince ourselves that it is better to get it all out than to allow our anger to boil up inside us, as the saying goes. Unfortunately, we are wrong on two counts for engaging in such behavior.

First, venting allows our thoughts and suspicions, our hurt feelings and offenses, to become solidified. We confirm our thoughts by justifying them, explaining why we are right and the other person is wrong, how we are wounded and the other is the cruel offender. Second, we pull the other person or persons listening to us into sin with us. We infiltrate their thoughts and perceptions, tainting the way they think and feel about the supposed offender. This is actually worse than the first wrongdoing, because we are not only sinning but creating a stumbling block for someone else.

It is an easy enough temptation to fall into, especially given that contemporary society encourages expressing our anger; it teaches us it's a necessary evil to pour out the poison in order to avoid blowing up. But since when has the authentic Christian embraced what the world teaches? Here is what Elder Thaddaeus teaches we ought to do to resolve our inner turmoil:

> When the period of warfare comes, we are overwhelmed by thoughts. . . . This is when we must turn to the Lord in our hearts and keep silence. If we cannot abandon the thought that is bothering us

immediately then we must keep silence. We should not think about anything. It is not ours to think. The Lord knows what we can take and what we cannot. Then, when we are in silence and our mind is quiet, we should give it something to do so that it will not wander [and return to the matter that is bothering us]. We should pray.[38]

When we are confronted by strong emotions and thoughts, instead of venting to someone else, we can apply the elder's advice. And then we go to confession. It is in confession that our venting can take place. Not that confession is an opportunity to accuse, slander, or even simply reveal the faults of others, but it is here in confession that we can reveal our honest feelings and perceptions. Most importantly, it is through confession that our erring thoughts are corrected and we receive consolation for our sorrow. A wise spiritual guide can help us discern where we are at fault in a conflict, or, if we are innocent, how we can bear the injustices done to us.

The sisters protected themselves and each other by committing to keep silent instead of venting. Silence doesn't mean the heart is at peace, but it does ensure that sin does not progress into action through word or deed. By their silence the sisters "silence the enemy and the avenger" of mankind (Ps. 8:2).

A Life of Perfect Love

GERONTISSA OFFERED to see us in her office. This was a first. We had never been inside her personal office before. But this new first was one of many now that Fr. John was an ordained deacon.

We entered Gerontissa's cozy office, and she insisted Fr. John sit in the most comfortable seat and I in the second most comfortable, while she sat on a simple wooden chair. We felt uncomfortable with this arrangement. We had been visiting for years and had grown accustomed to simply being "kids," as she often called us, in the presence of such a respectable Gerontissa. But once Fr. John was clergy, our relationship changed.

She had often told us, "The great schema is a calling; the priesthood is an office and therefore of greater importance." Now we saw for ourselves that she applied this way of thinking to practical situations. In the past we could barely persuade her to advise us; now she made sure to speak with us if we visited.

As a rule, it is better for us to avoid sharing the words told to us by God-seeing elders and eldresses. However, there are certain statements and general advice one receives which are appropriate to share, so long as they are not too personal in nature. Gerontissa spoke to us on a theme applicable to many: keeping peace between husband and wife.

"The evil one tries to tempt couples to bicker, to take offense easily, and to remember wrongs," she told us. "Couples need to be watchful, especially on major feast days like Christmas and Pascha, and always on Sundays. If something upsets you on those days, let it go and talk about it the next day, after you've had time to calm down.

"And be careful not to couple with thoughts. Thoughts are not sins until you accept them. If you accept them, you'll begin to think of all the ways in which the other person offends you, or has offended you, and then you become guilty of sinning. The evil one brings to mind previous incidents and heightens your perception of offenses against you so that you become hardened toward the person. So be mindful not to accept such thoughts.

"At the end of the day, during the Compline prayers, we bow and ask forgiveness from one another. We should never go to bed angry. There is a saying attributed to the devil: 'All day long I tie up monastics, causing them to be angry and argue with one another, but at the end of the day they ask for forgiveness and all my work is undone.' This is how couples should end their day as well, forgiving one another."

Her words spoke of struggling harder and forgiving faster, a practice all couples can benefit from. They remind me of similar words spoken by Gerontissa Makrina of Portaria: "God won't ask us why we fell down, but why we did not get back up."[39]

In the Orthodox wedding service, the priest prays the words, "If they walk this way, their life together will be one of perfect love." If we would follow Gerontissa's prudent advice, our life together would indeed be one of perfect love.

Edified by Silence

THE FIRST TIME I VISITED an Orthodox monastery, I was escorted into a small room to speak with a priestmonk. When I entered the room, I saw he was seated, his hands folded in his lap, while his elbows rested on the chair's wooden armrests. He wasn't wearing his monastic *skoufa* [hat], but he was wearing a priest's stole, which looked peculiar to me with the buttons holding it together in the middle, since I was used to Western stoles that hang on either side of the neck like a scarf.

His long black monastic robe grazed the floor, and behind him, leaning against the wall, was a wooden ladder. I don't know if it was placed there on purpose or was merely being stored there, but it nevertheless made an impression on me. Even though I wasn't yet Orthodox, the imagery of a ladder behind a father confessor was not lost on me: "For it is a ladder from the earth unto heaven that confers glory on the souls that ascend," the Kontakion of St. John Climacus says.

Approaching the priestmonk, I bent and touched the ground and kissed his right hand. (I had done a little homework and looked into basic etiquette at a monastery.) He gestured for me to sit on the floral-patterned couch.

I was incredibly nervous about speaking to him, not only because I felt I was speaking to an important person for the first time, but because I imagined this conversation as my opportunity to speak out loud my heart's desire to become Orthodox. (This was a potentially destructive desire for my relationship with my husband, who at that time, as I said above, was in the process of becoming an Anglican priest.) I saw this as my one chance to reveal the burning desire I had kept relatively hidden until that point.

Sitting down, I waited to see what the priestmonk would say. He didn't begin with small talk; he didn't ask how I was nor about my trip to the monastery. His first question, getting right to the heart of the matter, was, "How has your journey to Orthodoxy been?" That was all it took to start me sobbing. I managed to sputter, "Hard," in response but wasn't able to pull myself together to say any more.

Suddenly, while I was still crying, there was a knock at the door. The priestmonk quickly stood up and exited without saying a word. I continued to cry and take deep breaths, trying to compose myself. Time passed, and gradually fewer tears rolled down my cheeks.

More time passed, and I began looking at the icons lining the walls. I remember St. Katherine the Great Martyr, sitting next to a spiked wheel, hung on the wall opposite me.

I began thinking over what had led me to the monastery and what I was seeking from this experience. I managed to make a mental list of three things I wanted to speak to the priestmonk about. However, the more time passed, the more I began to wonder if something had happened to prevent him from returning. I thought of leaving, since it had been about thirty minutes since his departure, but I figured he would send someone to get me if he wasn't planning to come back. I decided to be patient.

Once again I began going over the three things I wanted to talk about. But as suddenly as he had exited, he entered and sat down again, saying nothing—*nothing*—not a "sorry about that" or a "something came up." He just sat down and looked at me, waiting for me to begin.

Those few moments of silence that passed between us deeply impressed me. *Never in my life have I met someone like this priestmonk!* I thought. I can't express how instructive this silence was for me. In the face of this silence, I felt that for the first time my loud, attention-seeking, talkative nature was revealed to me. I was filled with great admiration for him. I thought he must have had great humility to be free from the inclination to fill space with empty words. It was only later when I read the Desert Fathers that I learned the Orthodox Tradition holds silence in equal esteem with spiritual words:

Abba Theophilus, the archbishop, came to Scetis one day. The brethren who were assembled said to Abba Pambo, "Say something to the archbishop, so that he may be edified." The old man said to them, "If he is not edified by my silence, he will not be edified by my speech."[40]

That evening I was edified by the priestmonk's silence, and as a result I gained great insight into myself as well as learning the power of silence in place of speech. I have never forgotten his holy and passionless example.

✠ EIGHT ✠

Blessed Are Those Who Are Persecuted
for Righteousness' Sake
for theirs is the kingdom of heaven

Feeling the Heavens Breathing Near: 179 Martyred Monks

NOT FAR FROM ATHENS is an incredible monastery founded in the tenth century. It is called the Pantocrator Monastery (*Pantocrator* means "ruler of all"). The monastery is named after our Lord and Savior. In 1465 it was destroyed by Turks and later rebuilt only to have an even worse tragedy occur, soaking the ground in the holy blood of many martyrs.

The year was 1680, and although the monastery had a strong fortress built around it, Algerian pirates devised a plan to pillage it. They tunneled underneath, and on the evening of Pascha, while the 179 monks of the monastery were celebrating the Lord's Holy Resurrection, the pirates interrupted their celebrations and brutally killed every single one present.

The only surviving members of the brotherhood were a priest-monk and a novice who had gone to serve the Paschal Divine Liturgy in a nearby village before the pirates infiltrated the monastery. When the monks returned to the monastery, they found the fathers—their brothers—massacred. With the help of others, they buried their sacred bodies on Bright Tuesday, closed the monastery behind them, and moved elsewhere.

As years passed, the martyrdom of these 179 fathers was not forgotten, but the location of their graves was. And so it was that when nuns came to repopulate the monastery in 1960—the first time it had functioned as a proper monastery since the fathers' martyrdom, three hundred years before—the sisters did not know where the martyred fathers lay.

While the nuns were making renovations to the monastery's church, a number of the fathers' graves were found under the floor of the ninth-century catholicon. On their recovery, they began emitting a sweet fragrance. Yet the whereabouts of the rest of the martyred fathers' graves remained a mystery.

Once while St. Porphyrios, that great saint of the twenty-first century, was visiting the monastery, he told the abbess, "The ground we walk on is sacred ground; we are walking on the graves of the saints." St. Porphyrios had seen, as he often did, what other eyes could not. His sight was not limited by his physical vision; he had the gift of seeing despite obstacles or distances. Just as he had said, so it was. When excavations took place, many more graves were discovered.

Whenever I was in Athens, I would visit this monastery if I could. I heard the story of the fathers' martyrdom from the sisters who live there now. I listened to the sisters narrate many accounts of miracles attributed to the holy martyrs. I myself smelled the sweet fragrance and venerated their holy relics.

With the exception of one father whose relics reside in the narthex of the catholicon, the fathers' relics are housed in a small room. About six fathers are laid out in full monastic robes under glass covers. The rest, pieces of bone and skulls, are kept in glass cases. You can even see some of the skulls have holes right through them, a visible reminder of the physical suffering they endured all those years ago.

One Friday night I was traveling to this monastery with a friend to attend the vigil. It didn't start until around ten PM, if I remember correctly, so it was already dark when we set out for the monastery. As we drove through the winding roads, I was gazing out the window, not sure of exactly where we were. Suddenly a sense of fear took hold of me—a sacred fear. I thought, *We must be near the monastery*. It was the kind of fear that accompanies truly holy, sacred places, and just around the bend I began to see the entrance to the parking lot. It struck me just how powerful the unseen heavenly hosts are.

In a poem describing the Baptism of Christ, St. Nikolai Velimirovich says, "At once St. John was filled with fear, on feeling the heavens breathing so near." The heavens and the site on which 179 fathers shed their blood for Christ are thinly veiled. All who visit the monastery sense the sacredness of the place. When we took my mother and aunt to visit the monastery, my aunt, a faithful Roman Catholic, was transfixed by the holy relics of the father in the narthex. She didn't say anything, but we could tell from her countenance how affected she was by the holy martyr.

My words are feeble and my descriptions dry compared to the vibrant and sweet grace contained in that monastery on account of the holy saints who lived, died, and were buried there. It is an indescribable feeling to be in a place so sacred.

> As spotless lambs of the Savior, proceeding from various nations, the flock gathers together at Pantokratoros. Having been put to death by the rage of the barbarians, rejoicing you enter into heavenly pastures. Therefore holy martyrs of Christ, intercede on behalf of our souls. (Apolytikion for the 179 Holy Martyrs of Daou)

The Yoke of Monasticism

IT'S A WELL-KNOWN FACT that monasticism is chock-full of temptations. If one is thinking monasticism will be an escape from the world with its trials and problems, he will soon learn what a grave mistake he made thinking the monastery is a safe haven from spiritual and worldly obstacles.

Some who decide to become monastics encounter vast and extreme temptations. There are those who, even before arriving at the gates of the monastery, are faced with a variety of barriers.

The day my friend was to set out for the monastery he planned to join, he noticed a bush just outside his front door was engulfed in flames. When firefighters responded, they explained that the cause of the fire seemed to be spontaneous combustion in the mulch. To be clear, the city in which this friend lived is well known for fog and drizzle, so you can imagine the surprise of a fire starting all on its own.

Mrs. M traveled as far as the Holy Land to become a nun at the monastery of her choice. When she arrived, she called her daughter to tell her she wouldn't be returning home because she was entering a monastery. To her shock and dismay, her daughter told her that very morning she had woken up to find half of her body paralyzed. It turned out Mrs. M.'s daughter had multiple sclerosis and needed her mother to return home in order to take care of her newborn granddaughter. After consulting with her spiritual father, Mrs. M did in fact return.

Some monastic aspirants I know have encountered minor setbacks, like missing airplane flights, while others have met with parents who—though never showing signs of being controlling before—suddenly demand complete power over their child's life choices.

Others, however, experience divine confirmation when they or members of their family leave to become monastics. I know of a family, particularly the mother, who was initially quite devastated the night her daughter left to become a nun at a nearby monastery.

The next day a neighbor told the mother of the family, "That was some party you had last night with all those people in your home!"

The woman responded, "I didn't have any visitors last night. I don't know what you're talking about."

The neighbor insisted, "I saw your house from my balcony, and I could see there were tons of people in your home. But what kind of light did you have that was so bright it shone up from the roof of your house into the sky?"

At this point the mother of the family understood that although her daughter had left to become a monastic, God had sent heavenly visitors to her home as a consolation. I suppose God allowed the neighbor to see the invisible spiritual event taking place so she could relay it to the disheartened mother. Hearing the neighbor's description of the visitors to her home and the pillar of light the night before, she was comforted and no longer opposed her daughter's choice.

The idea that an angel is sent to minister to the family of a monastic in his or her absence is a story passed down in Orthodox tradition. I read in a *Gerontikon* about a monk who, on hearing his mother and sisters in the world were going through hardships, decided to leave his hermitage and return to his village to help them. On his way he met a stranger on the road, and they began talking. The monk revealed that he was leaving his monastery to help his family, while the stranger revealed himself to be an angel, the very angel in fact who had stayed with and protected the monk's family since the day he left to become a monastic.

Furthermore, the angel told him, "Since you are returning to your family to protect them and care for them, I will no longer minister to them." Hearing this, the monk became frightened, understanding that it was more advantageous for his family to have an angel as their guardian than to have him. He returned to his hermitage.

Such is the power of monasticism: it not only affects those monks and nuns who have laid down their life for the Lord, but even their family members benefit from their Christ-centered life in countless ways, seen and unseen.

The Glory of the Saints Contemplated in a Cellar

ST. TRYPHON WAS A VIRTUOUS and brave young man from Asia Minor. From his youth God granted him the power to cast out demons, prevent famines, and heal all manner of maladies. He even cast out a demon from the daughter of the Roman Emperor Gordian, asking only that he and his family believe in Christ God as "payment" for the good deed.

In Russia, St. Tryphon is considered a patron of birds because he once returned a lost falcon to a falconer of his namesake, Tryphon Patrikeiev, who later built two churches in honor of the saint. In Greece, he is implored for protection against insects and rodents. Thus it was that we found ourselves in a cellar of a women's monastery in Greece participating in a Paraklesis (Supplicatory Canon) in honor of St. Tryphon.

It was his feast day, February 1, and we had traveled to the monastery for a short two-day pilgrimage. Just as we arrived, a sister invited us to the cellar, where the nuns were about to begin an impromptu Paraklesis to St. Tryphon before a large icon of him which they had placed in the cellar as protection from all manner of unwanted critters.

It is not only in the large, frescoed, cruciform churches that one marvels at the glory of the saints, given by God as a reward for their good deeds, sacrifice, and endurance. Even in a stone cellar, when you hear the Canon being sung to a martyr, when you look upon his painted countenance, his youthful face, and his messy hair, even stony hearts can be moved.

St. Tryphon was in the prime of his life, boldly living out his faith in works, when Emperor Decius was informed of this youth's ability and success at spreading the Christian way of life. Having confessed his faith to the Emperor, the young saint was subjected to bodily torture, but even in the midst of this suffering the martyr endured, prayed, and even abstained from complaining. Being condemned to beheading, the saint prayed and gave up his soul before the sword even touched his neck. Having been informed by St. Tryphon in a vision where he wished to be buried, faithful Christians returned his holy body to his village to be entombed there.

Listening to the sisters chant hymns to this young martyr while

I stood with my back against the cellar's cold stone wall, I couldn't help but marvel at the honor given to the saints. Truly, God dwells in His saints, and we reap the benefit: we pray, they intercede, and we too are given the strength and conviction to confess Jesus Christ and have Him dwell in us and us in Him.

Holy Martyr Tryphon, pray to God for us!

Spiritual Warfare Is Not Won with Marshmallows

THERE IS AN ELEMENT of our Orthodox Faith—a reality of the spiritual world—that many don't like to think about: that demons exist and at times have control over people's bodies. This does not mean the possessed person is inherently evil or even necessarily at fault for the condition he or she may suffer from. But it is to say that spiritual warfare is very real. Demons not only exist but war against us, and at times—as the Scriptures themselves testify—they are given authority to enter people's bodies. Here are a few stories which, while disturbing, remind us that "we do not wrestle against flesh and blood, but against principalities, against powers, against the rulers of the darkness of this age, against spiritual *hosts* of wickedness in the heavenly *places*" (Eph. 6:12).

There was a young student who, although he was living in the world, lived extremely ascetically, eating very little and praying for many hours during the night. On account of his strict asceticism, he became like a skeleton. However, it was never clear whether his ascetic pursuit of holiness was taken on with a blessing or was based in self-will. One night his cousin came by to visit him and persuaded the young student to accompany him to a nightclub. Our young ascetic acceded and went with his cousin for a night on the town, where they met some young ladies. Unfortunately, this resulted in our young ascetic falling into sin with a woman.

The next day a friend tried contacting the young man, but he was evasive on the telephone. Sensing he was upset, the friend stopped by the student's apartment. Once there he tried to persuade his friend to leave the apartment and go out for a coffee to talk about what was upsetting him. However, the young ascetic, suddenly filled with rage, threw his friend up against the wall. Now remember, we said that on account of his asceticism he had become like a skeleton, and yet he exhibited great strength.

After this strange encounter, his friend became more and more concerned. The ascetic admitted to falling into sin with a girl, and the friend tried to persuade him to confess his sin to a priest. However, the young student—who at one time substituted vigil and fasting for a night's sleep—was not able to so much as enter a church. In fact, a group of strong men tried to help him enter in order for a priest to read exorcism prayers over him, but they were unable to assist him. Eventually, a priest was able to expel the evil influences, but the young student was never quite the same.

Do you see how easy it is for man's soul to fall from grace, despite so much prayer and fasting? This is why the Fathers teach us again and again to be careful and to take on ascetic practices with a blessing so that we do not become proud and fall into sin as a result.

Another story I know involves a young woman who was greatly tempted on account of her lifestyle. She had made a pilgrimage to a monastery, but when she ate a piece of bread the sisters had laid out for the guests as a blessing, she suddenly felt as though someone had stuffed a fabric softener sheet into her mouth. She had the sensation that someone was squeezing her around the waist to the point where she thought her ribs and lungs would collapse on account of the pressure.

That evening the pilgrim could not sleep. Seeing an icon on the nightstand, she picked it up and laid it on her lap. At some point she decided to hug the icon and pressed it up against her chest. However, as she herself related, she could not bear the weight of the icon. Although it was no more than eight by ten inches, it felt as though it weighed a ton and would crush her chest. She left it on her lap where it did not feel so heavy.

When the priest read prayers over her, she suddenly exhaled loudly and forcefully, without, however, having taken a deep breath first. After she had prayers read over her every day for a week, this temptation weakened.

These unpleasant stories, although certainly not things we want to focus on, are necessary to hear now and again in order for us to remember that our spiritual life is not a game easily won. As Elder Joseph the Hesychast says, the powers and rulers of darkness "are not fought with sweets and marshmallows, but with streams of tears, with pain of soul until death, with utter humility, and with great patience."[41]

These stories are a reminder of the care with which we must proceed in our spiritual lives. They also remind us that while demons do not have authority to read our thoughts, they have spent many years observing man turning away from God, and they have perfected their art in warring against us. They have the power—when and if God allows them—to possess people, and they do so because it pleases them to see man suffer. But this does not mean the individual who is possessed will be condemned; rather, by suffering this temporary chastisement they may very well enter the Kingdom of heaven, having suffered hell in this life so as to be saved in the next.

A Holy Fool for Christ?

THERE WAS A YOUNG theological student in Thessaloniki who was modest, pious, and from a family that raised her in the Church. She decided to become a nun. Although her family were "of the Church," as they say in Greek, they were dead against her decision. Despite this, she left her family and the world for Christ's sake and entered a monastery.

Instead of her family gradually coming to terms with their adult daughter's decision to become a nun, the more time passed, the more ferocious they became. They would go to the monastery and demand to speak with their daughter to persuade her to leave. They would call news stations and have them gather outside the monastery gates. It even reached the point where they would throw stones at the monastery to get their daughter's attention. The abbess must have prayerfully considered what was best for all involved, because she decided it was better for the young lady to leave the monastery and return to her parents' home.

The young woman returned to the world with her family, but she did not return the same. Soon, my friend—who was a friend of this young lady's— informed me, she began dressing differently. Whereas before she had dressed modestly, wearing only skirts and dresses, now she began dressing in the punk style, dying her hair all sorts of colors and smoking. She kept company with questionable characters and was often seen yelling profanities on the street at those passing by.

My friend was very saddened to see this transformation in this one-time monastic aspirant. She spoke of her sadness to another friend who told her a surprising story.

This young man had seen the former nun in the library one day walking around with headphones, head-banging. He approached her and took her headphones to hear what she was listening to. Would you believe it? It was an audio recording of the Book of Psalms. It wasn't heavy metal or any other kind of secular music. She was head-banging to King David's psalms! It was all an act, he assured my friend. The young lady's heart hadn't changed; only her outward ways and appearance had.

In the Scriptures we read, "Let no one deceive himself. If anyone among you seems to be wise in this age, let him become a fool that he may become wise. For the wisdom of this world is foolishness with God. For it is written, 'He catches the wise in their *own* craftiness'" (1 Cor. 3:18–19).

Since apostolic times we have had countless fools for Christ listed in the Synaxarion of the Church: St. Isidora, St. Andrew of Constantinople, St. Basil of Moscow. Many holy persons of later centuries, especially in Russia, have taken on foolishness for Christ's sake: Pasha of Sarov, Pelagia Ivanovna, Natalia Dmitrievna, and Maria Ivanovna were four holy fools all attached to the Diveyevo Monastery in Sarov in the nineteenth century, to make no mention of that great fool for Christ St. Xenia of St. Petersburg. St. Sophia the Righteous, the ascetic of Panagia, and Crazy John of Athens were holy fools of the twentieth century.

Whether this young lady I have described above, after being

forced out of the monastic life by her misguided parents, took on foolishness for Christ's sake is not something I can verify, but I was deeply affected by her story. It brought to mind many other holy fools whose wisdom far surpasses the wisdom of this world and who inspire us by their courage and soundness of mind and spirit to accomplish such ascetic endeavors, which truly obliterate the sins of pride and vainglory. Wherever she is, I hope and pray that her life is pleasing to the Lord.

Father Seraphim Rose and His Influence in Greece

IN GREECE Father Seraphim Rose is a very revered spiritual person. I doubt I could count the number of times I heard, "Oh, you're from America [since, as I've already said, Canada is more or less synonymous with America in the Greek mind]. Did you know Fr. Seraphim Rose?"

"Not personally, but I know his books," I'd explain, laughing inside at just how far away New Brunswick (where I grew up) is from California, to make no mention of the fact that Fr. Seraphim reposed before I was even born. And despite the distance between Greece and America—in thought and lifestyle as much as in miles—Fr. Seraphim's life and words have a great impact on Greeks. People read his books in translation and think of him as a contemporary elder. In fact, many refer to him as Geronda Seraphim Rose.

My family also has great reverence for Fr. Seraphim, since it was his biography that truly catapulted our entrance into Orthodoxy. Thus, we were happy to hear about a pilgrimage our parish priest in Thessaloniki told us he and a group of parishioners had made to America. One of their destinations was St. Herman's Monastery in

Platina, where they experienced a miracle at Fr. Seraphim's grave.

As the group was visiting the grave, a sweet-smelling fragrance began to be emitted. It wasn't only our priest who perceived it; everyone on the trip detected the scent. "It must be a gift from Fr. Seraphim because you're the first group of Greek pilgrims to visit his grave," a monk told them.

And that wasn't the only miracle attributed to Fr. Seraphim that we heard of. Once when my husband and brother were visiting the Holy Mountain with a friend of ours, a conversation took place at the skete where they were staying about whether or not Fr. Seraphim Rose was a saint. Some fervently believed he was, while others had doubts.

The next day, while they were at the port waiting for the boat to Ouranopoli, an unknown monk walked up to the member of the company who had doubts and said, "You know Fr. Seraphim Rose worked a miracle for us at the monastery! He's a saint." Having said this, he continued on his way.

I was speaking with a monk from a monastery in Palestine whom I greatly respect, and I asked him if he too considered Fr. Seraphim Rose a saint. He said, "Yes, of course. He had a saintly face in death. You can see it in photographs."

Fr. Seraphim said, "Everything in this life passes away—only God remains, only He is worth struggling towards. We have a choice: to follow the way of this world, of the society that surrounds us, and thereby find ourselves outside of God; or to choose the way of life, to choose God Who calls us and for Whom our heart is searching."

One of my favorite passages in the autobiography of Blessed Augustine says, "My heart is restless until it rests in you." Fr. Seraphim found rest because he found Christ, and not only found Him but struggled with all his might to acquire Him, so that now not only do his words remain to aid us in our own struggles, but his good works continue to the glory of God and the benefit of mankind, not only in America but throughout the Orthodox world.

May we have his blessing!

The Theotokos, the One Who Saves

IN THE CITY OF THESSALONIKI there is a modest church, nearly hidden by a beautiful garden, named in honor of St. Anthony the Great. It is located close to the site of the ancient hippodrome where St. Demetrios's disciple, the young Nestor, defeated the giant Lyaeus and suffered martyrdom. St. Anthony's is a *metochion** of the Holy Monastery of St. Theodora (a men's monastery in the center of the city). Here, in this small church of St. Anthony, is housed the miracle-working icon Diasosousa, which means "the one who saves."

The icon and its miracle are celebrated in conjunction with the liturgical feast of the Holy Protection of the Theotokos. This feast is typically celebrated on October 1; however, in Greece it is celebrated on October 28, "*Oxi* day": a national holiday. The feast of the Protection was transferred to this date some years ago in Greece because the people felt that it was through the intercessions of the Theotokos that they successfully withstood Italian troops (in cahoots with the Nazis), who in 1940 wanted to come into Greece and set up military stations in unspecified locations. Since Greece refused to allow this (they said *oxi*, no), the country was forced to enter the Second World War.

* Metochion: a dependency of another, usually larger, monastery.

The story goes that during this period of war, a group of five men from Thessaloniki were being chased by German soldiers and ran into the church of St. Anthony to hide. At that time St. Anthony's functioned as a monastery, and the abbot happened to be in the altar when the men entered, desperately seeking cover. The men told the abbot they needed to hide from the Germans; however, since the church is quite small, there was no obvious hiding place. The abbot told them all to stand behind the icon of the Theotokos, which at that time was located to the right of the iconostasis.

When the Germans came into the church, they looked everywhere for the Greek men: around the stasidia (seats), in the altar, everywhere, but they could not find them. Through the grace of the Most Holy Theotokos, they were blind to the five men standing behind her icon. After interrogating the abbot and learning nothing, the Germans left in great frustration, and the Greeks came out from behind the icon. Just then they noticed that the Theotokos's icon was covered in myrrh.

"She is sweating from the stress of having to hide you," the abbot told them. "Let's kneel down and say a supplicatory canon to her."

And this is how the icon came to be known as "the one who saves," since she saved the Greek men from the German soldiers. To this day the chanters at St. Anthony's sing each Sunday the kontakion that was written specifically for the miracle the Theotokos worked through her icon:

> Those who hymn thine icon, O Theotokos, who saves us from danger, find in thee shelter and protection, as when thou defeated the attack of the barbarians in the church of the godly-minded Anthony. In like manner shelter and preserve us from visible and invisible enemies, Champion Theotokos, the one who saves.

May she always hide and protect us from sin the way she hid those men from being captured by the Germans!

St. Ephraim of Nea Makri

IN 1384 A YOUNG MAN was born who, at the young age of fourteen, became a monk, taking the name Ephraim. For nearly twenty-seven years, he practiced strict asceticism in the mountain of Amoman in Attica, Greece, near a monastery in Nea Makri. In 1425 the nearby monastery was looted, and many monastics were beheaded by invading Muslims. St. Ephraim remained calm in the face of their brutality, which angered them all the more, and they imprisoned him, hoping he would denounce his faith in the True God. For months they tortured the saint, but to their frustration, the saint's devotion to Christ proved more difficult to damage than his physical body.

So it was that on May 5, 1426, the Muslims tied the saint's body to a mulberry tree upside down and continued their unspeakable, hate-filled torture. Having thought he had died, and yet still not satisfied with the blood they had spilt, they cut him down and continued to kick and beat him until he gave up his spirit, only after praying that God would forgive the sin of his enemies.

For five hundred years the life and sufferings of this worthy servant of Christ remained unknown. However, when an abbess, Mother Makaria, came to rebuild the monastery in Nea Makri—the site on which the saint had suffered five centuries earlier—her prayer for God to reveal one of the martyred fathers was answered. On April 23, 1999, she heard a voice within indicating where she should dig to find the remains of a holy martyr.

After some difficulties, the relics of St. Ephraim were discovered, and that evening while the abbess was reading Vespers, the saint appeared to her. He was tall with small eyes, and a beard down to his chest. He was holding a flame in his left hand and blessing with his right. Mother Makaria heard the story of the saint's life and martyric sufferings from his own lips.

From that time on, his holy relics began working countless miracles and healing many sick. Although he was only officially canonized by the Ecumenical Patriarchate in 2011, he has been revered by the faithful as a saint from the time the abbess found his holy remains.

While living in Greece, I had the great blessing of visiting this monastery a few times and venerating St. Ephraim's holy relics. Words cannot describe the grace the monastery exudes on account of the new martyr. I've gone to that monastery in the company of different people, and all attest to the profound grace one feels while within the walls of the convent.

The mulberry tree on which the saint was hung remains standing to this day. It is enclosed in a protective building in the monastery's courtyard. In the main church, laid out in a glass-covered coffin, are the grace-filled, fragrant relics of St. Ephraim. He is clothed in the monastic habit with a priest's stole prominently displayed on his chest, as he was a priestmonk. Indeed he was very tall.

No matter how many times you examine him, venerate him, smell the ineffable, sweet fragrance of grace emitting from his holy body, the awe you feel in his presence is never diminished. Truly he was a saint of God, a holy man, a prophet. He is alive in Christ and works wonders to this day. Whole volumes have been written detailing the numerous miracles he has worked in the years since the discovery of his relics. However, to my knowledge, only a few of the books about his life and works have been translated into English.

He is called a new martyr, a new example of the kind of asceticism, sacrifice, and dedication to Christ—even unto death—that the early Christians exhibited. His life, works, and martyrdom remained a silent testimony to our Lord Jesus Christ, but in these last years they have been revealed. His life and relics were uncovered for the benefit of today's Christians.

There is a commonly held belief in Greece and abroad that in the last years (however many God grants us), an abundance of holy relics of saints and martyrs (old and new) will be uncovered. We have seen this happening already. While the holy relics of both St. Demetrios the Myrrh-gusher and St. Savvas the Sanctified were stolen during the Crusades, in the 1960s they were returned—St. Demetrios to Thessaloniki and St. Savvas to his monastery in Palestine. In addition, the holy remains of Ss. Ephraim, Kyriaki, Akylina, Raphael, Nicholas, Irene, and Vassarion (just to name a few) have all been discovered in the last fifteen or twenty years in Greece.

These saints give us encouragement, strengthen our faith, and remind us—with their own fragrant remains and battered flesh and blood—that living and dying for Christ is possible and praiseworthy. They remind us that no matter what we suffer in this life, it is nothing compared to the grace and glory we can partake of in eternal life.

Once, when St. Euphemia the Great Martyr appeared to Elder Paisios the Athonite, he asked her how she managed to withstand the physical afflictions of martyrdom. She answered him, "If I had known what glory the saints have I would have done whatever I could to go through even greater torments."[42]

This truth is testified to by the life and person of St. Ephraim of Nea Makri, who dwells close to God on account of the unspeakable torments he suffered, and now we, the faithful, reap the benefits of the glory he experiences as a right reward for his martyric wounds and ascetic struggle.

Remaining Faithful to the End

ONCE, FR. JOHN AND I had the blessing of being introduced to an abbess from a small hesychastarion in Athens. She was very sweet and became visibly joyful when she heard we were from Canada and had plans to return to serve the Orthodox Church in our homeland.

"You need to take up the cross of Christ, but you need to do this *together*." Her face lit up as she began talking to us.

"No matter what, you *must* remain faithful until the end," she went on, conviction sounding in her voice. "There are heresies all around, distractions, falsehoods, but you must remain faithful. Didn't the apostles say they would be faithful until the end? Do as they did! Remain faithful! Even if the world is on fire, even if it is burning, you will remain faithful." She nodded, signifying she was finished. We rose from our seats and bowed to her, and she smiled at us as we took her blessing.

I often observed that not only monastics but priests and even laypeople we met while living in Greece very rarely advised us on tactics of how to run a successful parish, bring in new converts, or minister to the youth. They were always concerned first and foremost with encouraging us to hold fast to the Faith, struggle to live spiritual lives, and learn how to become witnesses of Christ's love to others—Orthodox and non-Orthodox alike.

Now that we have returned to Canada and served in a mission for over three years, their advice holds even greater meaning for me. We have no control over what anyone else thinks, feels, or believes. All we can do is be faithful to Christ and live our faith to the best of our ability. We must, as the abbess told us, be as the apostles were, faithful servants of Christ. For it was through their steadfast relationship to Christ that they spread the Gospel to the far ends of the earth and received the Kingdom of God for having done so.

The Power of Your Cross, O Lord

"WE SHOULD ALWAYS MAKE the sign of the cross, before we do something, before we speak," Sr. Silouani instructed us. "While caught up in a conversation, even if we can't make the sign of the cross over our mouth externally, we can do it internally, noetically, so as to be protected, to say what is necessary with the right words in an appropriate manner."

The symbol of the cross holds great importance for Orthodox Christians; we make the sign of the cross countless times a day. In a monastery, the respect and honor attributed to the cross is even more obvious. You cannot but notice the frequency with which monastics employ the cross, the great ensign "dread and most awesome in war" (Kontakion for Ss. Constantine and Helen).

Before beginning any task—even simple tasks like washing the dishes—a nun crosses herself; when cooking food in the oven, a nun makes the sign of the cross over it; when baking bread, a nun will cut a small cross in the top of each loaf. Monastics sew small, unobtrusive red crosses on their clothes (usually on the underside), as well as on blankets and pillowcases.

When they compliment or congratulate someone, they often cross the person as well. When they yawn or laugh very hard, the sisters mark their lips with the sign of the cross. They make the sign of the cross when they yawn to ward off sleep potentially induced by the evil one, while they cross their mouths when they laugh because they struggle to practice temperance even in regard to laughter. Before eating or drinking, they cross themselves as well as their food and drink.

Conversely, they do not sit with their legs crossed (over the thigh) out of respect for the symbol of the cross, nor would they put a cross pattern in a floor, because people would walk on it. In fact, it is said that Athonite monks used to check the soles of their shoes—and those of pilgrims—to make sure they were not walking on symbols of the cross. If they found cross patterns on their soles, they would cut those pieces out.

I once read in the *Gerontikon* that a monk was walking through the woods and saw two twigs on the ground in the form of a cross. He bent down and uncrossed them so that no one would trample on the sign of the cross. Such is a monastic's watchfulness and care for sacred symbols.

In all these ways and more, monastics try to keep the memory of the cross before them at all times, and not only the memory but the power of the cross. They look to the sign of the cross to help, enlighten, and protect them. As is said in an Orthodox hymn, "The power of Your cross, O Lord, is very great!"

We too should try to incorporate the sign of the cross into our daily lives as much as possible. To help inspire us to employ the sign of the cross and contemplate its great power, I will share the following stories.

When our friends were getting married, their *koumvaroi** wanted to give them a special present. They had been given a small relic, a piece of the True Cross—the very wood on which Christ was crucified. They wanted to share this relic with our friends in honor of their wedding. The only problem was they didn't know how to break a piece off. By the grace of God, such an action was unnecessary, for when they opened the reliquary they saw that the relic of the Cross had already divided into two pieces on its own, without anyone having touched it.

ANOTHER DEAR FRIEND OF OURS—more like a lay spiritual mother than a friend—had made a pilgrimage to a monastery for the Feast of the Theophany. During the service for the Great Blessing of the Waters, when the priestmonk placed the cross in the water, she saw the water bubble as though it were rapidly boiling each of the three times the priest immersed the cross to sanctify the water. She was astonished and looked around to see if anyone else was as surprised as she was to witness the physical manifestation of the spiritual reality. No one else seemed to observe this miracle, and so our friend waited to speak with the priestmonk after the conclusion of the service.

She told him what she had seen when he placed the cross in the water, and he told her, "That was a gift from God to prepare you for a great temptation." Needless to say, she witnessed with her own eyes the power of the cross.

---

* *Koumvaros/a/oi*: the Greek title for a sponsor, someone who is in good standing with the Orthodox Church and who supports the spiritual life of the married couple he/she is sponsoring.

WHILE WE WERE ON A PILGRIMAGE to the city of Xanthi in Greece, our priest told us about a holy patriarch, Joachim of Alexandria. At that time there was a king in Egypt of the region of Misiri. Despite his impiety, the king heard about the virtuous and venerable patriarch and began to admire the holy man. The king's servant, however, did not share his master's enthusiasm, and in order to demonstrate to the king that the patriarch was not as great as he seemed, he encouraged the king to invite the patriarch to visit.

When the patriarch arrived, the cunning servant proposed a debate, thinking he would defeat the patriarch. However, with ease the patriarch refuted all the servant's empty and false comments about the Christian Faith. Recognizing his defeat, the servant came up with what he thought was a cunning plan to humiliate the patriarch and demonstrate that he wasn't as holy as the King took him to be.

Knowing something of the Gospel, the servant challenged the patriarch to demonstrate the Christian ability to move a mountain with faith, promising to believe in the Christian God if the patriarch was successful. The patriarch requested a number of days to pray, and when he returned, he made the sign of the cross over himself three times, bowed, and invoked the name of the Lord Jesus Christ, and the mountain split into three parts and began moving toward them.

The King cried out in fear that they would be crushed and implored the patriarch to make the mountain stand still. (To this day the mountain is called *Dur Dag*, which means, "Stay still, mountain!")

Despite this miracle of faith, the wicked servant still refused to believe and instead proposed another test. He had also heard that the Gospel says that whoever has faith will not die even if he drinks poison. So once again he told the patriarch if he accomplished this feat, the servant would believe. But the servant, knowing something of the power of the cross, told the patriarch he could not cross himself.

When the cup of poison was placed before the patriarch, the holy man asked, "But from which place should I drink? From here, here, here, or here?" touching the four sides of the cup in turn. By asking this the patriarch cunningly made the sign of the cross over the cup of poison.

"Anywhere you wish," came the answer, and the patriarch drank down the poison and remained unharmed. The servant, thinking the poison must not have been strong enough to kill the patriarch, rinsed out the cup and drank from it. He, however, was not protected from the poison and fell down dead.

THE GRANDFATHER OF A FRIEND served as a soldier in the Greek army during the first half of the nineteenth century. He had a small piece of the True Cross sewn into his uniform for divine protection, and it worked a great miracle. The enemy opened fire on him, but he was preserved unharmed. To his astonishment, however, when he removed his uniform, he saw it was riddled with bullet holes. Such is the power of the Cross!

A YOUNG GIRL I KNOW also had firsthand experience of the power of the True Cross. She had gone to visit a priest from Crete who had in his possession a piece of the Cross. Countless people visit him in order to be blessed with the Cross, and many receive healing. Doctors had found a tumor in the bone of this young girl's leg, and when she was blessed by the Cross it stuck—of its own accord—to the very place where the tumor was in her leg.

Many people had similar experiences to this: the Cross would stick to the very place they had a health problem, sometimes healing the person on the spot; sometimes they would come back for multiple blessings. It's a wonderful reminder that even two thousand years after the death of our Savior, the wood of the Cross on which He suffered death for our sakes still works miracles.

Before Your Cross we bow down in worship, O Master, and Your holy Resurrection we glorify!

Confessing Our Faith in Spirit and in Truth

WHILE SPEAKING WITH HER SPIRITUAL FATHER about her workplace environment, my friend mentioned an incident in which her boss told a blasphemous joke against Christ in her presence. She explained that while it made her uncomfortable, she remained silent.

"One hundred prostrations," her spiritual father said.

"Excuse me, Father?"

"You will do one hundred prostrations," he clarified.

"One hundred prostrations?" she asked in surprise.

"Yes, one hundred prostrations, because you could have slapped him for saying what he did, but at the very least you should have said something, you should have protested."

Now, you may be thinking how outrageous it would be for Christians to go around slapping everyone who says blasphemous things, but St. John the Golden-mouthed was in fact a great proponent of such bold actions against blasphemers:

And should you hear anyone in the public thoroughfare, or in the midst of the forum, blaspheming God, go up to him and rebuke him; and should it be necessary to inflict blows, spare not to do so. Smite him on the face; strike his mouth; sanctify thy hand with the blow, and if any should accuse thee, and drag thee to the place of justice, follow them thither; and when the judge on the bench calls thee to account, say boldly that the man blasphemed the King of angels![43]

"Sanctify thy hand with the blow," St. John Chrysostom exhorts us. St. Nicholas the Archbishop of Myra did not shy away from such bold action, sanctifying his own hand with the blow he gave to the heretic Arius. Out of great zeal for the true Faith, and even greater love of the Lord—whom he worshipped in spirit and in truth—St. Nicholas slapped Arius in the face at the First Ecumenical Council in Nicaea on account of Arius's blasphemous beliefs and teachings, with which he attempted to infect the Church and confuse the faithful. Although Nicholas was initially removed from the council and stripped of his episcopal responsibilities for this action, God revealed to numerous hierarchs in a dream that He was well pleased with St. Nicholas's zeal. Thus he was restored to his rank as archbishop and has been praised ever since as a great defender of the Orthodox Faith.

Many times we are in the presence of people who make jokes or disparaging comments about the True God, His Mother, the saints, or the Church, and we—weak of faith and conviction—keep our mouths closed. If we have let the modern, syncretistic world dilute our zeal, then we often shy away from speaking up against such blasphemy.

We don't need to start throwing punches, but we should in no way stand idly by; we need to reclaim the boldness our Christian forefathers had. St. John Chrysostom goes so far as to say we should be so bold that blasphemers "may look round every way at each other, and tremble even at their own shadows, anxious lest perchance a Christian, having heard what they said, should spring upon them and sharply chastise them" (St. John Chrysostom, *Homilies on the Statues*, 1, 32).

It is for this reason that in the Slavic private morning prayers we pray, "Save, O Lord, and have mercy on . . . those of Thy servants that are persecuted for Thy sake and the Orthodox Faith by godless peoples, apostates, and by heretics." We ought to pray not only that we may be protected from their malicious blasphemy, but that God would establish us on a firm foundation so that we might stand up for our Faith when necessary, be willing to be judged foolish for our convictions, and proclaim with boldness that we worship the True God and will not suffer to hear, permit, or keep silent in the face of blasphemous words against Him.

I understand well that theory is one thing and practice quite another. I myself am hesitant to speak up when people curse with the name of Christ. However, I am also well aware that on hearing such things I must at the very least pray fervently. And when people on occasion apologize to me for saying such things, I always try to thank them for having the humility to apologize.

Not everyone, however, is as hesitant as I am. A dear friend of mine, an Orthodox theology student who was as faithful as he was clever, was walking in downtown Thessaloniki one day near Christmas when he noticed a few young American missionaries standing in front of a large screen they had set up. They belonged to a belief system similar to the Arian heresy that St. Nicholas warred against and the Church condemned in the early centuries. These missionaries were using the large screen to project their false beliefs to the passing crowds. So, the concerned, bold young theology student approached them and asked if he could write on the screen. They initially refused, but he persuaded them. ATTENTION HERESY! was what he wrote. They weren't too pleased, but he was glad to get the warning out, even if only for a brief moment before they erased it.

This is what is meant by being wise as serpents and harmless as doves, for we, the Orthodox faithful, are as much sheep among wolves today as we were in apostolic times. It was not only appropriate but commendable that this young man demonstrated such zeal for the faith. What a great thing it would be if we did not hesitate to exhibit such boldness when the situation called for it. In this way we "commit ourselves and one another and our whole life to Christ our God," just as our priests and bishops exhort us each and every time they pray the words of the Divine Liturgy.

Through the prayers of the great saints and zealots St. John Chrysostom and St. Nicholas of Myra, may we be sanctified through our effort to "stand well, to stand with fear" (Divine Liturgy of St. John Chrysostom), to safeguard, defend, and confess our Orthodox Faith. Amen, so be it!

Interior Martyrdom

AS I LAY AWAKE in the middle of the night, I thought about the three different dreams I recently had about suffering for my faith. I had three separate dreams, each featuring an unfortunate situation in which I got myself caught up with some people who were going to either maim or kill me for my faith. Each dream ended before the violence started.

When I woke up, I tried to put those dreams out of my thoughts, since we shouldn't trust our dreams. But the truth is, secretly, I did take them seriously. I had thought they might be an indication that I might come face to face with suffering. However, after getting off the phone with my spiritual father (in the middle of the night on account of the time difference between us), I was left considering that those dreams revealed something else: How easy it is to think, "I'd willingly die for Christ," but how hard it is to *live* for Him.

In the days leading up to that sleepless night, I had come to a crossroads and didn't know what to do, and so I asked my spiritual father's advice over the phone. Although his answer was what I expected, it wasn't what I wanted to hear. So here I was in the middle of the night struggling not to throw a temper tantrum while thinking about how hard it is for me to cut off my will and do not what I want, but what is blessed.

Can you stop yourself from doing what you want? Can you accept guidance when it doesn't correlate with your will? Despite often talking, even dreaming, about dying for Christ, do you live *for Him?*

The ability to fall asleep having long since faded away, I lay there struggling to control my emotions, and my thoughts turned to a story a dear monk told us.

One of the buildings at his monastery had caught fire, and he was responsible for taking the firemen through the old monastery so they could examine where the fire might progress. They had exited a window and were standing on the roof. To their right was the blazing fire, to their left a thick stone wall the fathers of the monastery had built many years ago, should such an unfortunate situation as this take place. The solid stone wall would act as a barrier so that in case of a fire, destruction to the monastery would not proceed past that point.

Unfortunately, wooden balconies had been added onto the monastery structure at a later date. Looking down at the balconies, the monk could clearly see that the fire would spread via the old, nearly rotted wood that encircled the whole structure. This would mean the entire monastery would burn from the outside in.

God, if the whole monastery burns, I'm going to lose my faith, he thought to himself.

"We need to cut this wooden balcony off," he said aloud to the firemen, pointing to the balcony below. "Go get your chainsaw and we'll cut it off so the fire will stop at the stone wall."

"We can't do that, we don't have permission to do such a dangerous thing!" the firemen protested.

"We need to or the whole monastery will burn!" the monk insisted. "If you don't get your chainsaw I'll get ours."

"Father, we can't. It's too dangerous. If we try to cut the balcony off, we could fall with it into the ravine below."

The monk knew this was the only sure way to keep the fire from destroying the whole monastery. But whether it was by good habit or by divine grace, he said within himself, *Paisios, don't insist.* And as he said this, the balcony, of its own accord, detached from the wall of the monastery and fell into the ravine below. It was a clear miracle: God allowed it to fall, and the fire was contained.

"The next day we went down and pulled the nails out of the old wood to reuse them. They were perfectly fine. The fire hadn't even begun to burn it," he told us afterward.

Lying there in my bed, struggling to swallow my will, my tears, my anger, my arrogance, I thought of this monk and his incredible story. And I said to myself: *This is struggle.* This *is martyrdom.*

Theirs is the Kingdom of Heaven

MANY ORTHODOX COUNTRIES in the last century suffered extraordinary hardships under the communist yoke. A great number of saints, confessors, and martyrs were revealed in these times of trial and temptation, and we have their blessing as a result. And not only their blessing, but we have their example as a fresh and constant reminder of what it means to suffer for the sake of Christ.

In Romania, a great many Christians—particularly students—were imprisoned for various reasons by the communist regime. However, it's not the reason they were put in prison but what they accomplished while there that is so praiseworthy.

At Auid, Romania's largest prison, in 1944, a group of imprisoned youths formed a kind of monastic brotherhood. This was during the time when the prison wasn't as strict as it would become in later years. The prisoners constructed a sort of monastery in which they kept a routine of prayer, reading, and confession of thoughts.

In a beautiful book entitled *The Saint of the Prisons* (which predominantly focuses on the holy person of Valeriu Gafencu), the spiritual work of these heroic young men is described thus by Virgil Maxim:

> We raised our minds to the level of divine meditation. We went down the road of holiness taken under the light of grace by *"the wise men of God, who served not the creature, but rather the Creator."* The Paterikon [writings of the Fathers], our fundamental guidebook, enabled us to intuitively understand how to put into practice the supernatural truths, saving our strength for the acquisition of virtue.[44]

What an inspiration! What courage! To become a saint, to seek virtue, even in the midst of persecution. The weak human soul would be tempted to say, "I am in prison; this is sufficient asceticism. My prison cell is my prayer, fasting, and Christian sacrifice." But instead these men sought virtue more fervently in prison. They sought opportunities not only to become rich in spiritual wisdom, but to actively do good as often as they could.

Listen again to this incredible description of the transformation of a prison into a great lavra, the transformation of young prisoners into holy ascetics:

> Our little community was a school of perfection. We learned that every passion can be replaced by a virtue, through which God is active in man. Our internal horizons broadened. We learned to love each other, to be tolerant with each other, to be patient with each other, to see ourselves within the framework of a broader human understanding, and, not allowing ourselves to stumble, we ran toward the ultimate goal of the glory of God. In this manner we achieved self-denial, the death of the ego. We forced ourselves, to be obedient to each other, to submit to each other in the same way as we submitted to God.[45]

There is no question that many of these young men became saints, a number even becoming martyrs. We are still learning about them, still struggling to preserve their memory and the memory of their sacrifice. The martyrs' bodies were thrown into a mass grave. Pieces of their holy relics have been collected from this grave and have already begun to work miracles and make their holy presence known.

While my husband and brother were in Romania for a friend's ordination to the holy priesthood, they received holy relics of the martyrs of Auid as a blessing. When they brought them back to Greece (where we were living at the time), I sought out small reliquaries suitable to house the precious relics. When I brought home silver reliquaries, my husband and brother told me the following story they heard while visiting the grave of the saints of Auid: Someone was planning on having a gold reliquary built to house the holy relics, but he had a dream in which the saints of the prison appeared to him and said, "No, don't use gold. Gold is what they used to build the idols; use silver instead."

Once, a Romanian priestmonk had some of these relics with him while he was traveling in a taxi. At some point the taxi driver put down his window and asked the priestmonk, "Father, have you been working with incense or myrrh? The scent is overpowering!" But, as the priestmonk had lost his sense of smell some years earlier, he had not noticed the aroma. When the taxi driver brought it to his attention, the priestmonk understood the holy relics must have been the source of the strong, sweet fragrance.

These are just two small examples of how the holy martyrs are making their presence known.

Valeriu Gafencu—possibly the greatest saint of Auid—had a heated conversation with one of the agents at the prison before he died. The agent was trying to coerce him into acknowledging that his life was in the regime's hands, not God's. If Valeriu agreed to acknowledge this, the prison would have allowed him to have an operation and receive medicine for his illness, but this statement would also have meant forsaking his faith and hope in Christ. He valiantly responded by saying:

"There is nothing under the sun that can survive without God. You cannot accept Christ. I cannot accept spiritual death."

. . . "Go and die with your Christ! I won't try and stop either Him or somebody like you!" [the agent responded].

"You can kill me now but no one can kill Him any longer. He is a stumbling block for all kinds of pride. Understand well that Christ is the only power that can deliver mankind from suffering and sin. . . . The truth is love that sacrifices itself for the poor and the persecuted!"'[46]

The holy Romanian new martyrs embody this last and greatest beatitude. Blessed are they, very blessed in fact, who were persecuted for the sake of righteousness, who gained the Kingdom of heaven, not only for accepting unjust suffering, but for seeking righteousness for its own sake, virtue, goodness, and holiness for their own sakes, while in the midst of suffering. May they inspire us to live for Christ as devoutly, as resolutely, and with as much zeal and love for His commandments as they did.

Epilogue

The great Serbian poet and saint Nikolai Velimirovich writes:

> Few have listened, O Lord, and yet there are those who believe.
> Few are those, who fix their eyes on their Lord and follow His
> gaze.
> I am searching for those who have listened, my Lord, and I share
> my joy with them. I tell them about Your ways and Your
> wisdom, and they confirm what I relate. And we multiply our
> joy and share it.
> I listen to the tale of those who have listened, how You removed
> the stumbling blocks before their feet, and I add my own
> story, and our room is filled with heaven.
> We strew all the events that have happened to us onto the fine
> sieve of Your law, and we call the chaff that falls out Yours,
> and we call the pure grain that remains Yours.
> We count all pains, all tears and all sufferings endured for the
> sake of Your name, as our gain.[47]

The Sweetness of Grace puts into print various stories, experiences, and lessons I took away from my travels in Asia, Europe, and North America. Throughout all of this, I have been seeking those who believe, those whose eyes are fixed on the Lord, those who have listened. I found many such ones, and to their stories I have added my own:

stories of trial and victory, of the sweetness of grace, and of a life of blessedness. While "From olden times David, with good reason, restraineth sinners like me from speaking the statutes of God" (Oikos for St. Andrew the First-called), yet here, on this isolated Atlantic island, I collect these stories and offer them to you, my reader, as a testimony to life in Christ.

Perhaps my adventures have come to an end; perhaps, after so many years of blessings, now only toil remains, and I am called upon to give back to the Master what He entrusted to me. These encounters I have recorded, the many holy people I met, and the rich depth of Orthodoxy I experienced have fanned the flame of my zeal, and I hope my relating of such events has done the same for you.

My zeal and love compel me to share the wonders of God, the inspiring words of abbesses and priestmonks, and the meaningful lessons I learned from faithful laity. I was eager to share what I have with you. And what I have are stories, simple stories that I hope and pray will strengthen, encourage, and inspire you to learn—through your own experience—that the uncreated energies of God, the sweetness of His grace, are liberally poured out on those who seek His favor.

In St. Jerome's letter to a Christian woman, Markella, he speaks of being wounded by the Savior's love, saying, "We shall say one to another: *I have found Him whom my soul loves; I will hold Him and will not let Him go.*" This collection of stories of conversations, encounters, and lessons from my experiences with monastics, priests, and laypeople is, in a sense, this exchange: us saying one to another, "I have found Him whom my soul loves; I will hold Him and will not let Him go."

I beg your prayers—not only for me, so that I might not remain "a teacher who teaches but doesn't practice what she preaches," as

Gerontissa Makrina has said—but for our mission here on Newfound-land. Please pray that all the blessings, wisdom, and encouragement bestowed upon us by those blessed ones we met in our travels may not go to waste, but be for the benefit of all the Orthodox and non-Orthodox souls God may put in our lives. I will finish with the inspiring words of Blessed Bishop Augoustinos of Florina (2009):

> Faithful souls, whenever earthquakes topple our world and whenever you see the ruins left behind by the faithlessness and corruption of our times, do not be disturbed. You have a rock upon which you can stand and an anchor upon which you can depend. . . . You have the sun that rose out of the tomb—Jesus, crucified and resurrected from the dead. Why are you afraid? What is there to fear? Come, let us worship and bow down to Him, Christ, the Victor over Death, the King of the Ages.[48]

May Christ, who is the true Light, enlighten and strengthen each one of us in our pursuit of a life of blessedness.

Notes

1   *The Sayings of the Desert Fathers*, trans. Benedicta Ward (Kalamazoo, MI: Cistercian Publications, 1984), p. 103.

2   Archimandrite Athanasios Mitilinaios, *Homilies on the Book of Revelation*, trans. Constantine Zalalas, vol. 1 (Bethlehem, PA: St. Nicodemus Publications, 2009), p. 290.

3   Saint John Chrysostom, Homily on Matthew 15, New Advent, accessed on January 21, 2017, http://www.newadvent.org/fathers/200115.htm

4   Gerontissa Makrina Bassopoulos, *Logia Kardias* (*Words from the Heart*) (Thessaloniki: *Orthodoxos Kupseli*, 2012).

5   Saint John Chrysostom, *Commentary on the Psalms*, vol. 2 (Brookline, MA: Holy Cross Orthodox Press, 1998), pp.135–136.

6   Saint Cyril of Alexandria, Homiletic Commentary on Luke 16:1–13, accessed on January 21, 2017, https://thedivinelamp.wordpress.com/2013/09/18/st-cyril-of-alexandrias-homiletic-commentary-on-luke-161-13/

7   Gerontissa Makrina Bassopoulos, op. cit., p. 533.

8   Abba Dorotheos, "That we should not judge our neighbour," in *Practical Teaching on the Christian Life*, trans. Constantine Scouteris (Athens: University of Athens, 2002), p. 137.

9   Gerontissa Makrina Bassopoulos, op. cit., pp. 598–599.

10 Elder Ephraim, *My Elder: Joseph the Hesychast* (Florence, AZ: Saint Anthony's Greek Orthodox Monastery, 2013), p. 94.

11 Op. cit., p. 333.

12 Abbot Nikon, *Letters to Spiritual Children* (Richfield Springs, VA: Nikodemus Orthodox Publication Society, 1997), p. 102.

13 *Desert Fathers*, op. cit., p. 83.

14 Archimandrite Sophrony, *St. Silouan the Athonite*, trans. Rosemary Edmonds (Crestwood, NY: St. Vladimir Seminary Press, 1999), p. 269.

15 C. S. Lewis, *The Last Battle* (New York: Harper Trophy, 1994), p. 213.

16 Archimandrite Constantine Zaitzev, *A Spiritual Portrait of St. John of Kronstadt*, accessed on January 21, 2017, http://www.fatheralexander.org/booklets/english/john_kronstadt_k_zaitzev.htm

17 "The Lives of Saints Cyprian and Justina" in *The Orthodox Word*, vol. 12, no. 5 (70) (September–October, 1976).

18 Elder Porphyrios of Athens, *Wounded by Love: The Life and Wisdom of Elder*

Porphyrios, trans. John Raffan (Evia, Greece: Denise Harvey, 2005), p. 203.

19   Pseudo-Dionysius, "The Celestial Hierarchy," in *The Complete Works,* trans. Colm Luibheid (New York: Paulist Press, 1987), p. 71.

20   *Desert Fathers,* op. cit., pp. 3–4.

21   Hieromonk Isaac, *The Life of Elder Paisios,* trans. Hieromonk Alexis Trader (Ormylia, Greece: The Holy Monastery of Saint Arsenios the Cappadocian, 2012), p. 415.

22   Gerontissa Makrina Bassopoulos, op. cit., pp. 467–468.

23   Abba Dorotheos, "On the Building and Construction of the Virtues of the Soul," in *Practical Teaching on the Christian Life,* trans. Constantine Scouteris (Athens: University of Athens, 2002), p. 220.

24   Saint John Chrysostom, *On Paul,* accessed on January 21, 2017 https://www. crossroadsinitiative.com/library_article/440/In_Praise_of_St._Paul__John_ Chrysostom.html

25   Abba Dorotheos, "That We Should Not Judge Our Neighbour," in op. cit., pp.134–135.

26   Saint Nikodemos the Hagiorite, *Exomologetarion: A Manual of Confession,* trans. George Dokos (Greece: Uncut Mountain Press, 2006), p. 136.

27   Saint Nikodemos the Hagiorite, op. cit., p. 140.

28   Elder Ephraim, op. cit., p. 503.

29   Metropolitan of Nafpaktos Hierotheos, *Orthodox Psychotherapy: The Science of the Fathers,* trans. Esther Williams (Levadia, Greece: Birth of the Theotokos Monastery, 1994), p. 162.

30   Priest Daniel Sysoev, *Instructions for the Immortal: Or What to Do If You Still Die,* trans. Deacon Leonid Mickle (Moscow: Mission Center, 2013), p. 18.

31   Saint Ignatius Brianchaninov, "On Spiritual Deception" in *The Orthodox Life,* vol. 30, no. 4 (July–August, 1980), trans. S. Karganovic.

32   Archpriest Seraphim Slobodskoy, *The Law of God: For Study at Home and School* (Jordanville, NY: Holy Trinity Publications, 1994).

33   Archimandrite Zacharias, *The Enlargement of the Heart* (South Canaan, PA: Mount Thabor Publishing, 2006), p. 174.

34   *The Matericon: Instructions of Abba Isaiah to the Honourable Nun Theodora* (Safford, AZ: St. Paisius Serbian Orthodox Monastery, 2001), p. 160.

35   Archimandrite Zacharias, *op. cit.,* p. 174.

36   Symeon Koutsas, *The Spiritual Father According to Orthodox Tradition,* trans. Constantine Zalalas (Bethlehem, PA: St. Nicodemus Press, 1995).

37   Abbess Thaisia of Leushino, *Abbess Thaisia: An Autobiography,* trans. St.

Herman of Alaska Brotherhood (Platina, CA: St. Herman of Alaska Press, 1989), p. 148.

38 Elder Thaddeus, *Our Thoughts Determine Our Lives,* trans. Ana Smiljanic (Platina, CA: St. Herman of Alaska Press, 2014), p. 116.

39 Gerontissa Makrina Bassopoulos, op. cit., p. 496.

40 *Desert Fathers,* op. cit., p. 81.

41 Elder Joseph, *Monastic Wisdom: The Letters of Elder Joseph the Hesychast,* trans. Ephraim Poonen (Florence, AZ: St. Anthony's Greek Orthodox Monastery, 1999), p. 51.

42 Hieromonk Isaac, op. cit., p. 260.

43 Saint John Chrysostom, *Homilies on the Statues,* 1, 32, accessed on January 21, 2017, http://www.newadvent.org/fathers/190101.htm

44 Monk Moise, *The Saint of the Prisons,* trans. Monk Sava (Sibiu, Romania: Editura Agnos, 2009), pp. 79–80.

45 Monk Moise, op. cit., p. 83.

46 Monk Moise, op. cit., p. 141.

47 St. Nikolai Velimirovich, XCIX in *Prayers by the Lake,* accessed on January 21, 2017, http://www.sv-luka.org/praylake/pl99.htm

48 Augoustinos N. Kantiotes, *Follow Me,* trans. Asterios Gerostergios (Belmont, MA: The Institute for Byzantine and Modern Greek Studies, 1989), p. 269.

About the Author

Constantina R. Palmer is from New Brunswick, a quaint province on Canada's Atlantic coast. She lived in Thessaloniki, Greece, for almost six years, during which time she received a Master's degree in theology from Aristotle University and studied Cretan-style iconography as well as Byzantine chant. Not one to simply learn from books, she also spent significant time at a number of women's monasteries throughout northern Greece. Currently, she lives with her husband, an Orthodox priest, in the province of Newfoundland and Labrador in Canada, serving the only Orthodox parish on the island of Newfoundland. She is also a social worker.

The Scent of Holiness
Lessons from a Women's Monastery

Every monastery exudes the scent of holiness, but women's monasteries have their own special flavor. Join Constantina Palmer as she makes frequent pilgrimages to a women's monastery in Greece and absorbs the nuns' particular approach to their spiritual life. If you're a woman who's read of Mount Athos and longed to partake of its grace-filled atmosphere, this book is for you. Men who wish to understand how women's spirituality differs from their own will find it a fascinating read as well.

Ancient Faith Publishing hopes you have enjoyed and benefited from this book. The proceeds from the sales of our books only partially cover the costs of operating our nonprofit ministry—which includes both the work of **Ancient Faith Publishing** and the work of **Ancient Faith Radio**. Your financial support makes it possible to continue this ministry both in print and online. Donations are tax-deductible and can be made at www.ancientfaith.com.

To request a catalog of other publications,
please call us at (800) 967-7377 or (219) 728-2216
or log onto our website: **store.ancientfaith.com**

ANCIENT FAITH RADIO

Bringing you Orthodox Christian music, readings,
prayers, teaching, and podcasts 24 hours a day since 2004 at
www.ancientfaith.com